Creating an Authentic Life

Other Books by Rob Reider

John Wiley & Sons, Inc. Professional Management Books:

Benchmarking Strategies: A Tool For Profit Improvement
Improving the Economy, Efficiency, and Effectiveness of Not-For-Profits
Managing Cash Flow: An Operational Focus (co-author with Peter B. Heyler)
Operational Review: Maximum Results at Efficient Costs
Operational Review: Workbook (Case studies, forms, and exercises)
Effective Operations and Controls for the Small Privately Held Business

Fiction

Road to Oblivion: The Footpath Back Home
Brother Knot

Creating an Authentic Life

The Storyteller and the Tale of Self

by
Rob Reider

SANTA FE

Sunstone books may be purchased for educational, business, or sales promotional use. For information please write: Special Markets Department, Sunstone Press, P.O. Box 2321, Santa Fe, New Mexico 87504-2321.

Book and Cover design › Vicki Ahl
Body typeface › Candara ♦ Display typeface › Ondine LT STd
Printed on acid free paper

Library of Congress Cataloging-in-Publication Data

Reider, Rob, 1940-
Creating an authentic life : the storyteller and the tale of self / by Rob Reider.
p. cm.
ISBN: 978-0-86534-657-4 (softcover : alk. paper)
1. Self. 2. Identity (Psychology) 3. Life
I. Title.
BF 697.R4175 2010
155.2'5--dc22
2009051828

WWW.SUNSTONEPRESS.COM
SUNSTONE PRESS / POST OFFICE BOX 2321 / SANTA FE, NM 87504-2321 /USA
(505) 988-4418 / ORDERS ONLY (800) 243-5644 / FAX (505) 988-1025

This book is for my wife Barbara and my three daughters
Kim, Michelle, and Heather—and myself
All of whom grew up differently but with much in common
Resulting in a different tale that each one tells

Contents

Preface

Our mind believes what we tell it—
and thus our story begins.

Many of us wonder why we continue to live the lives we have fallen into. If we were obedient children, we followed the societal rules laid out for us by our parents, community, schools, and peers. To be different would be risky; it was much easier to just go along—become part of mainstream society. Those who wanted to be different but weren't strong enough to fight the others may have wound up living a life of internal anger and depression. Those who were strong enough to dare to be different may have wound up feeling that they didn't belong, living as outcasts and exiles. Either way, we are all lost in the "tale" we have created for ourselves. Each of our tales has a prevalent theme that guides our behavior in a cycle of success or failure. For all of us the theme of our tale often encourages us to conceal or disguise our real selves. We become the storyteller of our own lives relating a tale about ourselves. Now we must unravel our tale to become who we are.

The tale a person tells to him or her self and acts out for others guides his or her behavior, choices, dreams and hopes. Unfortunately, some tales narrow choices, promote the repetition of counterproductive themes, and force the individual to maintain the predominant role determined by the tale. The tale drives the individual, making him or her victim to the tale rather than in control of the tale as author and storyteller.

There is tremendous power in uncovering your real tale—that is who you really are. Once concealment is removed a resulting opportunity or freedom allows one to become the author of his or her tale. Being able to direct the tale rather than being directed by it is the essence of choice. Refusing to play an undesirable role in someone else's story permits the individual to construct his or her own life in a way that is authentic for them.

Uncovering the real you is a difficult task. Children learn about whom they should be early in their lives. Such dictated roles are used as protection, a way of facing a world that demands certain behaviors and a way of being to survive. Some obey and conform to expected behaviors so that those around them cannot tell how frightened, lonely, and alienated they feel. As time passes, what is underneath these behaviors becomes less and less available to the individual; as a result, a tale is created that lacks possibilities for change. The person's life is lived through dictated behaviors, not from an authentic place within. For some, the tale simply limits his or her opportunity for optimum health, while for others being stuck in a counterproductive story leads him or her to unproductive behaviors. It is important that individuals recognize that their tale can be changed, and that they are capable of creating their tale in new and different ways.

The tale that parents and children bring with them can come together in ways that promote more risk. Parents, stuck in their own tale, may impose their own tale on their children. They then may blame their children (or spouses) for their own failures, or may refuse to deal with those whose tales remind them too much of their own. Some parents may without realizing ask their children to live out their tale for them. The parent or child then may become angry and reject those who cannot meet their personal need for success or control. Some stories of parents and children work well together. The parent, once in touch with his or her own tale, has the potential to assist his or her child to find their own voice and become the author of their own tale, thus reducing dictated behaviors and support their potential.

In looking at our own tales, we recognize the power of the individual in our lives and the freedom to be achieved when we can become our real self. Our dictated roles are used throughout childhood and well into our adult years. We may project confidence and control to others; or project inadequacy and self-depreciation.

For instance, if one does not do something well it is only because he or she doesn't care, not because he or she did not know how. Your behavior also informs others in your world that you are secure in what you want and that no one is going to tell you what to do. However, underneath may be feelings of insecurity, failure, and the belief that one is not smart enough. We are all caught in a tale that has to do with prevalent societal and family expectations of the time we were growing up. Some of us work hard not to submit to what we consider someone else's beliefs or instructions for our behavior that may include being an obedient child—male or female, marriage and children, and a career that is acceptable to the prevalent society or secondary to your husbands. Many of our choices are the result of the messages we have received from others and internalized for ourselves.

We all have a tale we tell about ourselves. Language, imagery and memory shape the tale over time. Some individuals see themselves as the author of the tale while others perceive themselves as victims. A listener also shapes a person's tale—telling a story about the tale he or she has heard. The story someone tells us about ourselves becomes linked with the tale we tell ourselves. Certain aspects of the tale stay consistent over time. They get told over and over again and become for the teller the truth, the absolute reality. The construction of the tale is made up of bits and pieces of connections, which when strung together seem like continuous events. Some of these connections, if disconnected, would appear illogical but to the teller there is logic and substance. It is rare that the teller challenges his own construction. The brain forges these connections in such a way that they become linked. The appearance of truth becomes truth. Because of this, it is rare that individuals' challenge the construction of their tale. The tale becomes the reality; the focal point of how each one of us lives our life. The reality that dwells in our minds affects the physical reality that we see and touch.

What the teller chooses to tell repeatedly is significant. It defines, in many ways how the person behaves in the world. It is the drama and the person is the prime actor. The actor accepts behaviors that support his or her drama and these behaviors become what interact with the world. What lies behind these obvious behaviors over time may become unavailable to the actor without assistance.

When a person's tale is fraught with defeat, feelings of unworthiness, victimization, and so on it is probable that the person will act as their old messages dictate, confirming the tale as reality. The possibilities for other behaviors and other tales become lost—with the individual seeking out those who validate their tale. Life becomes a set of defined instructions, with you as the actor performing your role to meet your own expectations.

Those considered at-risk for personal failure are often those whose tales guide them in counterproductive ways. These tales are often filled with negativity, hopelessness and a profound sense of not being able to influence the direction of their lives. There is little indication that these individuals see other possibilities to the drama they have created.

What happens to those who are literally stuck in their tale? When we tell our tale there is a psychological distance between the events in the tale and the present. This distance provides a space for examining the tale for content, patterns, and misconnections. With a more objective view, can the tale be written differently? Can the tale become a story with multiple possibilities for outcomes? What happens to those whose tales have no voice? Who validates and challenges these tales? What is the effect on the individual if there is no validation or challenge? Does this only add to the potential for being stuck? If a tale has no voice, it is likely the individual's feelings of alienation and powerlessness will increase. What if those considered at-risk changed their tale? What would make it possible for these individuals to uncover their own tales and look behind who they have become? What if in doing so they were able to begin re-writing their tale? What happens when the authority figure has a story that interfaces with the individual's tale in such a way to promote more insecurity? Can these tales come together to build reality?

This book addresses the power of the person's tale—for the teller and the listener. Through the examination of the interplay of the tale, space becomes available for building comfort or creating risk. To create tales to guide individuals towards success, he or she needs to understand their own tale as well as the story others tell about them. The tale guides behavior by fueling prejudices, feelings of failure or efficacy. The individual's learned behavior becomes the characteristic way of relating—the cover for what lies beyond.

Each tale in this book deals with a different aspect of the dance between the individual's story and reality. All the tales in this book are fictional, although some are based on fact or the author's observations. The tales depicted in the book present the basis for discussion in the analysis of the tale by the reader. To assist the reader in such an analysis, suggested questions or points to ponder are presented after each tale. Through analyzing these tales the reader should get a better understanding of their own tale as well as what they desire to change to move toward the life they have always wanted.

When reading and analyzing each of the tales in this book, pay particular attention to the *turning points* and *life determining decisions* affecting the course of the life and story of the subjects depicted in the narrative. Turning points are those places in our life where there are more than one route to take but the route taken has an impact on the remainder of our lives. Examples of such turning points include who your parents are (especially if you are adopted), where you live, the school you attended, your peer group, your ethnic group, your religious affiliation or not, and so on. Life determining decisions are those decisions that you make that have a lasting affect on your life. Examples of such life determining decisions include choosing your friends, taking school seriously, going to college, deciding who to marry, having children, choosing a field of work and who to work for, where to live, and so on.

You might ask whether we are all doomed to live as frauds in exile to the life we really want for ourselves. Hopefully, the tales in this book can help show the way others have been buried in a tale, and how they got there, and provide some insights as to how one might dig him or her self out from a tale that they find undesirable and suffocating or how to increase the benefits of a tale that is working for them—in both cases helping the individual to become the I that they want to be.

Life is in the head,
be it happy or sad,
angry or glad.

◇ ◇ ◇

I wonder why I wake up each morning
and I am still the same person
with the same story.
Will I ever be able to change my story
to become the person I want to be?

A Teacher's Story

As a teacher Joan only wanted to work with difficult children. Did she have this particular desire because she believed that she could serve these children well? Was she coming from a place of caring and concern? Would she make decisions related to the welfare of these children from her understanding of their needs and not her own? In retrospect, she realizes that her drive to teach such children had more to do with her own tale than with the children's tales. She wanted to teach where no one else wanted to go. She wanted to prove that she could succeed even in the midst of all the failure of inner-city education. From the outside her intentions looked good but it was really her tale and the messages contained in it that was driving her.

There was an opening in Joan's school district for a first-grade teacher. The members of the hiring team remarked that Joan, being small and slight, might not be physically large enough to deal with the children. They believed that the children would intimidate her because she was slight, a female, young, and inexperienced. With the tale that she was living that was all she needed to hear. Joan was not going to be told that she could not do something, especially something that she thought she wanted. To prove them wrong, she would teach in the urban ghetto in the most problematic school she could find.

Joan was hired to teach in her "dream" school in a poverty-ridden section of the city. She was totally unprepared for what she found. However, to keep her tale going meant that she was not going to quit. Her frustration at not being successful in the ways that she had imagined caused her to examine her motivation for teaching in this school. She asked herself why was she really there? What was making her face the problems of that classroom every day? What was really inside her that she could offer these children? This was her first experience that forced her to question and get close to her own tale. She wanted to work with these children but she was beginning to understand that her motivation was all wrong. She was more concerned with her success than the success of her students. Maybe it was the same thing but somehow when she recognized where her emphasis was it seemed different. She began to examine her own tale and where she was stuck.

Joan became curious about her students' tales. She was most concerned with the tales they would tell about themselves, not the tales she believed about them or others would tell about them. She began listening to her students more carefully, trying to look beyond their tales for the truth. For example, when asked what they wanted to do when they grew up they informed her that they would be on welfare—and that would be okay. For them, this was the only option, the only possible story line. Hidden behind these tales, however, were aspirations to be policemen, firemen, schoolteachers, and for one female child, a doctor. Other teachers in the school also had tales to tell about these children—they perceived these children as just stupid, unmanageable, and un-teachable.

Joan did not buy into the hopeless tales her students told about their future as welfare recipients. She also did not buy the tales that the other teachers told about them. She really believed that if these students could begin to have hope that their tales could change, and this would help them change their attitudes toward learning. By beginning the process of owning their stories, these children would develop a semblance of control over their lives.

Joan assisted her students in finding evidence that challenged their tales. She knew for some that it was the beginning of creating a tale with new possibilities. She was not successful with all the children but is grateful that for some a window of opportunity was opened. Joan does not know what happened to all of these children. She can only hope that they were able to continue to live tales that led them away from being just another school dropout statistic.

In the process of re-visiting her tale and the tales of her first students, Joan also re-visited the connections between her own tale and the choices she has made as a teacher and administrator.

Joan now believes that it is her professional responsibility to be as authentic as possible so that she is clear as to her motivations and responses to those that she teaches. Giving voice to your tale is the fist step in gaining the insight necessary for this authenticity.

Looking back at her own tale and the script that came out of it, Joan remembers that each piece of the tale placed a message in her life that has followed along with her as a beacon to who she is. While one can try to escape those pieces of their tale that they would like to forget, it is those pieces that seem to have the greatest impact upon us—and the ones most difficult to forget. These memories become the building blocks for our lives.

As a young child, Joan refused to talk to the teacher in front of her peers until she was in third grade. She was not sure why except that at home she was told she had a big mouth and was always getting into trouble by talking back to her dad. Based on this message, she didn't want to risk getting into trouble with another authority figure, her teacher. In first grade, she did write (or dictate to the teacher) plays that everyone in the class put on. She remembers thinking that she had something special and although she did not have a label for this "something" she now recognizes it as creativity.

Joan was a fairly good student but knew even in first grade that she was not in the smartest group. Funny how the color of a reading book sets kids apart. By second grade, she no longer held a high opinion of her academic skill. She was beginning to find out that conformity was the way to success and that conformity did not come easy to her. By fourth grade she had found her voice and it did, in fact, get her into trouble. She remembers telling her teacher that she did not want to go with the student teacher because she was bored with what he was teaching. Her teacher was very angry with her and told her she was disrespectful. Funny, this is what her father had said all along.

Joan's father also said that it was not very important for her to do that well in school academically because she was a girl. Her grandfather had different ideas and encouraged her, especially around creative writing. She loved to make up stories and read them to her grandfather. Her teacher liked her stories too, but told her that she would never have good handwriting because her mind went faster than her hand. To this day her handwriting is still not good. Could she have improved? She really doesn't know—she stopped trying at age nine.

Joan's family seemed okay that she often had a grade of "C" in math or science on her report card. She never thought she was any good in math and she felt that her parents supported that opinion, so she rarely put out much effort. She remembers in junior high school, her science teacher making it very clear that he thought Joan could do better than "C" work in his class. He did not lower one expectation for her and she got a "D" the first report period. This was her first "D" and she was devastated. She studied as hard as she could in this class and brought the "D" up to a "B" by the last report period. This was the first time that she realized effort and outcome were related!

Joan stopped seeing herself as incapable of learning higher-level math and with help from her uncle she did well in algebra and geometry. Math was still not her favorite subject but at least she felt she had some control over her grade. Following high school, Joan went to nursing school and was the first in her class. She studied all the time but she did it—recognizing the value of effort. She left nursing school for regular college and kept going until she completed a Ph.D. Her mother and father were college educated but found her interest in going to college (for something other than education—a girl's profession) a waste of time.

It was perfectly all right to attend college with the idea of marrying and maybe when the children were grown to teach. The school day supposedly ended by three and the idea was that as a mother and teacher one could be home when the kids got home. Joan's father could not understand why she would want a doctoral degree. It was unnecessary for a female and anyway she probably was not smart enough.

Joan didn't seem to use the same learning strategies as her classmates. She enjoyed ideas but had a hard time with a bunch of unrelated facts. She liked creating in her mind but never did well with an outline. She always felt that she was lacking somehow. Deep down she agreed with her teachers that outlines and a head full of facts was a mark of intelligence. She did not learn to appreciate the way her mind works until she was in her doctoral program. She finally realized that her way of thinking, creating, and learning was acceptable. It was wonderful to finally value herself as a learner but why did she have to wait until she was in her 40s to have this happen?

Points to ponder:

Many of the turning points in our life happen to us without our making a choice. For instance, the choice of parents, schools attended, teachers selected, peers available, and the neighborhood of our growing years. When we are finally old enough to make our own decisions, using the free will available in all of us, we make our life determining decisions based on our prior background, parental and other authority figures messages, values, and beliefs; and the life positions that we have accepted based on our experiences. Joan's tale depicts a life formed by such prior messages and beliefs where the subject finally begins to question the life she has fallen into.

1. Joan states that she only wanted to work with difficult children as a teacher—an admirable intention. Did her desire come from her concern about these children or something emanating from her own story? What was her real motivation?
2. Joan was told that she was too small, a female, and inexperienced to deal with difficult children in the inner city. What previous messages about herself influenced her decision to teach in the most problematic school?
3. Joan was totally unprepared for what she found in the inner city ghetto school that she was assigned to. This forced her to examine her own story to determine why she was really there—for the children or for her. What were her real motivations for wanting to teach in this school?

4. Forced to look at her own story, Joan became curious about her first grade students' stories. She was most concerned with the stories they told about themselves, not the stories she or others believed about them. What were the stories they told about themselves, where did they come from, and what was hidden behind these stories?
5. Other teachers in the school had a story about these children, that they were just stupid, unmanageable, and un-teachable? Where did this story come from?
6. Joan believed that if she could begin the process of helping her students own their stories and have hope that their stories could change their attitudes toward learning would change. Joan was certainly a turning point in the lives of these children, but what do you think the chances of her success were—and what factors got in the way?
7. Joan, in looking back at her own story, she recognized the messages that she had internalized to become who she was. What were some of those messages and how did they influence the decisions she made?
8. Joan refused to talk to her teacher in front of the other students until the third grade. One of her messages from her parents was that she had a big mouth that would get her into trouble. How did this message affect her relationship with her teachers?
9. In the first grade Joan realized that she was a fairly good student but not in the smartest group. Her group was given a different color-reading book than the smartest group. How do such subtle messages affect the self-image and subsequent performance of youngsters?
10. When living in a system of conformity that expects you to be an obedient child, what happens to a child like Joan who fights having her creativity stifled? How does this affect the decisions you make in your later life and who you become?
11. Joan's father told her that it was unimportant for a girl to do well in school; her grandfather encouraged her to do well. How do such conflicting messages affect one as they are growing up and then in later life?
12. Joan's parents accepted her grade of C in math and science subjects. The message she received was that she wasn't very good in those subjects, so she put out little effort. When she worked hard in junior high school, she was able to bring her grade up to a B. What did Joan

learn about herself from this experience?

13. Following high school, Joan decided to go to nursing school, a turning point and a life determining decision. By working hard and recognizing the value of effort she became first in her class. When she realized that nursing wasn't for her she transferred to regular college and eventually completed a Ph.D. How effective was Joan in dealing with these turning points in her life and making good life determining decisions?
14. Joan's parents, both college graduates, found her interest in higher education a waste of time—all right to find a husband and have children. When the children were grown it would be all right to teach school, so she allowed her parents to convince her to take education in college. Why do we allow others, especially our authority figures, to shape our turning points and coerce to make decisions that do not support who we really are?
15. Joan did not appreciate the way her mind works until she decided to enroll in a doctoral program, contrary to her father's opinion that it was unnecessary and that she wasn't smart enough, What changes did Joan make that allowed her to finally value herself as a learner and appreciate the way her mind worked?

The teacher teaches what
he or she has been taught.

People Who Need People

Artificial Barriers to Love

Sarah Wiedermann was born to Jewish parents on the Austrian side of the Munich border. Her parents lived in the Jewish sector of the city. Her father owned a grocery store with predominantly Jewish customers. Her mother helped in the store, but mainly took care of the children, Sarah the eldest, her sister Leah, and her brother Max. Her parents were quite sensitive to the power of the gentile world all around them, particularly in the aftermath of the First World War and the climate brewing for more hostilities between Germany and the rest of Europe. Sarah and her siblings were kept insulated from the gentile world; they were quite safe in the Jewish world. Luckily they also lived on the Austrian side, they would surely be protected from the German barbarians.

Sarah lived a sheltered life in the Austrian Jewish community. She was very bright and earned a scholarship to the University in Munich at the age of fifteen. Her parents wanted her to live at home and commute the 30 some kilometers each way to college. Sarah wanted to be on her own and persisted until her parents agreed to let her live at the university. However, she must come home each weekend and get the highest grades. Sarah agreed.

Gustav Guffmann was born to German Lutheran parents in Munich. His parents were strict Germans who tolerated no fun in life. Gustav was to study and make something of himself. He was to be a credit to the German race, an Aryan to be proud of. Gustav just wanted to be left alone, to love and be loved. Gustav's family, although they hated them collectively and individually, knew no Jews and had no contact with any of them. They were completely isolated in their German Lutheran world. Gustav's parents wanted him to go to college in Berlin where he could better strengthen his German heritage. Gustav, however, wanted to stay in Munich where all of his friends were going to the university and where he was most comfortable. He had never been away from Munich for more than two days in his life. He was happy in Munich; it was his home. Gustav's parents finally agreed, but only if he lived at the university so that he could become part of the German community on his own. He was to become an engineer like his father and help the fatherland become the greatest country in the world. They would show Europe what Germany was made of.

It was Sarah's first day at the university. On one hand she was feeling liberated to finally be on her own and away from the Jewish community. On the other hand she was deathly afraid, for she had never stepped into the gentile world on her own before. She was walking across campus to register for classes; she was to be a literature major. As long as she remembered, she had always read and her fantasy life resided in the world of books. Shakespeare sonnets, Jane Austen romances, Charles Dickens sagas, and so on. She was Jane Eyre walking across campus with her head in her fantasy. Not looking where she was going, she ran directly into a gawky, scholarly looking boy—it was Gustav.

They were both knocked to the ground, with Sarah falling on top of Gustav. Gustav who had never been this close to a girl other than his ugly cousin Greta was quite flustered. Gustav pulled himself quickly from the pile and blubbered. "Excuse me, I am too clumsy." He hurried off across the campus. He thought to himself what an attractive girl that is, but she'll never talk to me. Sarah picked herself up and laughed to herself. She thought what a silly boy. Momma has no reason to be concerned if all the boys are like this one.

One of Sarah's classes was German-Austrian Philosophers. Sarah was glad to have both German and Austrian heritage and she wanted to learn more about their great thinkers. As the professor was starting the lecture, the door opened and a male student entered carrying books up to his eyes. He walked directly into the professor's desk, spewing books all over the desk, the professor, and the floor. The class laughed, which caught Sarah's attention. Oh my God she thought, it is he, the boy I ran over.

The professor coughed to get the classes attention. "So, who are you, the book seller?" The class laughed. The boy blushed and looked away. He was so pathetic; he was cute.

"It is I," said the boy. The class laughed again—this wasn't getting better for him.

Sarah felt sorry for him—a klutz, but a nice klutz.

"And who is I, pray tell." The professor was working it now.

The boy flustered while he tried to pick up the books. As his arms loaded up, he picked up one book and dropped two or three. Really pathetic, thought Sarah, but maybe cute too. It was too funny, so no one came up to help him.

"It is I," the boy started, but the professor cut him off.

"So, it is I. No last name?" The professor looked at him over his glasses. "So?"

Sarah felt sorry for the likable klutz. She went up to help him. While she picked up the books, the boy got to his feet and faced the professor. He was visibly shaken, but stuttered.

"I am Gustav Guffmann from Kronsdorf Street in Munich."

"Very nice for you, Gustav Guffmann, from Kronsdorf Street. Do you think you can find a seat, so we can begin again the class?" The professor looked back at him over his glasses.

Gustav hesitated. "Please, next to last row—on the right. Mach haste."

Gustav stumbled to his seat. Sarah brought him the books she had picked up. They both looked away. Sarah smiled to herself on the way back to her seat.

Sarah had been to the university for about a month now. She had gone home every weekend as she had promised. Home, however, was not like it used to be. Where she used to enjoy her parents attention, she now found it constraining. She was quite involved at the university. She joined the philosophy club, the literature club, and was an apprentice member of the school newspaper. She had also made a good friend, another Jewish girl from Frankfurt named Gretchen. They lived in the same dormitory and spent most of their time together, either the two of them or the group of Jewish girls from the dormitory. There was Rebecca, Esther, Sally, the two Ruth's and so on. They had so much fun together, studying together and telling each other stories about their homes. They also talked about boys although none of them had a boyfriend or had even been with a boy except their cousins.

The first social event of the year, the harvest dance, was coming up and Gretchen was pressuring Sarah to go with her. It would be the first dance for both of them. However, it was on a Friday night and Sarah was expected to spend the Sabbath with her family. Sarah wanted to go to the dance with Gretchen, but what would she tell her family. They had always spent Friday nights together. Although the family wasn't overly religious, this was tradition to light the Friday night candles together. The dance was three weeks away and Sarah wanted desperately to go. With Gretchen there, it would be all right.

Sarah very rarely got sick. Gretchen, however, convinced Sarah that this was the only way she could avoid going home on the weekend of the harvest dance. Sarah was allergic to dairy products. Although like most children she loved ice cream, she could never have any at home except a spoonful on her birthday.

Gretchen and the rest of the girl's pooled their money on Thursday before the dance so as to be able to buy the large container of vanilla ice cream. They took turns feeding the ice cream to Sarah. In the beginning she enjoyed the treat, but now she was getting sick to her stomach, a horrible rash was covering her skin all over her body, and she was getting nauseous. She kept yelling, "no more, no more, please, no more," but to no avail. Gretchen and the girls just kept shoveling more ice cream into her mouth. Finally, Sarah gasped and threw up all over the girls.

"Now," Gretchen said, "you are ready."

They carried Sarah to the nurse's room. The nurse looked up from her paperwork.

"Yah, what have we here?"

Gretchen replied, "We have one sick girl here." They all laughed and left Sarah with the nurse. They gathered on the other side of the door to hear what was going on. The nurse put Sarah on the cot and began to examine her. Sarah looked up at the nurse, saw her white vanilla uniform, and threw up all over her.

"Oh my God," gasped the nurse, "you are one sick girl."

The girls put their hands over their mouths to choke back their laughter.

The nurse kept Sarah in her room under observation that night. The next day the rash had gone down, but Sarah still looked sick. The nurse sent her back to her room, but excused her from classes on Friday. The nurse knew that Sarah always went home on the weekends, but not this one. This was one sick girl.

The nurse said to Sarah, "You'll have to stay at school for the weekend. I'll notify your parents. You stay in your room and take this medicine and you should be all right by Monday."

"But I have to get home. I can't miss a Sabbath from my family." Sarah looked like she was about to cry.

"I'm sorry Sarah, but not this weekend. You'll have to have Sabbath alone."

"But my parents will be angry with me. I've never missed a Sabbath."

"I'll make sure they are told."

"All right." Sarah looked as sad as she could be.

Back in her room, the girls were waiting. "So, did it work?"

Sarah smiled. "Like a cherry strudel."

"Let's go celebrate," Gretchen said.

"All right," said Sarah, "but no ice cream."

That was how Sarah got to go to her first dance.

On the night of the dance, all of the Jewish girls were extremely nervous. Sarah's hives were back without the ice cream helper, Gretchen had chewed her nails to a pulp, Rebecca had unexpectantly had to go home, Esther kept asking the others what to wear, Sally spent the day trying to get into a borrowed girdle, and the two Ruth's had become one. This was their first un-chaperoned social event with boys and they were scared out of their pipics (belly buttons). While there would be some Jewish boys (the mensches), there would be many more gentile boys (the goys). What would they do if one of the goyish boys asked them to dance? This was forbidden in their communities and more than likely vice versa.

There would also be all the goyish girls looking them over, you know too much makeup, not enough makeup, breasts sticking out, skirts too short and so on, concluding that no matter what they did it wasn't right. It was all right for one of the gentile girls to dance with (or do other things) with a Jewish boy (as they made the best husbands), but not all right for a Jewish girl to dance (or even talk) with a gentile boy. It was enough to make one not want to grow up, and who needed boys anyway. Sarah was feeling guilty that she had allowed Gretchen to talk her into this. All she could think of was having a lousy, uncomfortable time and her parents finding out about her deception.

At the dance, the Jewish girls clustered in a circle, which allowed them to watch the boys but not for the boys to watch them. The girls would rate the boys (regardless of religious background) as they walked by. "He's cute, he's built, and he's nice and so on."

As time went by, all of the Jewish girls were asked to dance by Jewish boys of course, except for Sarah and Sally. Sarah was two to three years younger than the other girls and looked it. Although she was almost sixteen and developing into a woman, she was still far away. The other girls had developed obvious breasts and attractive legs. Sarah was still in the development stage. Sally, on the other hand, was too over developed; she scared the boys.

Sarah and Sally sat in chairs against the wall watching the other girls dance. Neither one of them was very happy, but they had to look happy in case one of them was asked to dance. Sarah wasn't very good at such deceptions and eventually her head started to droop. A number of dances passed by and the two of them still sat, with hope dwindling.

Sally poked Sarah in the side and said excitingly "That boy over there is staring at you. I think he likes you."

Sarah looked up and found Gustav across the room indeed staring at her. She stared back, but then looked away so as not to encourage him. Although she had become a little friendly with him as they shared three classes, she still considered him a mite weird. He was also of the gentile persuasion and her parents had taught her not to get involved with that kind. He had probably been told the same thing in reverse.

Sally poked Sarah in the side again. "Look, he's coming over here. He's still staring at you."

"Oh my God, Sal, what should I do?"

"Try smiling or hide."

Sarah decided to smile. Things couldn't get worse—so what did she have to lose?

Gustav was standing directly in front of her, still staring and it was scary. Gustav stuttered and stumbled over Sarah's chair. He was a cute klutz.

"Hi, Sarah, enjoying the dance?"

It was obvious that she wasn't enjoying the dance. What could she say? She hesitated and looked down at her shoes.

Gustav stood; Sarah sat—neither saying a word.

Sally finally spoke up. "She would love to dance. Thank you, Gustav."

Oh my God, thought Sarah, what was she doing? Do I have to dance?

Gustav said nothing but put his hand out, and Sarah took it. He picked her up off the chair with little effort. He was pretty strong for a thin boy.

Sarah looked back at Sally. "You sure you'll be all right? I don't have to dance."

"You go ahead, I'm used to this."

Gustav looked at Sally for the first time. "Wait a minute, I be right back."

Gustav came back in a minute with a rather chubby boy (well all right a fat boy).

Gustav bowed toward Sally. "This is Siegfried, Siegfried this is Sally. You two dance too."

They all went to the dance floor. The band was playing a swing tune. Sarah was amazed Gustav could dance so well (for a klutzy goy) and Gustav was equally amazed that Sarah could dance so well (Jewish girls didn't dance or enjoy life in those days). It turned out that both had practiced dancing with their siblings—Sarah with her brother Max and Gustav with his sister Greta. They danced together the rest of the night, without saying much at all to each other.

Gustav would bring her something to eat or drink between dances, but said very little. He continued to stare at her as they danced and between dances. It was awkward for Sarah, but she would rather keep dancing with Gustav than go back to her chair. Besides, Sally and Siegfried were dancing and laughing across the floor. She would be sitting by herself, about the only girl at the dance sitting alone. Sally and Siegfried were terrible dancers, bumping into and stomping on the other dancers, but they seemed to be having fun. So, why couldn't she and Gustav have fun as well? It was her first real time with a boy, but Gustav must have a lot of experience. He must be over eighteen.

It was the last dance of the night, typically a slow romantic number. Sarah didn't know what to do. Swing tunes were fine, but a slow dance. She didn't know where to put her hands or how to hold Gustav. She wanted to leave the dance floor, but Gustav held on. He pulled her closer to him and tried to hold her, but it was apparent that he was as awkward as Sarah. They finally just started dancing and their bodies came together. Sarah was amazed at how comfortable it felt being entwined with Gustav. He was really very gentle and gave her space to breathe. Some of the other couples were so close together, Sarah felt suffocated just looking at them.

After the dance, Gustav very awkwardly asked if he and Siegfried could walk Sarah and Sally back to their rooms. Before Sarah could say no, Sally said quickly "That would be charming." Sally and Siegfried walked ahead of them, holding each other very closely and laughing as they went. Sarah and Gustav walked behind in silence. Gustav tried to hold her hand, but she resisted. When they came to their building, Sally and Siegfried were already embracing and kissing. Gustav looked awkwardly at Sarah and tried to move closer, but

Sarah moved away. Gustav stumbled toward her and kissed her on the cheek.

"Thank you, Sarah," stuttered Gustav.

Sarah said nothing, but turned and ran into the building. She liked Gustav in his awkward ways, but didn't want to encourage a gentile boy.

As the days passed, Gustav became more and more attentive toward Sarah. He would carry her books (picking them up before she could gather them, as hard as she tried) for her between classes, walk her back to her room after classes, and meet her first thing in the morning at her building to walk her to their first class. They started talking to each other and found out that they had very much in common. They liked the same books, the same professors, the same healthy foods, quiet times, and were both solitary beings. He was a philosophy major; she was a literature major. However, Gustav liked literature almost as much as philosophy, and Sarah liked philosophy almost as much as literature. Eventually, they both had joint majors, philosophy and literature.

The other girls kidded Sarah about Gustav, her goy (instead of boy) friend. Sally and Siegfried were now going out steadily, but the girls didn't kid her, as Sally wouldn't care. Sarah, however, did care. She liked Gustav more and more, but didn't know what to do about it. They were spending almost all of their time together and she had started lying to her parents about not being able to come home on weekends anymore, too much studying, term reports and projects, visiting her friends and so on.

One night she had finally decided to tell Gustav that they shouldn't see each other any more. There was no place for this to go. Although they hadn't done anything more physical than kiss by touching each other's lips, she didn't know for how much longer this would be enough for Gustav. After all, he was a male, and a goy, and all they wanted to do was have sex with a Jewish girl. Gustav seemed different, but was he really?

They were sitting together on a bench outside of her building. Gustav put his arm around her. She moved quickly away.

"No Gustav, we have to stop this. I don't think I should see you any more." Sarah felt sad and ready to cry at any moment. Gustav had become her best friend—ever. It just didn't seem fair that they couldn't stay together.

"But," Gustav started and stopped. "But, I love you, you are my life. Without you, there is no life." Gustav looked stupefied. "I was going to ask you to come meet my parents this weekend. I know that they will love you too."

Sarah held back her tears as best she could, but tiny drops appeared at the corners of her eyes and slipped down her cheeks. "Oh, Gustav, don't you see, this can't be. I wish it could, but it can't."

Gustav was crying slowly now as well, fighting back the tears. "Sarah, what is it, you don't love me. That's all right. I love you for both of us. You'll see it will be all right."

"No, Gustav, it won't be all right. It will never be all right. Not a Jew and a gentile in our lifetimes, not in Germany or Austria. I'm sorry Gustav." The tears had taken over; Sarah didn't care.

"So, you don't love me, is that it? Not to worry." Gustav had stopped fighting his tears.

"Oh, it's not our love; its other's hate. They won't let us love. Don't you understand that?"

"Yes, Sarah, I understand. My parents don't like the Jews and your parents don't like the gentiles. But, you and me, we love each other, no?"

Sarah sank into Gustav's shoulder and cried uncontrollably. She tried to talk but only more tears came out. She was finally able to say choked full of tears "Yes, Gustav, I love you, but I can't. Too much love will kill us both."

They were both crying onto each other uncontrollably, each one dabbing at the other's tears, trying to make them stop. He was crying for what he wanted to do but couldn't, she was crying for what she could do but didn't want to.

"So, you'll come with me to my parents. I will tell them Friday night. All right?"

"Yes Gustav, all right."

They stopped crying and held onto each other desperately maybe for the last time. It was way past the university curfew, but neither one of them cared.

That weekend they went to Gustav's parents' house, six kilometers to the north. This would be the first Friday night Sarah had spent with any other family but her own—particularly a gentile family. Gustav had told his parents all about Sarah without mentioning too much of her background. Once his parents met Sarah, he was sure they would feel the same way that he did about her. How could anyone not like Sarah? She was so special and he loved her so much. They just had to like her; they just had to.

Gustav's parents, Mr. and Mrs. Guffmann, greeted Sarah with open arms. She was their oldest son's choice and they wanted to like her. Mr. Guffmann was an engineer at the local water works. Mrs. Guffmann was a housewife and mother, the traditional role for women at that time. They were the typical German husband and wife of the times; they could have been the poster couple for German family recruiting. Their house was very quaint with an elaborate collection of Hummel pieces and other German figurines and glassware displayed throughout the house. Sarah thought that the house could be a museum of German superiority in craftsmanship. Mrs. Guffmann walked with Sarah around the house while Gustav went with his father into the Black Forest like paneled den, for a man to son talk.

As Mrs. Guffmann showed Sarah the house she would point out each piece and describe how they had acquired it, the worth of the piece, its present inflated appreciated value, and how superior it was to other country's work. She would also question Sarah as they walked through the house. The questioning was casual, but very, very thorough.

"Sarah," Mrs. Guffmann asked, "what kind of name is that?"

"It's a biblical name," Sarah answered.

"Where do your parents live?" Mrs. Guffmann asked.

"Munich," Sarah answered.

"And which church do they attend? Maybe we know some

of the members." Gustav had told Sarah that his parents were strict Lutherans—his father being an elder in the church. They, of course, had expected their eldest son to marry someone from the church, maybe that nice Bronfmann girl. Her father was an attorney, and very well respected.

"Oh, they are not very religious," Sarah answered with a smile.

Mrs. Guffmann picked up a fine sculptured German made ivory carving of Jesus on the cross.

"But you must have Jesus in your home and your hearts."

Sarah answered too quickly. "No, no, we would never have that!"

"No, and why not. You are not a good Christian?"

Sarah could take no more of this charade. The hell with this pompous German Lutheran woman. The hell with her being Gustav's mother.

"Jews aren't good Christians." Sarah looked blankly at Mrs. Guffmann. There was nothing more to say. The yarmulke was out of the talus bag.

"Oh, my God, you're Jewish. My Gustav brings a Jewish girl for us to meet. This can't be so. Gustav knows this?" The ivory Jesus fell from her hands and broke into many pieces, but she didn't notice. Jesus couldn't help her with this one.

"Gustav loves me. It doesn't matter."

"Oh, it matters to us." Mrs. Guffmann called out so loudly that the angels in heaven or the demons in Hell could hear her. "Heinrich, Gustav has brought us a Jewess, come quick."

Gustav and his father rushed in, his father to his mother's side, Gustav to Sarah's side.

"Gustav, she is Jewish. You brought us a Jewish girl to meet?" He looked down sternly at his son.

"Poppa, I love her. I'm going to marry her."

Mr. Guffmann quickly and with malice slapped Gustav across the face.

"You marry who we tell you to. Now please take her from our house."

Sarah could see the finger marks across Gustav's face. He

struggled not to cry in front of her and his parents. He must stay in control.

"If she leaves, I go with her. I never thought I would be ashamed of you. You call yourselves Christian. Sarah is more Christian than the two of you."

His father smacked him across the face again.

"You leave my house immediately. And take your little Jewess with you. When you are ready to respect your parents, then you can return. This is still my house and you are my son."

"Sarah doesn't stay, I don't stay. Come Sarah, we will go."

Gustav and Sarah walked briskly toward the door.

"Gustav, who's going to eat the pot roast? I spent all morning cooking." Mrs. Guffmann couldn't comprehend what was happening. A visit from her son had turned into a shambles.

As Gustav and Sarah walked away from the house, Gustav put his arm around her and kissed her on the cheek. "I'm sorry Sarah, I didn't know."

Sarah looked up at him lovingly. "I knew this would happen, but you had to see it for yourself."

"Sarah, they are still my parents." The tears came running down Gustav's face, way out of his control.

Sarah took Gustav's hand and squeezed firmly. She reached up and kissed him on the cheek.

They walked in silence for quite some time. There was really nothing more to say. They were in love, but the world wasn't in love with them.

When they got back to school, Sarah tried not seeing Gustav. Gustav, however, was persistent. He would be at her door first thing in the morning, pick up her books after every class (even those they didn't have together), meet her at the last class to walk her back to her building and so on. Sarah wouldn't say anything, but he persisted in telling her how much he loved her. The more times he told her, the more adamant she was in her decision to not let this happen, she loved him too much to let him do this. She knew, if not in her heart, than in her head that he would be much better off with one of his own kind, a good, obedient, German Lutheran girl.

Sally and Siegfried, on Gustav's behalf, tried to work on Sarah. They talked up Gustav whenever they could and asked her to join them and Gustav just happened to show up. They, Gustav, Sally, and Siegfried, persisted in wearing her down. She finally agreed to go out with them and have Gustav come along, but they were to stay together as a foursome. When she met them at a club they all used to go to together, Gustav sat gloomily by himself. What a puppy dog, she thought.

Neither of them said much to each other the entire night. Sally and Siegfried got up to dance and Sarah went to the bathroom where she cried and washed her face, and then cried and washed her face again. It was the worst night she ever spent.

As they all walked back to the girl's dorm building together, Gustav took Sarah's hand. She neither pulled away, nor pulled closer. They walked behind in silence, as Sally and Siegfried jabbered in front of them. At the building, Sally and Siegfried entered and left them outside. Sarah looked up at Gustav to say good bye once again, she knew it just wouldn't work As she was getting ready to speak and run through the door, Gustav grabbed her and kissed her like he had never done before. She was consumed. Her first response was to run, for her life. However, she couldn't move. Her head knew better, but her heart knew what she really wanted. She kissed him back furiously like she was going to lose him and of course she was.

Gustav panted incoherently. "Sarah, I love you. Please marry me."

Sarah's breasts heaved, her heart raced, her pulse jumped, her body hair stood on end, she gulped to swallow, she kissed Gustav to save her life, and held onto him lest her legs buckle.

"Gustav, we just can't."

"We will have each other. The hell with the others."

"Yes, Gustav, the hell with the others."

That night they made love for the first time—on the ground in front of the dorm building. It was the best love for each of them.

It would and could not ever be the same.

Three weeks later the university chaplain married them. Sally and Siegfried and Gretchen were the only one's in attendance. They lived together from that day forth. Sarah was sixteen years old and Gustav was nineteen. They were still children, but they were together. Life was looking up.

Gustav never spoke again to his parents after that first visit to their house. He knew that his parents knew that he had married Sarah through his sister—the only one of the family he had contact with. They sent him a Hummel piece as a wedding gift. He smashed it into little pieces and sent it back to them.

Sarah sent a letter to her parents notifying them that she had married Gustav who was German Lutheran. They sent back a notice of her death and the sitting of Shiva—the Jewish tradition of mourning a dead family member. She knew this would happen. This was the price of love and she was willing to pay it. She was to never see her family again. So much for religious principles; and so much for humanity.

Points to ponder:

We all grow up being taught that our group is better than the others; be it based on ethnicity, religion, race, or income. Maybe this is a group defense mechanism or maybe just wishful thinking for survival. Regardless, while one group is spouting hate against the other and vice versa, individual members of each group may get lucky and find each other like Sarah and Gustav—taking the difficult path but maybe the right one for them. Here are some points to ponder from their story.

1. Sarah and Gustav grew up in different worlds—Sarah in a Jewish culture that was always fearful of the gentile dominant culture, Gustav as part of the dominant culture. Why do societal sub-groups, the dominant and the oppressed, tend to isolate themselves rather

than share the different experiences of diversity?

2. Sarah was brought up with the message to fear the others, while Gustav was taught the superiority of his culture. Why do societal subgroups work to maintain their individual identities rather than mix with the world in general?
3. In spite of societal and parental pressures, Sarah and Gustav found each other, even understanding the difficulties staying together would cause. Is learned behavior stronger than our basic instincts? Why does learned behavior keep us ignorant about others with a strong unwillingness to change our beliefs?
4. Sarah and Gustav found themselves in love, but neither set of parents approved of their union. Gustav's parents disowned him while Sarah's parents considered her dead. Can love really conquer all obstacles, especially inbred family and cultural hatreds?
5. Sarah and Gustav found themselves at a fairly early age, but felt strongly that what they shared was right. Can a sixteen-year old girl and a nineteen-year old boy experience a love that is counter to their adult world's belief system? Do they really know what they are doing and what is in store for them in the "real world?"
6. Sarah and Gustav found their own island of literature and philosophy that they felt was strong enough to sustain them. Can love, real love, be stronger than family and community ties? Can such love be worth forfeiting family and community?
7. Sarah and Gustav, both isolates in the social world, were able to construct their stories to exclude most outside influences. Can individuals and couples really isolate themselves from the disapproving world and family around them?
8. There are many influences and pressures that try to change an individuals thinking and actions making it easier to be accepted than to remain an outsider. Can an isolated life of literature and philosophy that Sarah and Gustav chose for themselves, or some other intense interest, sustain an individual or a couple for sufficient existence in today's ever changing world?
9. Sarah and Gustav tried to live as they desired, but eventually the others invaded their lives. Are we all vulnerable, in spite of our best efforts, to be pulled into the world of tragedy and danger?

10. Sarah and Gustav worked hard for the life they wanted and to forget the past as it negatively impacted on them. Can we ever totally forget our past and move on undisturbed? Is there really such a thing as starting over or beginning again?
11. Eventually Sarah and Gustav's past brought them to the reality that the others won't let you be who you wanted to be. Can you imagine a world without artificial barriers such as ethnicicity, religion, culture, class and level of income? What would it look like?
12. Sarah and Gustav married in spite of their parents' and society's dissent. When they have children, can their isolated world be passed on to that child without that child being touched by outside influences?

Why are we so afraid of "the other," when the other is us?

Karen's Story

Inheriting the Story

Seven month's after their marriage, Sarah and Gustav's daughter Karen, was born in Munich, Germany in 1923, between the two world wars—without grandparents. She was to be the only child of Sarah (nee Wiedermann) and Gustav Guffmann. As an only child, she was raised with all of the advantages that upper middle class parents could provide at that time. Karen's tale, like most people, began with her parents' story. Sarah and Gustav would not bring another child into this world; they could not. Sarah went on to get a doctorate in literature and Gustav a doctorate in philosophy. They loved each other deeply; they hated the world of intolerance. It was their first love, their only love and their last love. They lived in the world of ideas. They hoped they could save some souls from the Nazis of the world through their teaching. They won a few battles over the years but in the end they lost. They raised and protected Karen from the unloving outside world. She grew up among books, concerts, lectures, music and art lessons, nannies and tutors. She was a child of the intelligentsia, and knew little about the world outside. She had everything she needed for a healthy mind, but lacked an extended human family and a spiritual core. She was very happy in her world and that of her parents.

It was now 1939 and Karen was sixteen years old. While Munich remained the cultural capitol of Germany, the rest of Germany was in turmoil. Hitler and the Nazi party had taken over control of Germany and they were moving against Germany's natural enemies—the Jews, Gypsies, homosexuals, intelligentsia, people of color, communists, non-party members and so on. Sarah and Gustav were afraid for Karen, for in her protected life she knew nothing of life and its political realities. To the Nazis her worth was measured in terms of a Jewish mother and a non-Nazi professor of philosophy.

They made arrangements through their friends Sally and Siegfried, who had gotten married a short time after Sarah and Gustav (they didn't want to be left behind) to get Karen safely out of Germany to the United States to live with an aunt of Sally's in New York. Jewish Sally and Lutheran Siegfried gave up their family and religions, but they didn't care and were too selfish to have children. Siegfried had some friends in the Nazi party and they felt safe.

Sarah and Gustav planned to join Karen as soon as they could, but as devoted college professors they couldn't leave their students in the middle of a semester. They were both beloved members of the faculty community.

Karen was scheduled to leave on a Russian ship in October of 1939. However, within a week of the scheduled departure the Nazi party canceled the sailing date. No reason was given as none had to be given. It was suspected that this fleet of Russian ships was illegally transporting undesirables out of Germany. The Nazi party, so it seems, didn't want them there to despoil the real Germans, but didn't want them to leave either. They would provide their own solution to this problem, a more humanitarian solution.

Siegfried, who it turned out really had some connections with the Nazi party, but who himself insisted he wasn't a Nazi, was able at the last minute to get Karen on a Portuguese ship leaving that very night. They had to decide quickly. As they didn't know when such an opportunity would again present itself, they took it. Siegfried set it up that Karen would travel with a cousin of his, Lilly, who was desperate to leave Germany—for other reasons that the police knew. The cousin was over 20 years old, rather unattractive and would provide protection for Karen. As this was a freighter vessel, there wouldn't be many other passengers on board, but Siegfried assured them it was safe. For what they paid the Captain, he would make sure of their safe passage.

Karen and Lilly were given a cabin way below deck and far away from the crew. For the first three days and nights on board, the two girls kept to themselves. The only other human they saw was the deck hand, Stosh, who brought and picked up their meals.

He was somewhat retarded but nice. Karen, with her gentle nature, was sea sick a good part of the time. By the fourth day, they both needed some air, so they went up on deck. This was the first glimpse and knowledge that the crew had that any women were on board. The only other passengers were a group of twelve elderly male Lutheran missionaries. While the two girls were left alone on captain's orders, the crew noticed them.

Although Lilly was indeed unattractive, she was still female and the crew wasn't known in any ports to discriminate in their taste for women. Karen, although only sixteen, was developing and quite striking but she didn't know this or the danger that men presented. One of the crew, a rather interesting younger man, passed by and tipped his cap to them. Karen smiled at him. The name on his shirt said Tony.

As it was extremely hot in their cabin, the girls, after the first night, had relaxed into wearing nothing to sleep in. They were far away from the crew and the Captain had instructed them on how to double lock the cabin door and not to open it for anyone. They felt safe. For the first three nights they slept uneasily but undisturbed.

About three in the morning on the fourth night there was a knock on the door. The girls didn't hear it at first, but the knocking persisted and got louder. They sat up in bed and pulled the sheets over them and hid their faces under the sheets.

"Come on, I know you're in there. Stosh told me—it cost me plenty. Come on, its Tony, I'm your friend from the deck."

The girls cowered together on Lilly's cot-like bed. Karen was scared. This was nothing like Munich.

"Go away you ugly man or we'll tell the captain." Lilly spoke shakily.

"Go ahead, tell the captain. I only wanted to say hello."

"Sure," said Lilly, "Just go away."

"All right, but I'll be back."

They heard his footsteps as he left. They couldn't sleep the rest of the night; Lilly holding Karen close in her bed, but Tony never returned. The next day they told the captain and he said he would talk to Tony and not to worry, they were safe on his ship. Never been any trouble before in his eighteen years as a captain. Of course, there had never been any women on board.

The next night the two girls went to bed in their clothes. They couldn't sleep, so they talked about their new lives in America. Karen told Lilly about her parents and how much she missed them. She started to cry. To make Karen feel better Lilly told her story of parental abuse. How her parents were alcoholics and forced her into a life on the streets. When she got into trouble how her parents threw her out of the house. She told Karen of the horrors of living off the streets, never knowing whether she would ever eat again. When her cousin Siegfried approached her about going with Karen to America, she seized the opportunity. Anything had to be better than the streets of Germany in 1939. This was a part of Karen's education that she had missed.

As they were talking and hugging into the night, there was a scratching at the door. The girls' bodies tensed and they held each other more tightly. Karen was petrified, but Lilly put on her street face. They watched from the far reaches of Lilly's small cot as the bottom lock turned and opened. They shivered, knowing it was Tony, but thanked God for the double bolt on the top of the door. This would keep him out and he would eventually go away. The fear, however, did not go away.

There was a crashing at the door. The girls cowered into the corner of the room—Karen holding onto Lilly and her book of Nietzsche for her life. They heard Tony speaking through the door. Their worst fears were realized.

Tony was shouting. "Get back, let the big Polack do it. Come on Stosh."

There was a loud crash and the door burst and an enormous sailor fell into their small room and onto Karen's bed crushing it as he fell. Thank God Karen wasn't in the bed.

Tony, and four other men came into the room. They glowered and salivated at the girls. The girls moved closer to the corner of the room and cowered there. You can get out of Germany, but you can't get away from the Nazis of the world. Karen's parents were so right, but it was too late.

The room was really too small for all of them. Stosh had moved to the doorway to make room for the others, but there was still no room to move, nor for Karen and Lilly to escape. Karen couldn't stop screaming and crying. Lilly tried to be brave for both of them, but she knew it was hopeless.

"Leave us alone, you filthy pigs," Lilly shouted at them and spit at Tony.

Tony grabbed at Lilly, but she was able to push him off.

"Heinie, give me a hand here, I have a little German Nazi tiger by the tail."

Tony with Heinie's help pulled the two girls apart. They hit, kicked, spat, screamed, and fought as hard as they could, but they were no match for two hardened sailors. They would have their way and do what they wanted. Heine and one of the other sailors held Lilly down on her bed, while the two other sailors held Karen down on the floor. Stosh stayed by the door. Tony looked over his choices. He looked at Lilly and then at Karen, and looked again.

"Take the Jewess, leave me alone," Lilly screamed. Once again the gentile had betrayed the Jew and once again there was nothing the Jew could do about it.

"A Jewish virgin Christ killer, eh. I think I go for revenge this time. Age and experience can wait. I do the whore next." Tony looked back at Lilly. She knew he knew.

Tony moved toward Karen. She struggled as best as she could, but the two sailors had her pinned to the floor. Her parents had sent her off to safety, but where was that for a Jew at that time?

Tony moved closer, the sailors arms tightened about her, and her eyes left her head. Tony straddled Karen's body. She squirmed as much as she could, but there was no way she could get away from Tony. He had a knife in his hand with a long, sharp blade. One of the sailor's had his enormous hand over her mouth so she couldn't scream out loud, but she heard her screams in her head (and still does) until she lost her entire sense of reality. She watched terrified as if it was someone else as Tony cut her clothes off and stood back and savored her young body.

"Very nice, very nice indeed. Pure virgin meat. The best for Tony."

He ran the knife blade up and down her body, caressing but not cutting.

Tony jumped back suddenly and tore his clothes off. He stood naked casting a large ominous shadow over Karen's small body. Even Nietzsche couldn't save her from this.

Tony had an enormous penis and it was sticking straight out over Karen's face. She had never seen a penis before and had no idea they were this ugly. Karen couldn't imagine what he would do with that thing. Tony ran his penis over Karen exactly as he had caressed her with his knife. One was as terrifying as the other to Karen.

At Tony's signal, the other two sailors pulled Karen's legs far apart so that she was in extreme pain. As she screamed from the pain, Tony worked his fingers into Karen's vagina, she screamed even louder, but only she could hear. She screamed herself out of her mind and her soul died at that very moment. She lay there, but the "real she" wasn't there.

Karen had never felt pain like this, but Tony took his time. With each thrust into her, Karen lost a piece of herself. When Tony was finally finished with a long gasp and fell from her, there was little left of the Karen who had got on this ship of hope.

Tony nodded to the sailor holding her right arm and leg. Tony took his place holding her down, and the other sailor raped Karen. By this time Karen had lost all fight and they didn't need to hold her down or gag her. This allowed them to move around freely while two held down Lilly. They systematically repeatedly raped Karen until all the sailors, with the exception of Stosh, had their turn. As Karen moaned, they were able to leave her and start working on Lilly.

Tony went first, redoing his knife routine on Lilly. It went easier than with Karen as Lilly was far from a virgin. Lilly saw no way out, so she lay passively as each one had their turn. Getting raped was unavoidable, but at least she could give them the least pleasure possible. Men were pigs and they deserved no pleasure from her.

When they were all done, they left Karen and Lilly lying curled up on the floor. Only Stosh remained at the door. As Tony left he yelled over his shoulder "They're all yours Stosh," and laughed cynically.

When they had left, Stosh slowly moved into the room. He was at least twice as large as any of the other sailors. Karen and Lilly cowered at what was in store for them. Hadn't they had enough? If Stosh had his way, it would kill them. Stosh came over to Karen and looked down at her. There was pity and a trace of a tear in his eyes. He reached down to touch her and Karen instinctively pulled away in horror.

"Get away from her, you big dumb ugly Polack fuck. Haven't you shits done enough?"

Lily screamed over and over again.

Stosh moved closer to her. He had her clothes in his hands and was handing them to her.

"They shouldn't have done this to you. You're so beautiful. I shouldn't have helped them. They said you were both sick and couldn't get out. I helped them. I'm sorry." Stosh, the gentle giant, was crying.

Stosh helped them both get cleaned up and get their clothes on. He sat on the floor while the two of them slept. Stosh made sure none of the others would return. He did this each night for the rest of the journey. Stosh fixed the door and the locks. Karen spent her days locked in the room reading her books; her reality was better than the real reality. Lilly cowered on her bed and stared into space. The two of them never spoke to each other again. Stosh would come each night and sit by Karen's bed until the morning. They were left alone. They never told the captain. Tony would kill them as he had promised and the captain too.

Stosh walked Karen and Lilly down the gangplank, each one holding onto one of his enormous arms. Stosh made sure that they both got down safely and wouldn't leave their sides until they were safely picked up. The other sailors wouldn't bother them with Stosh protecting them; they were safe with Stosh.

Sally's aunt Sophie was waiting right in front of the boat with a bright red scarf tossed around her neck as promised. They recognized each other from photographs exchanged through the mail. There was no mistaking Aunt Sophie. She was an imposing woman, almost six feet tall compared to Karen's five foot one and a half inches. She was as big for a woman at that time as Stosh was for a man. Aunt Sophie hugged Karen so hard that tears came to Karen's eyes. When Stosh had Karen safely in Sophie's hands, he finally let go of her. Karen reached up and gently kissed Stosh on the cheek. He blushed and backed off onto the boat. As he went back up the gangplank, he waved feebly at her and then disappeared. Karen would never see him again in person, but forever in her memories and dreams.

An elderly weathered man picked up Lilly. They recognized each other by looking at photographs and searching the features of each other. More than likely the photographs were not recent ones. Karen learned later that this was a mail order-bride situation. This was the only way the German authorities would release her to Siegfried's custody and drop the prostitution charges against her. The elderly gentlemen seemed pleased with Lilly, even if she didn't quite match her photograph. Of course he didn't either. They walked off hand in hand, seemingly pleased with their deal. Karen never saw Lilly again. Years later she heard from Sally that Lilly had killed herself two years later.

Karen lived with Aunt Sophie in her little house in the Bronx section of New York City. This was to be the only neighborhood that Karen would ever know in the great land of America. Karen would sit for hours in her little bedroom in Sophie's house staring at the walls or reading one of the books her parents had given her for her journey. This was her one and only connection to the world. Sophie went to work each day and Karen took care of the house—an acceptable arrangement for both of them. In the evenings, after dinner prepared by Karen, they would sit in the parlor and talk about their days in Munich. Karen talked to no one else.

Karen would write her parents at least twice a week telling them how wonderful America was and all the things she had seen and done. The details were taken out of newspapers and magazines; they were all some other person's life. Her life was confined to Aunt Sophie's little house in the Bronx. Her parents wrote back telling her of their plans to join her, they loved and missed her so. However, each time they set a date to depart, something seemed to come up that prevented their departure. Sometimes it was a student who needed one or both of them, an obligation to the university, a birthday or anniversary, and so on. Munich was their home, their daughter was safe and well in America, and they were Germans above all, the Nazis wouldn't bother them.

Karen continued writing to her parents, as she had no one else. Life with them seemed like a faint memory, someone else's life. She lived her fantasies of the American life through her letters. Nothing was true, but what did it matter. They continued to write about their plans to join her, but now she didn't want them. Her life was over. Her parents couldn't protect her now.

It was now 1942 and the war in Europe was accelerating. There were rumors that the Nazis were rounding up all of their internal enemies in Germany and the countries they had conquered and were putting them into concentration camps. There were stories of mass murders and atrocities. Karen should have been more concerned about her parents, but she found it difficult to care about anything anymore. Her soul was dead, only her body survived.

A little after this, a letter arrived from her Aunt Sally. She hadn't heard from her since her initial arrival in America. She was afraid to open the letter. What could she want? It was a short note, probably written and posted in a hurry. The note said simply:

"Your parents have been taken by the Nazis. Jews and intellectuals are no longer welcome in our homeland. We are escaping to France tonight. God bless." The letter was signed simply Sally. No last name and no address.

Karen never heard from her parents again. They were finally

together in their world of ideas and she was alone. She never read another book again. She ripped up her parent's books page-by-page—and fed each page into the fireplace. This was the end of the world of ideas and ideals—literature and philosophy. She was now all alone, a Jew in a Nazi world. She was to stay in this house the rest of her life. She sat and waited in fear for the Nazis to come and take her.

Points to ponder:

If we are lucky we have good parents who protect us. But, sometimes through this protection they make us vulnerable to the evils and unforeseen events of the world. When one knows the dimensions of a real or imagined fear it may be less or more threatening when the individual ultimately faces it. Some try to survive with outward strength like Lilly, others try to survive with inward strength gained from books and literature like Karen, and others are unprepared when disaster strikes.

1. Sarah and Gustav decided on an isolated life of literature and philosophy; reacting from parents and a world that had turned on them. Why do parents, especially those who bear negative feelings about society, feel the need to protect their children from the dangers of the world that they perceive as parents?
2. Sarah and Gustav helped their daughter Karen to lead a safe and protected life away from mainstream society that could negatively impact their daughter. Are children safer by developing their physical strength, knowing that there are always others who will be stronger than them; or are they safer by developing their inward strength and self-confidence?
3. Karen grew up in the world of books, being saved from dealing with the mean cruel world by her parents. Why is there a tendency for individuals to be persuaded into believing and fearing the evil ones rather than welcoming the righteous ones?
4. While Sarah and Gustav tried to live their tales and that of their

daughter Karen's within their own world eventually the Nazis came after them. What delight do people derive from subjugating and witnessing other's fears, degradation, pain, and shame?

5. Karen, having been brought up in a safe protected world by her parents knew little of the evils of the world. However, this only made her more vulnerable for someone like Tony to take advantage of her. What makes a bully and gives them the right to use their power, physical or psychological, over others?
6. While Tony and the other four sailors had their way with Karen and Lilly, Stosh stayed by the door. When the others left Stosh befriended them and protected them until they left the ship. Where do righteous thoughts and behaviors, like Stosh's, come from in an otherwise non-righteous climate of negative group behavior?
7. Karen watched unable to do anything about it as Tony and the others violated her body. What affect does such bodily torture and shame have on the soul of an individual? Can the soul die before the person physically dies? What is the soul?
8. When Tony and the other sailors came after Karen and Lilly, Lilly gave up Karen by telling them to take the Jewess first, hopefully to save herself. Are we all susceptible to giving up the other, as Lilly did to Karen, to save ourselves, regardless of the consequences to the other?
9. Stosh, the slow witted large Polack, was coerced by Tony to tell him where Karen and Liily's room was under the guise of them being sick. In the end, it was Stosh who protected them from further attacks. What is human instinct, such as what surfaced in Stosh that allowed him to rescue Karen and Lilly? Do the dim witted have more compassion than those whose thinking is intact?
10. Karen, as a result of what happened to her on the boat, lived a life of fear and solitude in Aunt Sally's house. Can a traumatic fear such as that experienced by Karen guide the remainder of your life? Can such a trauma effectively stop one from functioning normally again?
11. Karen loved her parents and what they had done for her. However, when they were no longer available to protect her and the Nazis seized them, she rejected them. Why does one either embrace or deplore the attributes, beliefs, behaviors, and values of their parents? Why do such beliefs become turning points in one's life?

12. Karen tried to live her life from her parents' belief systems. When she was raped and then realized that the Nazis had taken her parents, she turned on these beliefs by burning the books that represented them. Can parents implant upon their children those characteristics that they desire for them? Are such characteristics able to be changed?

Wait long enough and do nothing
and they will come after you.

The Birth of the Angel's

Old world, New world

Giovanni Santangelo was born in a small Italian village about 100 miles south of Rome to working class parents. His father was a stonemason and his mother was a peasant woman who took care of the family of eight children. Carmen Petrazinni, of the same village was also born to working class parents. Her father was a storekeeper of a small Italian grocery and her mother helped in the store while raising their six children. Giovanni and Carmen both had very little growing up as their village was poor and it took quite a lot to raise such large families. The Santangelo and Petrazinni families were on very friendly terms and the children all played together. Giovanni and Carmen were friends almost from birth as they were born within a month of each other. They never knew life without each other. They were raised to be hard workers and had to contribute to the family from the time they were about eight years old. Giovanni would help his father in his stonemason business or when there wasn't any work he would find work running errands for one of the merchants in town. Carmen was expected to help in the store with the other children so that her mother could get some rest (particularly during one of her pregnancies) or so that her parents could have some time together.

As teenagers, Giovanni and Carmen would sneak off and meet whenever they could. They both talked of getting away from such an oppressive life filled with too much poverty and too many children. He was a very serious and studious boy. The other siblings in his family were forced to quit school when they turned twelve years old. His mother, by withdrawing her body from her husband, convinced her husband to allow Giovanni to finish school. He would be the first in the family to finish high school. Carmen, on the other hand, being a girl had no choice but to quit school after the fifth grade. Giovanni would talk to Carmen about what he was learning and she would fantasize about a world where she and her children would be free to be educated. There was no doubt by either one of them that they would be married as soon as they could and get away from this village.

Giovanni finished high school when he was sixteen years old. His father expected him to help in his stonemason business. Giovanni was a strong boy and with his education he would be able to help the business grow. Giovanni knew that no matter what he did the business would not grow. Their village was too small and too poor. His family and he were doomed to poverty and hard work if they stayed there. Giovanni knew that his father would never let him leave—he owed his father for allowing him to finish school.

The summer after he finished high school, Giovanni worked in his father's business. It was hard work and long hours. Giovanni grew more depressed and irritable. When he was able to see Carmen even for a short time he would argue with her as if she was keeping him there. Carmen would plead with him to get out of there with her before it was too late, before he became too much like his father. He was already talking like him and bemoaning his fate. It wouldn't be too long before he too was stuck in the village of despair.

Carmen had an uncle, her mother's brother, Antonio, who lived in Rome. All of her life she had dreamed of living in Rome, the land of opportunity. When she would visit her uncle in Rome she would dream of her life of plenty, shopping at the markets buying fresh meats and produce and nice clothes and sitting in the cafes sipping espresso and talking about the world. There would always be enough money to enjoy the good life. What a difference 100 miles could make. Carmen wrote her uncle about Giovanni and pleaded with him to find a way for the two of them to escape while they could. Her uncle, who was a civil engineer for the state, wrote back that he could get Giovanni an apprentice position with the state. While it didn't pay much for now, it was an opportunity for Giovanni to become part of a profession. Giovanni could also go to the university in the evenings and obtain a degree in engineering. Antonio would be able to obtain admittance to his college for Giovanni. It would be hard work for a few years, but in the end it would pay off for them. Carmen and Giovanni, if they were married, could stay with Antonio and his wife Carmella and their two children in the small room in the back of the house. It wasn't luxurious but they would have their privacy and they would be together.

When Carmen received her uncle Antonio's letter she was excited. It wasn't much, but it was better than what they had here and it meant escape and hope. Her excitement died quickly when she showed the letter to Giovanni. He read the letter and spat on the floor. He couldn't leave his family for this—his father needed him. Carmen spat back at him. If he didn't leave his family, she was leaving him. Until he was ready to leave, she didn't want to see him again. She was leaving in two weeks and she expected him to go with her. It was her or his family. Giovanni knew what he had to do, but he couldn't.

As the time grew near for her to go, Giovanni still hadn't decided what to do. He was afraid to go and afraid to stay. The night before her planned departure, she came to say good-bye to him. She was sad, he was angry. He didn't want to see her. She told him she would be on the seven AM bus to Rome. If he was coming she would see him there. If not she would be in Rome. She put her uncle Antonio's address in his hand and left. She cried throughout the night—what would life be like without Giovanni? She would only bring her hate with her to Rome.

Carmen waited until the last moment to board the bus for Rome. She hoped to see Giovanni running for the bus, her, and freedom at the last moment but he never showed up. She cried against the bus window all the way to Rome. Although it was less than 100 miles to Rome, Carmen could only afford the local bus that stopped at every village along the way. It took her over six hours to get to Rome. Uncle Antonio and Aunt Carmella were at the bus station to meet her. She fell into Antonio's arms and cried desperately. Her Uncle and Aunt took her bags and she cried against Antonio's cheek all the way to his house.

Uncle Antonio carried her suitcases to her room while Carmella prepared some tea and cakes in the kitchen to cheer up Carmen. Antonio returned from her room with a grim look on his face. He didn't like to see his favorite niece so sad. When the tea and cakes were ready, Carmella insisted that Carmen eat them right now, they would keep her company. The tea and cakes would make her feel better. Antonio ignored Carmella and put the tea and cakes on a tray to take them to her room. "Come" he said "you'll be much better in your room."

She followed her uncle to her new room in the back of the house. It didn't matter to her. She didn't want the tea and cakes anyway. She just wanted to be alone. Uncle was right. He went in the room first and placed the tray on the small table by the bed. She stopped at the door.

"Come, Carmenita, this is your new home." She entered the room. Antonio watched her face turn from gloom to gladness. She was crying a different kind of tears now. There on the bed was Giovanni.

Giovanni had taken the express bus and beat Carmen to Rome by two hours. When Carmen had left that morning, Giovanni wouldn't get out of bed. His mother came into the room and put an envelope in his hand. He opened the envelope and found enough money for the trip to Rome on the express bus and for them to live for around six months in Rome if they were thrifty. Giovanni looked at his mother and cried. "Momma, I can't take this. This is your savings." His mother opened his closet. She had packed his clothes. "Giovanni you are the only one with a chance to leave this life. Go, Carmen needs you. She can't live without you and you can't live without her. Go, run." His mother moved the suitcases from the closet and placed them next to him. "I take care of Poppa. You go. This is what I save for."

Giovanni got up from the bed and held his mother tight and they both cried. His mother pushed him away. "Go. The express bus leaves in fifteen minutes. Go, before your father returns." She put a bus ticket in his hand. Giovanni took the suitcases and ran from the house. He looked back. His mother was lying on his bed crying into his pillow. He hesitated to stay but then ran as fast as he could, as it was his life.

Carmen ran to the bed and Giovanni. They embraced, crushing their bones against each other. Antonio closed the door quietly behind them. They made slow passionate love for the first time. When they were done they devoured the tea and cakes as they had devoured each other. Two days later they were married. In their eyes, if not the eyes of their church, they were still virgins.

Giovanni finished college in three years at night as a civil engineer. He still worked for the state, but now he would no longer be an apprentice. He would be a professional engineer. Carmen was pregnant with their first baby. They wanted to finally move out of uncle Antonio's back room. They needed more money, possibly more than Giovanni's promotion would provide. This was a time of reconstruction throughout Italy. The department that Giovanni worked for was responsible for countrywide renewal projects. One of these projects was to rehabilitate all of the old bridges that were in need of repair in the small villages that were so important for the villagers' existence. It would require quite a lot of travel, but it would move him up three more positions in the pay scale and the department would pay their living expenses while away from Rome. Giovanni and Carmen discussed the opportunity and while they would have preferred to stay in Rome, this was an offer that they couldn't refuse. They would wait until the baby was born. He would do this for a year and then they would return to Rome with enough money to get a good start for their family. A month after their first born was born, a boy whom they named Marcus, they left Rome for Giovanni's new job.

Less than a year later, their second child, another boy they named Augustus, was born. As this birth was unexpected, Giovanni would have to remain at this job a little while longer. Carmen gave birth in one of the little primitive villages where medical assistance was unavailable. The birth was a difficult one as Augustus was turned the wrong way in the womb. The only assistance available in the village was an elderly midwife. She tried to be helpful, but she was limited in her capabilities. She had never encountered a birth such as this. In such cases, they allowed the mother to die to save the baby. Giovanni wanted them both to live, but if he had his choice it would be Carmen. The midwife with Giovanni's help was able to turn the baby around, but not without extreme pain to Carmen. Giovanni would hear her screams the rest of his life. Carmen vowed to have no other children, Catholic or not, let the Pope have the children, and to leave such a country where people had to live like this.

Marcus and Augustus became the best of friends due to the closeness of their ages and the moves from village to village. Giovanni and Carmen made sure that both sons were properly educated, in the village schools or by them. They were both bright boys and assimilated easily into each village where Giovanni was working. They were accumulating money each year, but at the end of each year they would agree to one more year. At the end of that year, they would have enough money to return to Rome and live in the manner they desired. This went on until Marcus was twelve and Augustus was eleven. At that time, Giovanni was working in a very small primitive village. He had been assigned to help the villagers repair the four bridges that joined the village to the main roads. During the course of his work, the two boys would swim in the little rivers and creeks that ran under the bridges. Fortunately, his two sons had always been healthy strapping boys. However, lately Marcus was always tired and slept too much. Normally, both boys would jump out of bed at six in the morning with their father and walk him to his job.

Marcus would complain of body aches and just want to stay in bed. The only medical assistance in the village was a self-taught homeopathic doctor who treated everything with herbs and potions usually with some limited success. It was now over three months since Marcus first showed signs and he was not getting any better. Augustus would stay with him and read to him all day, but Marcus now never left his bed. Carmen was getting increasingly worried and decided that enough was enough. She decided that she would take Marcus to Rome where they had proper medical treatment. The family left immediately. Uncle Antonio had set it up with a specialist in children's disorders to examine Marcus. At the Rome hospital, they took test after test, but Marcus continued to get worse. They couldn't determine the cause of his illness and therefore knew no way to treat it. Uncle Antonio learned of an American doctor who was visiting Rome and was studying the type of illness that Marcus had. When the American doctor examined Marcus and ordered the right tests it was quickly determined that Marcus had contracted polio. The polio was too far gone. The American doctor did what he could with treatment, but Marcus died three weeks later. The American doctor was saddened, as was the family. If only he could have seen Marcus six weeks earlier maybe something could have been done—the doctor was sure of that.

Carmen was tired of a country with such a large population that lived in poverty without the basics for life. She refused to let Giovanni return to his work in the little villages. He agreed to return to Rome and take a job in the department. It would be less money and they would have to pay for their own living expenses, but they would manage somehow. Carmen refused—she wanted out of such a country altogether. They would go to America, the land of opportunities for good employment, proper education for Augustus, and adequate medical care. One of Carmen's cousins had moved to America only a few years ago and they were already living in their own home with their own automobile. They would do the same. Carmen and Augustus would go. If Giovanni wanted to, he could come with them. Carmen would not argue about this. They all left the next month. Giovanni knew better then to argue with Carmen when she was ready to leave.

They arrived in New York at Ellis Island, the temporary home of all new immigrants at that time. They were asked for their names. Carmen didn't want to be identified as Italian immigrants. She knew a little English. When she was asked for their names, instead of Santangelo she told them that their last name was Angel and that her husband's name was Johnny. When the inquisitor pointed to Augustus and asked how about the little guy, she nodded her head. That was how Johnny and Guy Angel were born.

They moved to Hartford, Connecticut where Carmen's cousin was living. They were their sponsors and knew no one else in America. Johnny tried to get a job as an engineer, but his lack of sufficient English and the reluctance of American companies to accept his Italian engineering degree made this impossible. Their money was running out and Carmen's cousin Maria and her husband Mario were getting edgy as to when they would be able to move out on their own. Their three-bedroom row house was too small with three small children as well as the three Angels. The Angels were all sleeping in the small living room.

While Johnny was actively looking for employment, he had taken to tinkering with Mario's car. He found that due to his engineering background, he was adept at automobile repairs, with the help of the owner's manual. The reading of the manual also forced him to learn more English. Mario, in his desperation, suggested that Johnny look for a job as an auto mechanic. He would talk to his mechanic and see if he could use another worker. Johnny was hired immediately on approval, as good auto mechanics were difficult to find.

Johnny took to auto mechanics quickly. It allowed them to move out of Mario's house and get their own small apartment in the neighborhood. Johnny would only do this until he could find proper work as a professional engineer. Johnny became an excellent auto mechanic to the extent that he was always in demand. He was making a lot of money for his boss, but not enough to buy the house that they wanted or an automobile. He was an auto mechanic without an auto.

One of his customers, who had some money, told him how stupid he was to work so hard to make money for his boss. The customer offered to stake Johnny to the money necessary to open his own shop; they would be equal partners. Johnny jumped at the chance. In no time, the business was making more money than his previous employer. However, Johnny was doing all the work, but he had to share half the profits with his partner. Johnny finally understood the arrangement, the American had taken advantage of the immigrant, and he didn't like it but a deal was a deal.

In spite of the arrangement, the garage prospered and the Angels were finally able to buy their own small row home. Johnny bought a new Chevrolet. Now they had everything but their own business. Guy was now fourteen and had started to help in the garage. He picked up the art of auto mechanics very quickly. Johnny saw his son one day working in the business with him. Carmen saw her son going to college and becoming the engineer that her Johnny couldn't be in America. Her son wouldn't have to work so hard and come home dirty every night. His wife wouldn't have to get into bed with a dirty body.

Johnny wanted to have his own business for his son. He approached his partner to see if he would be willing to sell his share to him. His partner who had made a substantial return on his investment in Johnny's garage was not an entirely greedy man. He agreed to sell his share to him for ten years of future profits. Johnny felt this to be excessive, but he wanted to have a business for his son, so he agreed. He didn't have that kind of money so he had to obtain a loan from a bank. Johnny had never dealt with a bank before in his life. To get the loan, he had to collateralize his business. If he missed one payment, the bank would own the business. Johnny made the deal. He worked harder than he ever did. In the next four years, he had the loan substantially paid off. Guy worked with him in the business after school, on weekends, on holidays, and during summer vacation. Guy was ready to graduate high school and Johnny expected him to work in the business so the loan would be paid off in no time, Carmen expected him to go to college.

Points to ponder:

The immigrant story is that if you have the courage to leave an oppressive life, by getting out of there and moving to a "land of opportunity" life will be beautiful. Rarely do the immigrants understand what they are getting themselves into—the changes and hard work necessary to be successful in their new life. And, when they have children, they want their children to have it easier and better than they had. Sometimes, within one or two generations, the children forget what the old country signified and only want what the new country offers. In addition, the parent's desire for a better life for their children sometimes precludes the life the children want themselves. This was very much the theme of this tale. Sometimes, it becomes difficult to know whose story you are really in.

1. Carmen recognized the oppression in her life and knew she had to get away from it. Giovanni on the other hand accepted his oppression and his script from his father. What allows some people to easily recognize the oppression in their lives and gives them the ability to do something about it? What factors impact on others to accept their tale of oppression without questioning the possibility of change?
2. Carmen and Giovanni were expected by their parents and their community to accept life as what was in their little village. What subtle and other pressures do the family and community place upon individuals to remain in what could be for them an oppressive tale rather than to support them to get out of such a situation?
3. Carmen's uncle in Rome supported Carmen's desire to get out of her oppressive village. In turn, Carmen tried to persuade Giovanni to do the same and leave with her. How did Carmen's story interface with Giovanni's? Is it easier and necessary to deal with and leave an oppressive situation when there is a strong person such as Carmen and her uncle to support you? Without Carmen, would Giovanni's tale have been the same?
4. Carmen leaving the oppressive village she was brought up in and Giovanni being helped to leave by his mother helped obliterate their parent's tale of what life had to be in their little village. What is the threat to a parent's story when the child negates the value and validity of that tale?
5. Carmen and Giovanni were willing to work hard to change their lives once they had escaped their village and those of their children by

hard work and necessary sacrifices. As these immigrants of the past were willing to work hard to change their situation and make life easier for their children, do you think present immigrants are willing to do the same? Would Carmen have taken the same action today and would Giovanni's mother react the same?

6. Carmen and Giovanni stayed in Italy even when the poor level of health services contributed to their child dying. Why do people such as Giovanni and Carmen kid themselves so that they delay making the decisions they know they have to make? Turning points often open spaces for changing the script that guides the story—why do individuals and couples resist such script changes?
7. Carmen and Giovanni held onto the belief of being Italians and not leaving the country they were born into. However, a disaster such as the death of their son Marcus many times becomes the turning point that forces one to take action, such as Giovanni and Carmen moving to America—why is this so?
8. Carmen and Giovanni, in spite of the myth, did not find America's streets paved with gold. In fact, initially it was a hard life necessitating starting over again. Why do some people adjust to their new country or surroundings, fighting off the reality of despair, while others allow themselves to succumb to a new oppression?
9. Carmen was adamant in leaving the oppression of her village in Italy and making her new life in America successful. What are the characteristics that made Carmen strong so as to keep moving forward in spite of the hand she was dealt?
10. While Carmen maintained her beliefs of a better life, Giovanni tended to be accepting of whatever life dealt him. Do individuals such as Giovanni always need a pusher such as Carmen to move forward? Why are some people leaders and others followers?
11. Giovanni worked hard in his father's stonemason business in Italy, his life as an engineer in Italy, and his work in America as an auto mechanic. Where do our value systems come from, for example the hard work value of Giovanni's?
12. Carmen and Giovanni tried to pass on their old world values of hard work and integrity to their child in America. How can we effectively pass on the values and experiences that we have learned to our children? Why don't our children believe them? Why do parents expect

their children to want what they want? Why can't they grant them the freedom to choose for themselves?

The grass is always greener
until you get there,
and then the grass is greener
somewhere else.

Guy Angel

Filling Large Shoes

Guy Angel started state college in the fall, in the engineering program, as his mother Carmen wanted. He worked with his father Johnny after school and on the weekends in the family auto mechanic business. Guy had become interested in girls in high school. He was a well-built boy with Italian good looks. During his senior year in high school he started hanging around with an attractive Protestant girl one year younger than he named Anne Browne. A little stuck up, but desirable for a poor Italian Catholic kid. He had little time or money to take her out properly, so they would meet after he finished work at the garage and go parking in his father's Chevy. To have a car in his neighborhood was a big deal. Anne was impressed and the other girls were envious of her. If her mother knew she was seeing an Italian Catholic, she would put a stop to it. So Anne had to sneak around to see Guy. In high school they would make out in the back seat of his car going only as far as second base. She would let him play with her breasts but nothing below the waist.

When Guy started college and he would pick Anne up at high school, she really became the envy of the other girls. Guy was pressuring her to go all the way—he would be careful, he would pull it out in time. Anne wasn't quite sure. She didn't want to lose Guy, but she didn't want to lose her virginity either. Who would marry a non-virgin in those days? Probably not even Guy Angel. During their make out sessions, Guy would complain how much his penis hurt, his case of terminal blue balls, and did she want him to have to masturbate. Anne finally started feeling sorry for him and she was becoming aroused as well. One night he had her so excited that she forgot (or did she?) to stop him. She had never felt like this. This was the night that Guy first penetrated her. It hurt severely, but Guy was hardly inside her when he came out. As he pulled out, he sprayed them both.

They continued this way for the next three months, three times a week whether they had to or not. Anne and Guy weren't sure that they really enjoyed doing this, putting it in and pulling it out quickly, but this was what they were supposed to do at their age. Anne reported to Guy when she got her period so that they could relax for the next month. On the third month, Anne didn't get her period on time. They didn't know what they were going to do. Guy stopped seeing Anne. She was alone and frantic. By the next month she still hadn't gotten her period. By the following month she started showing—at least to her. Her mother was concerned that she was putting on weight and Anne had never been heavy. She finally couldn't take her mother's prodding and she had to tell someone, so she told her mother. Her mother pushed her to tell her who the father was and she finally told her it was Guy Angel. Her mother gave off a sigh of relief; at least it wasn't one of the dagos in the neighborhood with a vowel at the end of their names. Anne didn't know what to say to that.

Anne and her parents arrived at the Angel's door one night unannounced. Anne was getting too big to go to school without the other girls knowing about her condition. Guy's mother Carmen was the only one home. When she heard the whole story she sat down at the dining room table and cried into her hands. When Guy and his father came home, they were all sitting around the table. Guy saw Anne and her family and tried to bolt, but his mother's scream stopped him. When Johnny heard the story, the first thing he did was smack Guy hard on the back of his head. He had never hit Guy before in his life. He was mad at Guy for ruining his life so young. The families agreed that Guy and Anne needed to be married immediately. As they were underage, both families would have to sign for them. Johnny assured them that Guy would be there. They were married in two days. The baby was a boy and they named him Roberto but Anne called him Bobby. Both families were happy to be saved from disgrace, but maybe not Guy and Anne. Guy had to quit college and work full time in Johnny's garage. Carmen wasn't happy about this but she had a grandchild. Johnny secretly smiled; he had a new partner.

Guy worked at Johnny' s garage while Anne stayed home to take care of little Bobby. Guy was eighteen and Anne was just seventeen. She couldn't go back to high school, but her mother encouraged her to get her GED, which she did. She received her high school diploma before her graduating class. Guy would come home from work tired, expect his dinner on the table, play with Bobby for a while, and then go up to bed. Anne would be left with feeding Bobby and cleaning him up afterward, giving him his bath, changing him into pajamas, and getting him off to sleep. When she came up to bed she was exhausted, but Guy was replenished. He would want to make love, but Anne was ready for sleep. She would let Guy have his way with her as it was easier that way and then he would fall back to sleep and so would she. This became their daily habit. Soon she was pregnant again. They had another boy, which Guy named Alphonse and they called Ally. After the second birth, Anne was more forceful in denying Guy and made him wear a rubber. Guy insisted that this was against his Catholic religion, but Anne knew he had no religion. Anne insisted that it was well within the dogma of her Episcopalian religion, but Guy knew she had no religion. This discouraged Guy and he left Anne alone. Guy became a father to the two boys as they became older. They were going to be his Italian stallions.

Anne came to America from England when she was four years old. She remembered very little of her early years. Her first memories began in their house in Hartford. Her father was a claims adjuster for the Hartford Insurance Company. He prided himself on being a white-collar worker. The Angels were quite beneath their social standing. Anne's mother was a stiff upper lip type English lady who still had tea at four o'clock every afternoon. Both she and her husband projected a slight British accent when they talked. Guy felt that it was a put on. Anne's mother hoped that Anne would go to a good college and marry a man of some substance and a white Protestant. She couldn't hide her shame as to what Anne had done, getting pregnant by an Italian, having to marry him, and now having a second child within a year. Her mother didn't know what she had done wrong. As she was their only child, her hope for raising dignity through her child was dead. Anne's mother claimed that they were Episcopalian, although they never attended church. Anne, while she was growing up, was forbidden to play with the Irish and Italian Catholics in the neighborhood.

Anne was able to keep Guy at bay for over three years while he fathered the two boys. They were definitely his sons—dark, rough featured, and roughhousers. They were definitely of Italian descent and the apples of Johnny and Carmen's eyes. During the third year, Guy was getting restless working at Johnny's garage. The hours were hard and long and Johnny wasn't willing to pay Guy any more than when he started. He would tell Guy that when he was gone Guy would have the whole business. They were building a business for Guy and the grandchildren. In the meantime while Guy was getting the business, Johnny was getting the money. He was also getting tired of Johnny yelling at him, telling him he couldn't do anything right except get Protestant girls pregnant.

Guy needed to take more money out of the business than his father Johnny was willing to give him. It was obvious that Johnny was going to live for many more years and Guy couldn't wait. Johnny yelled at Guy. Told him how ungrateful he was, and that he should try to get another job as good as this one that paid so much. Guy left angry. He'd show the old man. Guy knew a mechanic who had taken a job with a boat repair business in Newport, Rhode Island. They were looking for a good inboard motor mechanic. The pay was almost double what Guy was getting from Johnny. Guy went down to talk to the owner on his day off. The owner, Dominic Baggio, was an older man in his late sixties, an Italian from the old country. He liked Guy immediately. He offered him the job as well as the opportunity to buy him out. In his anger at Johnny, he jumped at the chance. When he told his dad, Johnny offered him more than Dominic with a full partnership, 50/50 sharing of the profits. Guy would have jumped at this two days ago, but now it was too late. His honor wouldn't let him renege on Dominic, and he had something to prove to his father. Guy moved the family down to Newport the following month.

Guy surprised Anne by buying the corner row home, a premium location because it came with a side yard. At the time, it was in the best Irish/Italian neighborhood in Newport. Anne wasn't impressed. Frankly, it wasn't good enough for her.

Guy made sure that his sons went to the parish parochial schools. The nuns would give them a good education. They both turned out much like Guy—tough Italian kids who knew everything. Each of them attended state college for one year. They partied as hard as they could and each in turn flunked out. You can't pass a class if you don't go to the class. While Anne was disappointed, Guy was happy to have them in the business.

Points to ponder:

Parents, usually the father, sometimes work hard to make life easier for their children. They build a business for themselves but in the back of their mind is the hope that the children will one day take over the business. However, selfishly they want to hold onto the business as long as they can to protect themselves. Sometimes, the child doesn't want the business; it is a noose around their necks together with living under the control of the parent. So they rebel, many times outsmarting themselves in the process.

1. Carmen and Giovanni (Johnny) wanted their son Guy to have a better life in America than they had growing up in their small village in Italy. They wanted their son to be an American. In spite of this Guy went his own way. Why do children rebel against their parents and their heritage, desiring the forbidden fruit rather than what comes with their heritage?
2. Guy didn't want to be a typical Italian American and live according to the custom that had him marrying an Italian American girl and having plenty of children. Instead he was attracted to Anne, an American

Protestant. Why do individuals find "the other" more desirable? Why do they see such a conquest as a prize?

3. Anne wasn't attracted to Guy because he was an Italian American, but because the other girls desired him. In fact, her parents had warned her against Italian Americans. Why do individuals find someone more desirable because others do? Do others' envy make someone more desirable? Is there an added attraction and pull toward a specific group when you're told by your parents to avoid them?
4. Guy and Anne's relationship eventually led itself to sexual relations. What is the pull to sex in such a relationship? If sex weren't so forbidden by adult society, would teens and young adults treat it more reasonably so that unwanted pregnancies could be avoided to a greater degree?
5. Anne was raised with the message that a girl's virginity should be saved until she is married and that no man will marry a non-virgin. How did the pressure of this message impact upon Anne's dilemma of getting pregnant? Is virginity as important today as it was in previous times—to the female to keep it until marriage, to the male to marry a virgin?
6. Anne's parents wanted her to marry a cultured male with a background like their own, not someone of Italian descent with a Roman Catholic background. Guy's parents wanted him to marry within their culture. Why do we judge individuals by their backgrounds, such as Italian Catholic and English Episcopalian, rather than by individual traits? Does such prejudice cause unnecessary problems?
7. When Guy got Anne pregnant, he wanted to run, but his parents forced him to do the honorable thing (even though they were against it) and marry Anne. Is a forced marriage ever advisable? Are there better solutions that you can think of?
8. Carmen wanted Guy to go to college, to be better than they were. Johnny wanted Guy to come work with him in his auto mechanic business. When Guy started college Carmen was elated. When he dropped out of college and came to work with him Johnny was elated. Why do parents believe that they have the right to control, judge, and criticize their children no matter how old they get—but don't allow the other way around?

9. When Guy and Anne got married sex continued to be very important to Guy in his relationship with Anne, but less important to Anne. How important is sex in an intimate relationship based on real love of the individual? Are there any scars to the male and female from the societal pressures placed upon them as to sex as they grow up?
10. Guy and Anne, after the birth of their first child Bobby, continued to have sex that would result in more children. Why do young parents have children in the first place? What are the internal and external pressures? Do children enhance or encumber a marriage? What impact does cultural conditioning have on the drive to have children?
11. Guy was the apple of Johnny's eye while he was growing up. However, once Guy started working for Johnny, Johnny became quite critical of Guy and refused to compensate him fairly. Is it inevitable that parents will push their children away as Johnny did to Guy—is this a natural phenomenon or can it be prevented?
12. Guy treated his two sons, Bobby and Ally, as his Italian stallions, his children and not Anne's. What subtle pressures or messages do parents put out that perpetuate what they really want from their children—as Guy succeeded in having his two boys grow up just like him and work with him in his boat business?

Whoever you are,
the other always looks better,
until you become the other.

The Farm Boy

Changing Your Story

Charles was raised on a small family farm in a rural area of Wisconsin. From the time he was a youngster, around eight years old, he was responsible for doing chores on the farm. He woke up early to feed the livestock before school and cleaned the barn after school. He prided himself on always getting his work done. He was an obedient child with a high work ethic—his parents were proud of him. On top of his chores, it was expected that he do well at school. His parents were strict with him, but he always knew that they loved him and wanted the best for him and his three sisters and two brothers. Charles was one of the middle children. His parents didn't want any of their children to have to work as hard as they did—farm life wasn't easy. The older children helped the younger children and they all worked together. Charles needed no other people than his family for support.

His eldest sister, Anita, was the first person in the family to go to college and graduate from an eastern school as a nurse. She worked in the intensive care unit at a large hospital in Milwaukee. The next eldest, his brother Ronald, graduated with a business degree from a small college in Michigan and took a job with one of the large accounting firms in Detroit. Charles was the next in line. His older sister and brother helped him financially get through college. Charles decided to attend the University of Wisconsin in Madison. As it wasn't too far from the farm, around 80 miles, he could come home on weekends and help out. He had never been away from the family and wasn't sure that he would like living away from them. His safety net was coming home on the weekends.

During his first year at college, he came home every weekend. The big university and all those people scared him. He was comfortable with his family, but not with strangers. He was used to receiving orders and knowing what he had to do that he could do well. He wasn't used to being on his own and being self-responsible to get things done his way. The freedom of university life wasn't for him. He talked to his parents about leaving school. They made it clear that this wasn't acceptable. Now he had a clear parental order. He would be a good obedient child.

He didn't know quite what he wanted to take at college, with returning to the farm always in the back of his mind, so he signed up for a liberal arts curriculum the first year. He was enjoying the classes, but he didn't know how this would get him a job or help him with his farm work after college. His parents would need the help with Anita and Ronald gone and the younger three leaving for college themselves.

In his literature class, there was a very nice girl, not too attractive but nice, who sat next to him. She made it a point to talk to him before and after class. She tried to walk with him after class. He was shy with girls, other than his sisters, and tried to avoid her, but she was persistent. Her name was Sandra Barski and she was from the Milwaukee area. She seemed alone like him.

He saw Sandra around the school, coming and going to other classes and walking around the campus. She always gave him a big wave. He waved back shyly. Sometimes Sandra was with another girl or two, but Charles was always alone. He didn't make friends easy, as he was much too serious and overly sensitive about being a farm boy. He developed a routine of going to classes and then returning alone to his dorm room. His roommate, Larry something, from a big eastern city, was very rarely there. When his roommate was there, he had very little to say to him. They lived in peaceful co-existence, each in his world. When Friday came, he couldn't wait to get home to the farm. He left as soon as his last class ended. He returned to school on Monday morning just in time for his first class. He spent as little time as possible on campus. He didn't mind driving back and forth and this way his parents had the use of the pickup truck for farm work on the weekends.

He was studying alone in the library one day when Sandra

came in. She looked around the study area as if she was looking for someone. He kept his head buried in his book. She spied him and came over. "Hi," she said. "Can I join you?"

"Sure, it's a free library." He was trying to be funny, but everything he said came across too serious—he wasn't good at making jokes or talking to people.

She sat down next to him and started talking. He would ordinarily be annoyed, but somehow he found her pleasant and he didn't know how to be rude.

"So," she began, "you're Charles. I'm Sandra." She put her hand out.

He took her hand meekly and released it quickly. He wasn't comfortable holding a girl's hand. She just started talking. The students at the next table shushed her. She talked lower.

"Students. All they ever want to do is study. No fun."

He nodded his head. "Yeah." That was all he ever did was study.

"So, where are you from?" she asked.

"Three Rivers," he said.

"Oh, I know that place. Beautiful farm country. I spent one summer near there. Quiet place."

"Yes it is."

"So, you like it there?"

Others were starting to shush them again. One of the students sent the librarian over. She asked them to be quiet.

She looked at him. "You want to go get something to drink?"

He really didn't want to, he was too shy and scared. Somehow he said "sure."

They went to the campus canteen. and took a table in the back away from other students. She asked him all about the farm and his sisters and brothers. He had never talked so much to anyone in his life. Before he knew it, it was getting dark outside.

"I better be going," John said.

She looked at her watch. "Oh shit. I missed early dinner—again."

"Me too."

"Why don't we eat here? It's not much, but it's food."

He had never missed a meal in the college cafeteria. He was on the prepaid meal plan and if he missed a meal that was it. He had very little spending money; he was on a tight budget since his sister and brother were helping his parents pay for his tuition and room and board (as he would do for his two younger sisters and brother), he felt guilty if he wasted any money. He wanted to remain sitting here with Sandra, but he couldn't afford to buy his dinner and hers. He said nothing.

"Come on," said Sandra "it'll be fun."

"Okay."

She ordered a full dinner plate with soup and desert. He cringed. He ordered a hamburger with the works at no extra cost and a glass of water. She looked over, but said nothing.

Sandra had a voracious appetite. She ate quickly as she continued to talk. Charles ate slowly and said little, periodically nodding his head. Eventually Sandra finished eating and stopped talking, waiting for Charles to speak. Charles found it easy to talk to her, to tell her about his life growing up on the farm. It was obvious that he loved his parents and his sisters and brothers and his life on the farm. He talked about returning to the farm after college. He had never talked so much. Sandra listened and nodded. The waitress brought the check; he stared at it. It was more money than he had with him. He stopped talking. She looked up at him. He said nothing.

"You okay?" she asked him. She seemed genuinely concerned.

He said nothing, but his eyes kept looking down at the check. He couldn't help it. She followed the path of his eyes. She said nothing. She looked at him. As she did, she opened her pocketbook and took out enough money to pay the bill and a tip. He tried to push her money back. He didn't know what he would do, but he didn't want a girl paying for his dinner. He wasn't brought up that way.

She held his hand. "Charles, it's okay. You buy next time." She explained to him that her parents were divorced and she was the only child. Both her mother and her father felt guilty, so they both sent her money. Money wasn't her problem. He felt awful as they had spent all this time talking about him and his family and he hadn't asked her one thing about herself.

He walked her back to her room. He felt sheepish about not paying for their dinner, but was grateful that she had. As they walked through the campus, she held him by the arm. He felt awkward, but he didn't pull away. She moved her hand down his arm and held onto his hand. It felt good to him, but strange. He had never held a girl's hand before. At the entrance to her dorm, she stopped and turned around to face him. She looked up at him, stood on her tiptoes, and kissed him softly on the cheek.

"Thank you, Charles. It was a lovely evening. The next time we'll talk more about literature and less about us."

He nodded his head, put his head down, and walked slowly away. She watched him walk away. A strange boy she thought but I like him. It was better than being alone and lonely.

Charles and Sandra spent a lot of time together after that first meeting. After a few weeks, he stopped going home every weekend. He was relieved. The farm would survive without him, and Sandra was relieved. When the end of the school year was approaching, they didn't want to part. Sandra really had nowhere to go, either to her mother in New York or her father in Milwaukee where she was raised. Neither one really wanted her; she would only be in their way and alone. Charles talked to his parents and asked them whether Sandra could spend the summer with them. He knew Sandra would love the farm as much as he did. Since Anita had left they had missed having an older daughter. Sandra would be just fine.

In the rural farmland of Wisconsin nice young unmarried people didn't sleep together—at least not at Charles's parents farm. So, Sandra slept in Anita's room on the third floor that summer, while Charles stayed in his room on the first floor. However, with the big summer Wisconsin sun and moon, romance continued to blossom. Sandra loved to walk with Charles around the farm, especially in the early morning and at dusk, hand in hand. He was the first real friend she had ever had who made her feel safe.

She wished she could stay like this the rest of her life. His parents and siblings quickly loved Sandra and made her one of the family. She had never been part of a family before. When summer was coming to an end, neither one of them wanted to go back to college. They would be back in the dorms and away from each other. They had gotten used to having each other in the same house.

Two weeks before college was to begin again, Sandra took Charles for a walk into the fields at sunset. She lay down on a pile of hay and pulled him down with her. She rolled toward him and kissed him hard on the mouth. She held him hard. "Oh Charles," she said. "I don't want to go back to college. Let's stay here. I love your family."

He pressed her against him. She always provided strength to him when he held her close. For a big strong farm boy, he was a social weakling with other people. He said nothing for a long while. She waited. He finally spoke.

"I can't. I have to finish college. I'm expected to. Once we finish, we can come back here. I was planning to anyway."

She looked at him. "Charles! Is that a proposal?"

He hadn't thought about it. "I guess it is. I don't want to lose you."

She kissed him again, this time excitedly. "Oh, Charles. I was hoping this would happen. I don't want to lose you either."

They hugged each other. She kept kissing him all over. They wanted to make love, but they knew they shouldn't.

"I know," Sandra said."Let's get married now. We can stay together in the married apartments then. Going back to college will be fun then."

He didn't know what to say. He was only twenty years old. He knew he would get married some day, but not so soon. He was afraid his parents would be angry and unhappy. He would be the first child to be married.

"Let's go tell your parents!" she said.

His parents were ecstatic. They had grown to love Sandra as a daughter. They didn't think twenty was too young; they had been married when they were both eighteen. Charles and Sandra were married in the local church the following week. Her parents came in for the wedding. She had to keep them separated, but they otherwise behaved. Charles kind of liked them both but he wasn't sure, as he didn't know many city folk. After the wedding, they drove to college and had their honeymoon in the college apartment.

They were inseparable. She had never been so close before and had never had a family before. Now that he was married, Charles wasn't sure it was such a good idea to continue with liberal arts and then return to the farm. He knew Sandra loved it there and his family but he now wanted to have a life of his own. He talked to Sandra about this and she suggested that he transfer to business. Her father was a production supervisor and he loved his work. She was sure that her father would talk to him about it. After talking to Sandra's father, he was sure. He would switch to business and learn all he could about it. Sandra would be the liberal arts person in the family; one was enough.

They spent the school year studying together and staying in their apartment. They made few friends. The single students were too young and the other married students were too old. They were happy and they needed no one else. In the summer, they went to the family farm and stayed in Charles's old bedroom. They were happy and very much in love. They both hoped that nothing would ever change.

During their third year of college, Sandra missed her period. They had always been careful with birth control, but sometimes they wanted each other too much and they would forget. Charles told her not to worry; it couldn't happen to them. They were always so careful. When the second month passed and still no period, he started to worry with her. The last thing they needed right now was a child. After they finished college, maybe, but not now. They were so involved with each other, neither thought that they could share a child. Neither said anything about this to the other.

Sandra finally got up enough nerve to see the campus doctor. She didn't want anyone else to know how dumb she was. Charles went with her. The doctor confirmed what they already knew. The good news was that the baby wasn't due until July. They would be able to finish the school year. By September the baby would be big enough to allow Sandra to return to school or so they hoped. Or they could leave the baby with Charles's parents; they would love that.

Sandra continued her classes, but was exhausted at the end of the day. She was experiencing horrible morning sickness and severe trouble sleeping at night. Charles urged her to see the campus doctor, but she didn't want to spend money needlessly as they would need all the money they had when the baby arrived. She told him that everything would be all right, he would see, it was just natural. She was now in her fifth month and her condition hadn't gotten any better. He insisted that she go to the doctor. Sandra liked when Charles insisted and told her what to do—it didn't happen very often.

She went into the examining room, while Charles waited outside. A few minutes went by quietly as he read a back issue of *Farm Magazine*. All of a sudden the doors burst open and a stretcher pushed out in a hurry. Sandra was laying on it in severe pain. Charles rushed over and looked down at her. She was crying. Charles, I'm so sorry." The nurse pushed her out the door toward a waiting ambulance.

At the hospital, they tried to save the baby, but it was too premature. The baby had formed sideways in her womb and they couldn't dislodge it without damaging her uterus. If only she had come to the doctor a month earlier. She wouldn't be able to have any other babies.

Charles held her tightly and kissed her softly on the cheeks. "It's okay, we still have each other."

"Oh Charles, I love you," she said.

He said quietly, "I love you." It was the first time he had said that to anybody. They cried together.

When Sandra came out of the hospital, she was required to rest for about six weeks. While she was resting, Charles continued to go to his classes, and she tried to keep up with her classes at home. It was during this time that Sandra started calling Charles "Father" and Charles called Sandra "Mother;" just like his parents.

She tried to keep up with her schoolwork, but she felt too depressed to do anything. She spent most of her time sleeping even when Charles was there. He suggested that she drop out of school for the semester and she accepted. She could return to school in the fall, giving her the summer off. But she never returned to school. She would concentrate on being a good wife to Charles and making it up to him for the lost baby. Charles became her life and her eyes to the outside world.

Charles and Sandra didn't go to his parents' farm that summer. She couldn't face his family. She knew how important it was to them to have children and she felt that she had robbed them of their first grandchild.

When Charles graduated the following June, he wanted to go back home and apply his business education to running the farm. He thought it would be good for Sandra as well. But she wanted to get out of Wisconsin as it had bad memories for her. The last place she wanted to live was Charles's family farm. Her memories of their time on the farm were too happy and she didn't feel that she deserved to be happy again. She would punish herself, since Charles couldn't do it. He applied for a number of industrial positions. With his academic record and recommendations from his professors, he received a number of offers. Most of them were to come into the company's training program. He was looking for an immediate position as a business problem solver. At that time not too many companies were hiring college graduates for such positions directly out of school. Defense industries had greatly expanded as a result of increased government orders and it was the only company that offered him such a starting position but it was at their Tennessee plant. Charles dismissed it as too far away and too foreign to him. Sandra said that they should take the offer. Nothing could be too far away.

Charles started as a systems analyst at the Tennessee plant.

He was the youngest member of the staff. The senior analysts assigned him work. He did exactly as he was told and did each assignment excellently, the right job at the right time. He was much in demand by the other systems analysts. Each senior member wanted him on his team. He liked doing work at his desk, while the senior analysts worked with the employees on the shop floor and in the office. He had minimal contact with the other twelve analysts other than around work. They were a serious group and so was he.

He would leave their apartment before Sandra would wake up. He would have his breakfast and then make breakfast for her. He would leave it on the table for her. He would go to work arriving a half hour earlier than the starting time. He would do his work, working through breaks and lunch, so that he could leave exactly at quitting time to get home to Sandra. When he got home, she would be attractively dressed and waiting for him. She would greet him at the door, embrace him, and kiss him full on the lips as passionately as she was able to. The neighbors called them the lovebirds. They expected them to have many children the way they loved each other. She wasn't ready to get back into life, so most of the time she didn't prepare dinner. She just cried to herself instead. They would go out to their favorite diner in the neighborhood. Charles felt these were happy times, but Sandra was still depressed.

This became their life for the next two years. He suggested that they purchase a house. She resisted as she was afraid of a new venture. He prevailed and they moved to a new development in the suburbs. When they first moved in, she would sit facing the window while Charles was at work and watch the young mothers wheel their young children past. She cried silently.

Two of Charles's co-workers lived in the same development. The three of them would car pool to work. One of the co-workers, Horace Bechtel, was an older man in his forties. He and his wife, Betty, were childless just like Charles and Sandra. Horace befriended Charles; told him that Betty couldn't have children. They had adjusted. Betty volunteered at the school library. They were looking for another helper, would Sandra be interested?

With the Bechtel's assistance, Charles was able to convince Sandra to try it. She and Betty became friends. Sandra liked working in the library, dealing with the students, and having a life of her own. No longer did she have to live through Charles. Now when he came home from work, she had dinner waiting on the table. She would talk all through dinner about her day at the library. Charles's job had become just what he did so that they could pay the bills.

They settled into a very prescribed life. He went to work at the plant, and she went to work at the school library. They came home, had dinner together, read some, and then went to bed. They held each other closely, but the passion in their sex life had diminished. They saw Horace and Betty once in a while socially, but otherwise shunned the other young couples with young children in the development.

Points to ponder:

We are all victims of our birth and upbringing. Charles was born to a rural farm life with parents possessing solid family values. His parents taught him the value of work and being independent. His upbringing kept him socially isolated on the family farm, producing a solid self-sufficient individual who was improperly socialized. Sandra was born to urban parents, both from New York, who had settled in Milwaukee, Wisconsin when Sandra was quite young due to a job transfer of her father. Sandra was raised in an urban environment, with summers spent in New York with relatives, resulting in a somewhat sophisticated but lonely child always seeking security. Both Charles and Sandra found what they lacked in the other.

1. Charles was raised on a mid-western farm with a very close family—somewhat isolated from the world. Sandra grew up in Milwaukee with a divorced mother feeling pretty much alone. What impact do family and the environment in which one is raised have on the development of the individual—for example, Charles and Sandra?
2. Charles's parents wanted him to go to college, to make something of

himself in the world and get away from the farm. Charles just wanted to spend the rest of his life on the family farm. This was enough world for him. Why do parents make decisions for their children based on their desires for the child rather than on the child's desires? Do parents always know what is best for their children?

3. Parents tend to praise their obedient children who do things the way they want them done and agonize over the children who rebel and want to do things their way. What messages do these obedient children such as Charles learn and what messages do the rebellious children such as Sandra learn? How is free will compromised for each of these children?
4. Sandra, having grown up on her own to a great extent coming from a divorced family, turned out extremely independent. Charles, having grown up in a very circumscribed environment on the family farm turned out fearful of people and very dependent on the family. What are some factors that make some children fiercely independent, such as Sandra, while other children, such as Charles, become almost totally dependent?
5. Sandra, a take-charge independent individual, attracted Charles, a rather shy non-people person. Why do we seem to be either attracted to those who are most similar to us or those who are opposite to us? What was each of them looking for in the other?
6. Both Charles and Sandra have experienced turning points in their lives; Charles leaving the farm, going away to college, and meeting Sandra; Sandra moving to Milwaukee, her parents divorcing, going to college, and meeting Charles and his family; which have impacted their lives. What are some of your turning points and how have they affected your life?
7. Charles only wanted to go back and work on the farm. Sandra really had no place to go back to, but she was attracted to Charles and his family and the family farm life. What are some of the motivators that pushed Charles and Sandra to marry young?
8. Sandra realized how important it was to Charles and his family to have babies. Losing her baby and not being able to have another baby caused enormous depression for Sandra. A trauma like this, such as losing a baby for Sandra, can affect the rest of a person's life. What affect did losing the baby have on Sandra? On Charles?

9. Charles always wanted to finish college if he had to and then return to the family farm under the guise of applying what he had learned at college. Instead he took a job he really didn't want in Tennessee. How does one get pressured to do something they don't want to do and how does it affect the reminder of their lives?
10. Charles and Sandra went to live in Tennessee, with Charles doing his job and coming home each night, and Sandra helping out at the local library. Was this normal adjustment or were they merely playing out the life that was handed to them? How do we adjust to traumas in our lives and get ourselves to move on? Why do we hold onto such traumas, making them life threatening, waiting to be rescued?
11. Charles and Sandra fell into a circumscribed life, going through the day-to-day motions, by holding on to each other. Why do people settle for an otherwise undesirable prescribed life when their dreams point them in other directions?
12. Charles performed his job well, as he had been taught at home. His hard work earned him an excellent reputation from his fellow workers. He could probably have a job at the company for the rest of his life. How does one allow one's self to settle into such an existence which may go on for years with little change?

Even when we think we know what we want,
life gets in the way of our real plans.

The Wife's Story

Growing Up is Hard to Do

Betty was 32 years old, married to Eddie Stern, an engineer with ELB Industries, when he was transferred in his job and the family moved to Michigan. Their children, Stuart (nine years old), Ned (almost seven years old), and Arlene (five years old) were fairly close to being on their own. The two boys were in school, and the daughter was to start regular school in the fall. Their lives had begun; she was waiting for hers to start. While she was living in Syracuse, she tried to have the life she had never had. Growing up in New Jersey, she was chubby and considered herself unattractive. As she matured after marrying Eddie as a safe risk and a way out of her family's house, she suddenly found herself becoming physically attractive. Where she had been shunned and ridiculed by the boys as she was growing up, she was now very much desired by males. She had fun with her new sex appeal in Syracuse, enjoying men being attracted to her. She realized that she couldn't continue in that role in Michigan as the wife of the chief engineer. She would have to become someone else.

She didn't want to move to Michigan, she was having too much fun in Syracuse. She resisted the move like a child wanting to be irresponsible for the rest of her life. When she realized that her husband was moving ahead without her, she decided that it might be time to start growing up. It was difficult for her to give up the childhood she had never had, now that she was having it. In the end, she became the wife and mother that was expected of her. She never liked it; she always resented it.

Prior to actually moving herself and the children to Michigan, she had to change. She gathered her short skirts, tight tops, overly high heels, and bikini panties, the costume of her acting out teen-ager, and took them to a friend of hers, Sally Bevins. Sally had three teenage daughters. Sally told her that she was extremely grateful to get the clothing; her girls would just love them. Sally's daughters all thought that Betty was great, the most beautiful and sexy woman their mother knew. They envied her. They wanted to be just like her. When Betty left, Sally threw the three bags of clothing in the trash. She wouldn't let her daughters walk around like that.

Betty didn't get rid of her skimpy bikini bathing suits, as she felt that she needed something in her life. Right before the move, she had her hair cut short. This was the first time since she was sixteen that she had her hair cut. Since that time, her blond hair had always been long, reaching down to her waist. It was very attractive to men when she wore it down with one of her bikini bathing suits. She knew how to use it. But she had her hair cut conservatively to look like one of the Michigan country club matrons. She hated it.

She replaced her mini skirt centered wardrobe with a more conservative one. She went shopping with one of the wives, who helped her pick out appropriate clothes for the wife of a corporate executive. They covered her arms and they covered her legs down to the ankles. She looked like her mother on a dress up day. She hated it.

By the time she and Eddie, and the kids, moved into the big house in Michigan, her transformation was complete. She was the corporate wife she thought her husband wanted her to be. Eddie never said anything.

During the day she looked like any other ordinary wife of a wealthy socialite. Her clothes were shapeless—with no way to know what kind of body existed underneath. She was just another rich suburban housewife and mother. She wanted her husband and children to be proud of her. They may have liked her the other way, but no one said anything. At age thirty-two, she had said good-bye to her youth. She had joined the club of corporate wives.

During the first summer in Michigan, she took the kids to the pool at the company country club. She continued to wear her skimpy bikini bathing suits. The men at the club noticed and she noticed them noticing. She smiled to herself. She hadn't given everything up just yet. Her two sons noticed her and the men noticing her. They were proud of her, but ashamed. They wished she could be like the other mothers, fat and matronly, but were glad she wasn't.

She was one of the youngest women at the club other than the young wives and mistresses of the rich older male members. She didn't want to be associated with them. They would lie around the pool in groups, displaying their bodies for men to see. Their husbands loved it when the other men envied them for possessing such a woman. They would sun bath on their stomachs with their tops off showing off the sides of their breasts. They gloried in male attention; it was what they wanted. They made Betty's bikinis look like full cover. They might as well have been nude. Betty was no competition for them. They made her feel like an undeveloped schoolgirl. She stopped wearing her bikinis. What was the sense; she might as well be comfortable. That was the last trace of her former life; she was now one of the matrons.

In the fall, when the children started school, Betty had most of the day to herself. She wanted to go to work to use her university degree in English Literature but she knew that wasn't acceptable for a corporate wife. She would even volunteer to work in a museum, her real desire, but she wasn't sure that she could do it. Instead, she joined a number of committees at the country club. She was much in demand. The older members much preferred Betty. Most of the show-off wives were of short duration anyway, while they sensed that Betty was in for the long haul. She became a member of the social, women's activities, social action (an annual visit to a public school), and special event committees. This required a weekly luncheon meeting and a monthly social get together. Her committee commitments together with her twice a week trips into Detroit and the little time she had to spend with her children made a complete activity schedule for Betty. She hated most of it.

Eddie worked late every night including Friday and all day Saturday. Saturday night was their night at the country club. Eddie came home on Saturday as late as he could and got ready to go to the club. As chief engineer, there was an unwritten rule that he be active at the country club. The company was paying for it and they expected him to pursue business contacts—money begets money. He didn't even have time to himself on Saturday nights and Sunday. But on Sunday he was expected to be part of a golf foursome, weather permitting. Each Friday he was sent a memo from the company president's office as to which table he would be sitting at on Saturday night and which foursome he would be golfing with on Sunday. It was expected that Betty charm the other men and befriend their wives. She hated this part of their lives, but never said anything. She pretended that she enjoyed it.

The dinner dance at the club was one activity left to Betty where she could still have fun. The expected attire was formal evening gown, which allowed her to dress up. She would choose form fitting evening gowns that accentuated her figure. At the dance she could be competitive with the trophy wives. She could look classy; they looked trashy.

Eddie was content to sit at the table and talk business. He would typically find some of the other men who were also interested in talking business. Betty and the other women found it boring—Betty found the other women boring. There were a number of men at the club who waited to dance with Betty, others who waited to watch her dance. As she got older, she only got better. She would dance and flirt most of the night, as Eddie would talk business. Betty and Eddie said very little to each other.

Her life continued like this until Eddie became a vice president. Eddie started to travel and she was on her own day and night. While he had been chief engineer, he at least came home every night. He slept in the same bedroom with her and when she needed to be close she could still get into his bed with him. Now that he was away at night, she was alone in the bedroom and she was becoming lonely.

She would talk to her friend Agnes about this. Agnes suggested that she take a lover. There were plenty of candidates at the club. She would have loved to do this, but she couldn't, as sex wasn't her thing, closeness was. And, she was a married woman with three children. She would have to divorce Eddie. She couldn't take the financial risk. She decided to stay with the life that had been chosen for her.

Eddie bought her a Mercedes convertible when he was promoted. She loved the car, but she really wanted him. She settled for the car. It was bright yellow, the color of her hair. When she got out of the car, she knew she was being watched. She would make sure that her skirt or dress hiked up when she exited the car, hoping there were men (or boys) still watching her. There always were. She loved driving her car with the top down. When a trucker pulled next to her, she would pull her skirt up so that the trucker could look down at her and whistle. She found the little fun that was left wherever she could. There wasn't much.

With Eddie as vice president, she had to become even more mature and matronly, the demure wife. She danced less, showed less leg, and flirted less; she was boring herself. She was a respected member of the community. She had become Mrs. Edward Stern and the mother of his children—how awful.

Once Betty lay naked alone in her bedroom spread across the immense king-sized bed thinking of making love to another man—that smarmy smoothie from the club, Roy Rodgers. It made her itch all over. She thought that it should be her; she just wasn't sure whether she wanted it to be Eddie or Roy. She thought of when Eddie came home from work, in or out of town, and how he went right to work. They still slept in the same bedroom, but it was mainly sleep. The few times that she slept close to Eddie, it was just to feel close to another human being—it usually didn't work.

She wanted what Agnes had; she was jealous. She didn't want to wait until Eddie died; she wanted it now. She was living a slow death. She was living someone else's life and waiting for her own to begin.

Betty was now 38 years old. She had always thought of herself as young, with everyone older than her. Now people, at the club and in the community, were younger than she. She saw 40 approaching and felt that her life would be over if she didn't do something about it. In the meantime, she would go on being a corporate wife; she actually did it very well.

She watched the children get older and agonized through each of their problems as they moved through their teenage years. She felt paralyzed to do anything for them. She was caught up in her own life. She had seen her dream come true, to be rich, and it hadn't made her happy and now she had no dream. This was worse than having a dream unfulfilled. She resolved that this was to be her life. She was the wife of a vice president and she would always be Mrs. Edward Stern. Where had her life gone, when would her life really begin. She had fully become her mother and she didn't like it one bit.

Points to ponder:

As youngsters growing up we all have dreams and fantasies about how our life is going to turn out. Lower middle class individuals like Betty from a working class family dream of being rich and having all the material things their parents never had. Should they achieve such a position in life, does this bring them happiness from a dream fulfilled or does it shatter their dreams and leave them empty?

1. Individuals, like Betty, carry their childhood images (in this case chubby and unattractive) with them as they get older. Sometimes they perpetuate this image, and other times they work hard to create an opposite image. How do such childhood images affect our life and play out in later life?
2. Betty grew up being told to marry successful—it is just as easy to marry a rich man as a poor man. While it is wonderful to marry the one you love and live happily ever after, this rarely happens. Why do individuals get married and what do they hope for as in Betty's case?
3. Betty had finally found herself and her lost adolescence in Syracuse. It is said that most people live where they live because of family or

a job. Why would Betty move to Michigan to a life she didn't want?

4. Betty found her lost adolescent years in Syracuse. She was having the fun she should have had growing up. She was living the life of an attractive popular teenager. Why did she feel she had to abandon this identity when they moved to Michigan and Eddie became chief engineer?
5. Betty decided on her own to become the wife she thought Eddie wanted as a corporate wife when they moved to Michigan. She was thirty-two years old and she allowed herself to become a country club matron. Why did she make this assumption rather than talking to Eddie?
6. Eddie, seduced by his promotions, became a workaholic corporate follower, allowing his bosses to dictate how he should live. What would coerce one into leading such a life? What affect does this have on your life and the role you are asked to play?
7. Betty found herself in a life that she didn't want, that of a corporate wife and a country club matron. What kept Betty faithful to Eddie? Why couldn't she move on her own impulses to have fun and seek out other men? Why couldn't she leave Eddie?
8. Betty settled into her life as a corporate wife and Eddie settled into his life as a corporate executive. As couples get older. why do they forget what is important to the other mate? What is the significance of the yellow Mercedes convertible—for Betty and for Eddie?
9. Betty was unhappy with her life, so she envied her friend Agnes's life, not knowing whether Agnes was really happy or not. Many times we live out our fantasies through others such as Betty did through Agnes. What might have been her motives for envying Agnes?
10. As Betty grew older she was still attractive, especially to other men. While Betty fantasized about being with other men, she never acted on her impulses. Why did Betty hold herself back, creating resistance and reluctance to get involved with another man? What kept her with Eddie?
11. Betty continued being depressed about living a life she hated and envying others. How could Betty allow herself to grow older living a life she found so distasteful? Why didn't she do something about it?
12. Betty knew she had to do something about her life, but yet she did nothing, allowing herself to go through the motions of her role as a

proper corporate wife. What was Betty holding onto with Eddie? Do you think Betty or Eddie will ever change? If not, what keeps them together? Why do people allow their lives to just go on in a boring repetitive cycle?

Before you know it you are in a life you didn't want
playing a part you didn't audition for,
unable to change the role.

Divorce, Divorce

The Goose and the Gander

Alice and Will Sparrow met in college where they both were marketing and advertising majors. Will was president of his fraternity while Alice was a cheerleader and sorority member. Will had always been popular—it seemed from the day he was born. He was a three-letter man, in soccer, wrestling, and track. While these were not the popular sports, the three letters on his varsity sweater only served to increase his popularity, especially with the women. Alice's popularity mainly came from the size and shape of her breasts. They served to make her popular but they also denied her the freedom to develop social skills. She was severely insecure socially; she let her breasts do the talking for her.

All the girls in Alice's sorority had their eye on Will, as he was the campus catch. Alice found him self-indulged and arrogant. In reality, she was afraid of him, as he appeared to be so socially together. While she worked hard to give him the cold shoulder, she was secretly in awe of him. He really scared her, and made her feel incompetent. When she was around him, everything she said made her feel stupid. She was sure that Will wasn't interested in her.

Since Alice and Will shared the same major, they found themselves in some of the same classes. While all the girls in the class tried to get his attention, Will sat staring at Alice. When Alice caught him staring, she would turn away. She was sure that he was only looking at her breasts. She always wore tight shirts or sweaters with a push up bra to emphasize her assets—life was marketing. Sometimes Will stopped her before or after class to ask a question. She looked down at the floor and stammered an incoherent answer, turning red in the face. Will smiled at her and walked slowly away, looking back over his shoulder. She watched him walk away, as she got goose bumps on her breasts.

It was a homecoming party at Will's fraternity house that first brought Alice and Will together. Alice had come to the party with Roger Glock, an upperclassman. Most of the boys at school were petrified to ask Alice out, as they were sure that she would turn them down. There was nothing worse for the male ego than to be rejected by a girl. Roger, as the scion of an extremely wealthy family, didn't care, as there were too many girls after his money. He liked Alice because she didn't seem to care about his money. He was right about that. Alice liked Roger because he made her feel safe and she knew he wouldn't try anything. It was enough for Roger just to be seen with Alice and give the impression that something was happening.

While Roger went off to get her a drink, Alice stood at the old bathtub of gin sitting in the middle of the floor in the downstairs of the frat house. She felt a tap on her shoulder.

"Alice, how nice to see you," Will said as he stared at her chest. Alice blushed and turned away.

"I won't bite you," Will said.

Alice smiled.

"Would you care to dance?" he said.

Before she could answer Will was holding her hand and gently pulling her toward the dance floor. When the music changed, Will kept her on the dance floor. They danced silently with Will trying to dance closer and Alice trying to keep him away. She looked around for Roger and saw him holding two drinks and looking in her direction. But she continued to dance with Will and soon noticed Roger going upstairs with Natalie Cox, one of the so-called "bad girls." She felt better—Roger was in good hands. She snuggled closer to Will.

When the band finally took a break, Will took Alice by the hand and led her upstairs and she didn't resist. Will took her to his room. He said nothing as he slowly started to undress her. Alice knew she should stop him, but she couldn't. When she was fully undressed, Will stood back and looked at her with a gentle smile. "Exquisite," was all he could say.

Alice wanted his hands all over her but she couldn't move.

She took his hands and placed them on her breasts—what all the boys wanted to do. Will pulled his hands away. "Not yet," he said.

Will slowly ran his hands over her body, making sure he didn't touch her sexual parts. Alice was burning up, as she wanted Will. As Will continued, Alice couldn't take it any longer. She hurriedly pulled Will's clothes off and coaxed him toward the bed.

"Please," she groaned. It was the first words she had spoken to Will.

Will gently made slow love to her. Alice knew she was on unsafe ground, but she couldn't stop herself.

When Will and Alice went back downstairs, most of the crowd had left. Alice looked around for Roger but he had already gone.

"Come," Will said, "I'll walk you home."

At the sorority house, Will took her hand and kissed her gently on the cheek, then walked slowly away.

After that Alice saw Will from time to time walking around the campus with other girls on his arm. Neither of them said anything about the night in his room. In fact, they hardly talked to each other. Alice, although missing the thrill of Will, crossed it off as another frat boy conquest.

Three months later Alice found that she was pregnant. She was petrified to confront Will as he still scared her. She couldn't talk to him so she told her best friend Adele.

A few days later, Will came over to Alice's sorority house. He took her by the hand and led her out to his car. He sat across from her in the driver's seat and smiled.

"Alice, why didn't you tell me?"

Alice looked down at her lap. She wasn't showing so Adele must have told him.

Will handed her a piece of paper.

"What is this?" she said.

"What we need to do to get married." He smiled over at her.

"Will, I can't do this."

Will smiled at her again. "Yes you can. It was my fault. I'll see you on Tuesday."

After Will drove away, many thoughts ran through Alice's head. She had hardly said more than three sentences to this man and now she was going to marry him; a man she was still afraid of, but he was still the campus catch.

When Alice and Will graduated from college a few months later, and two months before the baby, Will took a corporate marketing job and Alice became a stay at home housewife and mother to her baby daughter. Will thinking quite a lot of himself, set the rules for the marriage, for Alice's behavior, and for the children. Alice obeyed; she was afraid not to. Will had one affair after another, as he was still attractive to women. Alice continued to be a good wife and mother, eventually having two more daughters.

Will and Alice had very little to say to each other. Will was still fascinated by Alice's body but partook of it less and less. As Alice had actually never really been that interested in sex this didn't bother her greatly and she didn't miss Will as she didn't really know him. She stayed faithful to Will as she was bound to her own value system. She couldn't be disloyal and she couldn't disgrace her husband by having sex with another man. Will would leave her in an instant and she would get nothing.

Ultimately, Will met Julia, who wanted more than a casual affair or just to have sex with him. After two years of a torrid affair, she gave him the final ultimatum—leave your wife or leave me. This was after sixteen years of marriage to Alice. Will was quite comfortable with his situation, a devoted wife at home, and devoted girl friends and sex partners out of the house. Life was working for him. He was ready to give Julia up and move on to his next conquest. However, when it came time to confront Julia, he couldn't do it. For the first time in his life it was more than just sex; he actually liked Julia as a person.

Alice became a rich woman through the divorce. For her it was poetic justice for the years she had spent with that monster. Within six months Will was married to Julia. He continued with his affairs.

But Alice was devastated, as she had always assumed that

Will would always be there. Now she was alone with three teen-aged daughters. Even divorced she couldn't be unfaithful to Will. Old values and fears die hard.

Alice spent considerable time with her best friend Gladys, who had been divorced from another ogre a number of years before, and other women at the club. Membership at the exclusive country club was a fringe benefit from the divorce. Alice looked to Gladys for consolation as a recently divorced woman and Gladys, as a fellow veteran of the marital wars, felt obligated to help her. Gladys would spend many late nights with Alice, sometimes at Alice's house, sometimes at her house. Alice was accumulating sympathetic women friends, but she was distancing herself from male friends.

It was about this time, around two years after the divorce, that Alice first took a lover. Not really a lover, but a male partner. His name was Peter Helfand. He was an environmental lawyer. Alice had met him at a party in her condo building. She had not even considered another man since her divorce, as she still hated Will and all men for what Will had done to her. Alice and Peter started their relationship as concert and museum partners. He had been divorced for over twelve years with one married daughter and was sour on women. She felt physically and sexually safe with him. They were able to have a good time without any sexual overtones. Alice was 43 years old at the time and Peter was 47, they weren't kids anymore, they just felt like it.

Gladys urged Alice to give love a try but she felt she wasn't ready. Gladys and others had fixed her up on dates a number of times, but she never went out with any of them a second time. They all wanted to get close to her immediately and take her to bed, as she was still a very attractive woman with the breasts of a much younger woman. Gladys was becoming a full time counselor.

Peter was finally pushing for more than a platonic relationship. Alice was still happy being just friends. Gladys told her that it was impossible for a man and a woman to remain just friends as sex was always ultimately there. If Alice didn't do something about it, she would lose Peter.

Gladys invited Alice and Peter to her house for dinner one night. It was just the three of them. Gladys had a champagne cocktail hour, free flowing wine with dinner, after dinner aperitifs, and brandy cake for desert. By the time dinner was over, they were all feeling beyond mellow. They went into the den to listen to music and sip on brandies. Gladys took the single chair, which forced Peter and Alice to sit together on the small love seat. Romantic classical guitar played on the stereo.

As Peter held Alice's hand and Alice leaned her head on his shoulder, Gladys got up to go. She looked at the couple enviously. "Good night, you two," Gladys said as she started to leave the room.

"Oh, don't go," whispered Alice. "Please."

Peter looked over at Gladys knowingly. They nodded to each other.

"I'll see you both in the morning, she said as she left."

Alice got the point and gave in. Upstairs, in the room Gladys had prepared for them, they both came quickly as it had been a long time for both of them. She cursed herself for waiting. But, she could still see the son of a bitch watching her; her ex-husband wasn't letting go. She was free when she was having sex with Peter, he would just have to continue doing that.

Points to ponder:

Couples get married for various reasons, sometimes due to an unwanted pregnancy, other times to avoid being lonely, and sometimes out of desperation so as not to be left. Sometimes the arrangement works, other times it is a terrible mistake and a cataclysmic disaster. Guilt and fear of leaving the other one may keep the couple intact physically, but psychologically one or both of the partners has already left; creating a living prison and maybe hell.

1. Alice was a popular sorority girl and a cheerleader. But, she was never sure whether her popularity came sincerely or due to her large well shaped breasts. This made it easy for her to attract boys. How does

one ever know what is attractive to them? Does the ease of physical attraction make it easier or more difficult for one to learn how to socialize?

2. Will was a three-letter man, in soccer, wrestling, and track. While these were not the popular sports the three letters on his sweater impressed the girls and the girls in Alice's sorority considered him the campus catch. His social arrogance scared Alice, but something about him attracted him to her. What are some of the attributes that attract us to a member of the opposite sex? Are they always rational feelings?
3. Alice always wore tight shirts or sweaters with a push-up bra to emphasize her breasts. However, she always felt uncomfortable when she caught a boy, especially Will, staring at her breasts. What were some of the conflicts Alice had with her endowment of breasts? Why do girls want to display what they know the boys are interested in even if makes them uncomfortable?
4. Alice didn't have many dates as the boys at school were afraid to ask her out, assuming she was already going out with another boy or that they would be turned down—and such rejection would kill their egos. Due to Alice's social ineptness, she tended to go out with safe dates such as Roger Glock, who was satisfied just to be seen with Alice. Why do young males and females play such social games rather than being honest with each other?
5. Will held Alice's hand and gently pulled her toward the dance floor and then led her upstairs. He undressed her and eventually made slow love to her with each one barely saying a word to each other. While Will knew exactly what he was doing, Alice knew this was not what she wanted to do but she couldn't stop herself. What is it that males and females want from a sexual relationship—is it similar or are there differences?
6. After Will seduced Alice, neither one of them said anything about it—they hardly talked to each other. Will went on with other girls; Alice merely dismissed it. What is that boys really want from girls and vice versa? How important is the sexual conquest?
7. Alice found out that she was pregnant from her one night with Will. She couldn't confront Will, so she told her best friend Adele, who told Will. Will came over and negotiated the marriage. It was his fault and

he was willing to do right by Alice. They still hadn't said more than three sentences to each other. What are the motives for a couple to marry? Did Will do the right thing for himself and Alice? When a young girl realizes that she is pregnant, is marriage always the best solution? What are some other possibilities?

8. Upon graduation Will accepted a corporate marketing job and Alice became a stay at home housewife and mother. Will became the dominant spouse and set the rules for the marriage and Alice. Alice obeyed, as she was still afraid of Will. Why do women (mainly) accept such domination and oppression from their spouses?
9. During the marriage Will had one affair after the other. Alice continued being a good wife and mother to her now three daughters. Will, still fascinated by Alice's body, had less and less sex with her. Alice couldn't have sex with another man as Will would leave her and she would get nothing. Why do women and society allow such a double standard to still exist today? What are the reasons that Will and Alice stayed together?
10. Ultimately Will met Julia, who was more than just sex to him. He divorced Alice, making her a rich woman. After six months with Julia, Will continued with his affairs. Alice, now divorced and alone with three daughters, still couldn't be unfaithful to Will. Once a couple, either one or both, realizes the disaster that marriage has caused them, why do they stay together? Is there a proper way to split and divorce?
11. Around two years after her divorce, Alice found a male partner, Peter Helfand. They were able to have a good time, as concert and museum partners, without sexual overtones. Alice's friend Gladys invited them to her house and set them up so that they finally consummated the sexual act. Why does sex play such an important part in a relationship for a couple—be it the male and/or the female? Are there other important parts to a relationship? What are they? Why did Alice have such trouble consummating her relationship with Peter?
12. Alice finally found out that sex with the right person was all right and a healthy part of a male-female relationship with Peter. What are some of the messages that become part of our story about sex that result in retarding a healthy sexual relationship?

Why do the oppressed allow the oppressors
to oppress them, needing the oppression
to create their own identity,
and missing the oppression when it stops?

Poor Boy Does Good—

Or Does He?

Marty Scargill was the son of a working class itinerant carpenter and his wife. His father drifted from construction site to construction site; never having a permanent job as he had problems getting along with others especially bosses. If the construction boss told him to do something that wasn't his way or criticized his work he would tell the boss off and leave the job. Marty remembered too many times when his father was at home drinking away his sorrows and cursing at "those idiots" who ran the world and construction sites. Marty remembered more of these times than times when his father brought home a decent pay check. His mother put up with it until she couldn't do it anymore—lying to the landlord, the grocery owner, the electric company and so forth. She went out and got a job making more money than his father ever did, and a steady job. It was his mother who took care of the family and made sure that they ate regularly—Marty and his two sisters.

Marty grew up in Rye, New York, his family moving from place to place, one step ahead of the landlord and the bill collectors. He vowed that one day he would have enough money so that he wouldn't have to live like that. Due to the many moves Marty made few friends, as he knew he would have to leave them soon. He avoided attachments; his life was easier and better that way. Upon graduation from high school, he worked with his father as a carpenter. He knew of no other options. But Marty was polite and kept his jobs, continually persuading the boss to give his dad another chance. To keep Marty, they ignored his father's bad behavior. College wasn't a consideration for boys who couldn't afford it and whose parents saw no value in a college education. His father didn't have a college degree and it never held him back. Marty hadn't even considered it as schoolwork wasn't his thing. He was bright and smart but not for school. He would succeed in spite of not having a degree and in spite of his father's legacy.

When America entered the Vietnam War, Marty was one of the first to be drafted—he was then 20 years old. Marty spent three years in the Army overseas seeing heavy combat. He would never talk about those years; it was as if he was ashamed of what he did and what he saw. When he returned to the states, he drifted around New York City looking for a thread to his life—any thread. Ultimately, he applied to Cornell University in Ithaca, New York upon the advice of a good drinking buddy and alumnus as a way of ending his senseless days of drinking and womanizing. The GI bill would pay for his college, and maybe he could get a life back—any life other than what he had left in Rye.

Marty was accepted into the Cornell school of hotel management. He didn't know what he wanted to do. Hotel management seemed as good as anything. All he knew was a little carpentry and a lot of killing. Taking care of people might be a welcome relief. It would also bring him in contact with a better class of people. At Cornell, being one of the older students, he kept to himself. He rented a small shabby apartment off campus. He went to classes and came back to the apartment. He drank alone and slept alone. He craved company but without any demands. In the meantime, he was very much alone. He preferred life that way; no demands and no one telling him how to lead his life.

In his first year at Cornell, Marty took up with a girl named Rhoda Petrowski who worked in the school cafeteria. At that time, very few girls, particularly poor girls, went to college. Rhoda was from town, a "townie," and took the best job she could find out of high school. She wasn't popular nor did she get good grades in high school. She saw her life as hopeless. She would get a better job later; she knew she would. Her family was far from rich; they lived on the poor side of town. She was flattered that a college boy was interested in her. She didn't particularly like Marty; he was too uptown and too uptight, but her family encouraged the relationship. A college boy was better than gold to a family from the other side of the tracks.

Marty didn't particularly like or dislike Rhoda. After Vietnam he didn't want to get close to any other human being. With Rhoda it was easy, he didn't have to perform, he just had to be there. He was attracted to the possibility that there was no future here. She would keep him from his loneliness without making any demands. He could hide with her; fill his time and get through the days and nights. He liked girls, and people, who made no demands on him.

Marty had no real money to speak of. This was partly what kept him from seeking the acquaintance of his classmates and dating a richer girl. He would meet Rhoda in the cafeteria after classes and she would get dinner for the both of them. They would then go to his room off campus, and smoke and drink. When they had both gotten sufficiently high (or drunk) they would make love on his little bed. Marty would lose his anger as he climaxed. Rhoda never climaxed. It was all they could do to keep from falling on the floor. Neither one enjoyed the sex part, but it kept them from being alone. Rhoda had been a virgin before Marty. Rather than be alone or go home to her parents at night, she preferred to spite them through sex with Marty. She became pregnant during Marty's first year. She didn't care; this was the way it was supposed to be. Marty figured that this also was fated; he didn't care, so he agreed to marry her. They had a baby girl, Hope, that March. Marty was 24 and Rhoda was 19.

He graduated in three years—he had years to make up—and was offered a position with a hotel chain as assistant manager in Albany. It was while with the hotel that Marty learned the value of people, both customers and employees. He was taught by his boss Tom Ketchum that each customer was their business and that each employee was valuable; it was the ignored unhappy customer and the unappreciated low paid employee who could kill your business. Marty learned to be a "people person" and that appearance was everything. He became a performance artist who loved everyone. He could help and befriend people; he just couldn't get close to them.

Marty enjoyed his job. He loved dealing with people and solving problems. In his second year on the job, Rhoda got pregnant again. Hotel chains didn't pay much and Marty was concerned as to how they would make it with two kids. One of his frequent customers at the hotel, Warren Bennis, was an executive at a large manufacturing company. When he visited the plant in Albany he always stayed at Marty's hotel. Marty had gotten to know him well after solving a lost luggage problem for him. It seemed that Warren had arrived in Albany, but his luggage had gone to Rochester. Marty was able to retrieve Warren's luggage the same day.

Warren took Marty out to dinner and they became road friends. Now when Warren came to town, he and Marty would get together, sometimes the two of them, sometimes with Rhoda. Warren had grown fond of both of them. They were like his family away from home. When Marty told Warren about the impending baby and his financial concerns, Warren told him he would see what he could do.

A week later Warren called Marty and offered him a job at his company's Albany plant as assistant to the plant manager. The plant manager was a traditional dictatorial SOB of that time and the employees detested him. Marty would be the "people person."

Rhoda gave birth to another girl, Faith, just as the offer came. Marty didn't hesitate to take the job; it paid over twice what he was making. He never looked back and they never had another child. He didn't want to be in this position again. He had a new job that would keep him from getting close to Rhoda and the kids—a perfect position.

Marty knew nothing about bronze manufacturing, but he knew a lot about people. The plant manager, Leroy Grindel, was of the old school—if you don't watch those bastards all the time they'll steal you blind. Marty quickly became the confidant of the employees. They would do anything for Marty, but nothing for Leroy. Marty learned quickly what he had to know about manufacturing. When Leroy finally pushed the plant employees too far and they resisted his pushing and shoving, plant production started to drastically decline. Management decided, as a way to get Leroy out of plant operations, to promote him to an administrative staff position at headquarters. That was how they removed senior plant employees who had outlived their usefulness. Headquarters top management wanted to replace Leroy with another plant manager in their system, but Warren fought for Marty and he prevailed. Marty became the Albany plant manager ending his money worries and ensuring that he stay away from his home. This was a perfect set-up that allowed for Marty to continue hiding.

Through his appearance (Marty was six foot two inches tall and built broadly and he always wore a suit with a flower in his lapel from his hotel management training) and his people skills, he was able to bring production results to new record highs. Six years later he was transferred to the larger Toledo plant; where again he was quite successful in increasing production results. He has been there as plant manager ever since. Based on his success as plant manger, he has been expecting the promotion to Cleveland plant manager, the flagship and largest plant of the company's empire. He has consistently been told that this would happen as soon as they could find a replacement for him at Toledo. In the meantime, three plant managers came and went at the Cleveland plant.

He has been at Toledo for sixteen years and it is time for him to move on. If it wasn't now he would spend the rest of his career in Toledo; which was a fate worse than death for him. Work and the company had become his life. They wouldn't disappoint him. Three weeks later, Marty picked up a memo from headquarters announcing the appointment of Steve Hill as the new Cleveland plant manager. He was 26 years old with an MBA from Harvard. Marty lost out to affluence and education. He was destined to spend his life where he was. To Marty, his life was over. He began drinking and bemoaning his fate, staying out as late as he could, resisting going home. The nut hadn't fallen far from the tree; it only spoke and dressed better.

Points to ponder:

There is a tendency for individuals to either embrace their parents and their heritage or to turn their backs and embrace the opposite set of values. Many times such parental and cultural messages, for and against, provide the pivotal focus for the individual to conduct his or her life. Sometimes it takes an individual time to realize what his or her real prime mover is in life; sometimes the individual never realizes what really motivates him or her and just moves through life as it happens; accepting his or her fate, not knowing why.

1. Why do some parents, like Marty's father, abdicate their role as father allowing their own psychological needs to overpower their own selfish needs to be irresponsible?
2. When one parent, such as Marty's father, lets the family down, why is it that the other parent, such as Marty's mother, assumes the role of rescuer, enabling the spouse to continue in their role of irresponsibility?
3. What is the effect of adversity or shame on a youngster such as Marty when he grows up, such as Marty's family moving from place to place and always having money problems?
4. What effect does one's family life have on the ability to obtain friends and keep them, expecting other people to like the individual or not? Consider Marty's situation.
5. So much of what we embrace emanates from our own family's values. How did these values affect Marty in his decision not to go to college and become a carpenter like his father?
6. The individual does not always make his or her own decisions such as Marty being drafted for the Vietnam War. How does an individual deal with such twists of fate? Do such experiences test the individual's value system? In what manner?
7. Many times it is merely serendipity that helps an individual to make a life decision such as Marty applying to and being accepted to Cornell University's school of hotel management. How do we convince ourselves that such decisions are all right?

8. What are the factors that form the way we decide to live? Consider Marty's experience in the war, drifting around New York, going to Cornell, living a reclusive life, taking up with Rhoda (a poor local girl), getting her pregnant and marrying her.
9. What pressures and values drew Rhoda to Marty? Why was she willing to engage in sex with Marty? Why would the two of them marry primarily because of Rhoda becoming pregnant?
10. What transposed Marty from a reclusive individual into a people person at his job as assistant hotel manager? Had he really changed or was it merely a performance piece?
11. Many times our lives change through the introduction of one significant person? What effect did Warren have upon Marty and his getting Marty a job at the manufacturing company?
12. How did work provide a hiding place for Marty, keeping him from looking at what was really happening to his life?
13. How do decisions not made effect us in our later life? Consider Marty getting a hotel management degree, and then working in another field, and finally being passed over for youth, affluence, and education.
14. Why do we accept our fate, such as Marty being stuck at the manufacturing company, and sometimes judge it as bad, resulting in adverse behavior such as drugs and alcohol, ignoring your family responsibilities, and becoming that bad role model from the past—that is Marty's father?

Leaving our fate to outside forces
keeps us always on the outside.

The First Born

Momma's Boy

Derek was born when his parents, Tom and Jane, were both 23 years old. Many would say that this was much too young to start having children; others might ask what were they waiting for. In this case, Tom was mature (and adult like) from a work and professional standpoint. This was the world he hid in. However, from a social and emotional standpoint, he was very immature. His problems in relating to other people were very damaging in his work and personal life and crossed over to his relationship with his wife. He really didn't relate, but possessed Jane as a source of security and someone to take care of him. Jane, on the other hand, may have been hiding from her own reality, that of an unattractive, unpopular child. Tom may have become the hiding place that gave her security from an unfriendly world. These then were Derek's young parents; maybe no more or less dysfunctional than other first time parents, with their own set of dysfunctional characteristics which would have a profound effect on Derek. His parent's genes as well as their psychological and emotional patterns would help form Derek.

Derek was born a physically healthy baby at seven pounds and six ounces. Jane's pregnancy had gone without any major complications. She was thin and tried to stay thin during her pregnancy and that may or may not have had an effect on the baby. Who really knows? Derek was a long thin baby with wisps of blond hair. He had a long angular face with a fairly sharp chin. He was not cute and cuddly as might be said for other babies. In truth, he was closer to an ugly baby; but who would call a baby ugly. Derek looked just like his mother, the image of her when she was a baby. He was Jane's son.

When Derek was born, Tom was at work. That was not unusual. The first male to pick Derek up and cuddle him was his Uncle Nick. It was instant bonding between adult male and baby.

But when Tom first came to the hospital and was given Derek to hold, Tom held him tentatively and gave him back to Jane as quickly as he could. There was no immediate bonding between father and son. It was just the opposite. From the first day, Derek preferred his Uncle Nick to his natural father. The bonding between father and son remained a problem.

Jane had trouble calling the baby Derek, but she had agreed with Tom that he would name the baby boys and she would name the baby girls. Tom had no family names to fall back on. He picked the name of an actor. It was a name that he thought brought distinction, breeding, and upper class attachments. It would give his son an advantage when he entered the world of business and commerce later in his life Tom thought. Tom was sure he would want to follow in his footsteps. Tom didn't allow nicknames or shortened versions of names, so the baby had to be called Derek in his presence. Uncle Nick called the baby Dicky (and always would), but Tom would cringe when he heard it. Jane got into the habit of calling the baby Dicky as well. Her mother said to her, "what kind of name is Derek for a baby?" So, what's in a name; only Derek would know the suffering of such a name.

Derek grew up as his mother's son. In the early years, she took him with her everywhere she went. She didn't trust him with his father. But when Nick came to visit, she left Derek with him. Derek was always glad to be with his Uncle Nick, but not with his father as he was too fussy and strict. Uncle Nick was always fun. After the first six months or so, Tom got uncomfortable with his son getting too close with his Uncle Nick. He believed that Nick as a laborer was a bad influence on his son. It was better to cut it off now then to have a larger problem later. Tom asked Jane to discourage Nick from visiting. She thought it was just Tom's male jealousy, so she agreed. Tom never told Jane what his reason was and she never asked.

Derek's earliest memories were being with his mother and Uncle Nick. In his mind, this was his earliest family unit. Tom became the man who forbid or stopped him from doing things. Tom wouldn't, and couldn't, get close to his son. There was no hugging, kissing, or

"I love yous." He expected Jane to raise the son he wanted, someone like him, but he didn't see himself having any role in such raising. In Tom's mind he wouldn't have brought another child into this world. If Jane wanted children that was fine with him, as long as it didn't interfere with his work. Work would always come first; life would be second.

Tom kept away from his son as much as possible. Having a son interfered with his work, which was always most important. Tom designed his life to have as little contact as possible with his son. When Derek would want to be with his father, Tom would call for Jane to come get him. It wasn't that Tom wanted to be a bad father; he just believed that if he tried to be a father that would be worse than not being a father.

So Derek spent his first few years primarily with his mother. There would be infrequent trips to visit his mother's parents and brothers. He remembered his grandmother as being more concerned that he wouldn't make a mess in her house than about him. His grandfather would hold him and make baby noises at him and say, "he definitely is Jane's son—looks just like her." He would put Derek down quickly and Jane would quickly gather him up and rescue him from her father. Jane would tell him, "You are whoever you want to be." His mother's older brothers would try to rough house with him, to make him a real man. When Uncle Nick was there Derek would go directly to him and they would play on the floor for hours. His grandfather and older sons would be relieved and go down to the basement recreation room.

Derek from birth was a tall, thin, frail child. He had been nurtured as a baby through Jane's breastfeeding and ate well as a toddler. Jane tried to feed him the right nutritious foods, but he didn't seem to gain weight or get much heavier. He was destined to be tall and thin like Jane, with the same type of long face. Jane had always been over protective due to his frail physical condition and sensitive nature. Tom was also concerned about him hurting himself, as he wasn't built for endurance in the real world. Physical activities were de-emphasized; academic endeavors were encouraged. Tom was already programming Derek's career in business and upper middle class society. Derek could play later; now he would learn.

Derek, just like his mother, took to books and learning easily. Even at four years old he was learning to read, write, and solve math problems. Tom was proud of his son. He knew he was going to be just like him. Jane was concerned that he was going to be just like her, too much books and not enough fun. She wanted her son to have a more normal childhood, maybe even to enjoy it. She would have to accomplish this in spite of Tom.

The following year Derek was to start regular school. The public school that the children living in their development went to was only two years old. It was in a suburban school district that was considered the best in the area. Jane thought it would be best for Derek, both academically and socially. Tom looked into private schools that would ensure Derek a spot in one of the best high school prep schools. Tom had Derek graduating from college even before he entered elementary school. Tom found a private school, Edgemoor Academy, which boasted of many graduates who had gone onto impressive careers in business. Once again, Tom prevailed. Derek, with his sensitive nature, would be much more comfortable in an academically oriented private school; kids in public school could be so cruel.

Derek excelled academically at school and with that accrued popularity with the other studious kids. While this was good for Derek, he really craved popularity with the more popular athletic kids. This didn't come as easy as popularity in this group was based more on physical capabilities such as ball playing, swinging, running, skipping, and so on. Derek wasn't very good at these things and always stayed on the periphery.

Derek became alienated from the neighborhood children. He was an outsider to the other kids—the rich private school kid. They started to call him names such as "sticks, pole, slats, mantis, and Dicky Rich." Jane heard her son being called such names and she felt for him; it was her childhood all over again.

Derek would be the only kid picked up by his private school bus in their development. Some of the other kids, particularly the older kids, would taunt him as he got on the bus. Slowly, he made friends with some of the other kids at his school. They were more like him. Sometimes he would go home with them and sometimes they would come back with him. Jane would try to make them comfortable. Many of the kids at Edgemoor came from the wealthiest and oldest families in the area. It made Tom beam when he heard the names of the children Derek brought home. Derek tended to go to the other kids' homes, as they were much larger. He was becoming ashamed of his own house and his mother who did everything around the house. Most of the other kids had maids, butlers, and chauffeurs.

When Derek was eight years old and in third grade, the other kids started to tease him. First, they teased him about his mother, rather than a chauffeur, driving him and picking him up and in a station wagon. Then they started to call him names, not so endearing nicknames, such as rails, lurch, skeleton, and bones. Derek retreated with a few friends who also were the butt of the other kids jibes. They formed an exclusive academic circle. Derek didn't particularly care for these kids, but they were the ones he was left with. He really preferred to come home alone and read his books and do his homework alone in his room. Jane insisted that he go to other kids houses and that they come to their house. They stayed inside and read or played games. Tom was pleased; Jane was quite concerned. They did nothing about it.

In high school, Derek found a group of similarly minded non-social boys as school friends. They might get together to go to the library or study together, but had little contact outside of school. This was fine with him and it was safe. When he wasn't at school, he would stay in his room and read. Where he once looked healthy, he now looked sallow and sickly. His high school, Hawthorne Academy, prided itself on developing well-rounded young men of the upper middle and affluent classes. They stressed socialization as well as academics. In their minds they thought they were preparing young men for what they would face in the real world of privilege and upper class entitlement.

As part of the schools social program, they required each student to learn social dancing and graces with the opposite sex. To practice such social graces, the school had a series of weekend dances, some at the school, others at nearby girls' private schools. It was expected that each student attend these dances, either with a date or without. Derek was uncomfortable with girls, especially at that time when some of the girls were taking the lead in the sexual dance. He could go without a date and face his vulnerability to female persuasions or find a safe date for himself where the other girls would leave him alone and the other guys would leave his date alone.

There was a girl named Penelope Prentiss in his neighborhood. The other kids preferred calling her Penny, but she preferred Penelope. She had had her eyes on Derek since she first saw him five years before. She had invited Derek to a number of parties and social functions, but he had always refused. She was extremely skinny, gawky, long faced and wore glasses. Derek found her unattractive and a pest. Now, however, he saw her as an ideal date for the required school dances. He would be safe from other girls and needn't worry about the other boys trying to steal his date.

Derek went through high school in this manner. He would go to school, come home and read, and date Penelope. There was nothing really happening anywhere. Derek had other boys call him to go over homework or talk about school projects, but he never socialized with any of them outside of school. Tom took pride that Derek was turning out more like him than Jane. He would turn out all right. Tom was sure of that.

Derek got mostly A's in high school. Tom was expecting Derek to follow in his footsteps and attend his college. When the time came to apply for colleges, Tom applied to his college for his son. As the son of a graduate, and with Derek's academic record, he was readily accepted. Tom was pleased, but Derek was not. Tom wanted him to study business economics just like him. There would be a position at Tom's company ready for him. Derek wanted to study literature and philosophy, just like his mother. He had applied to colleges on his own and had been accepted at Princeton, Yale, and Columbia.

Tom tried to argue with Derek, but he got nowhere. Derek wasn't worried about a job or making money. He had always been taken care of by his parents and had never really wanted for anything. He assumed that would continue. He neither knew, nor cared, how one made money or how much was needed to live in the manner that they lived. Jane had protected him from all that. She gave the impression that you just lived. He had no idea what his father had to do to make the money. He had very little contact with his father. He knew that he didn't want his father's life; he wanted his mother's. It was his mother who continually told him "be whatever you want." This is what he wanted. Nothing, not even his father's pressure, would change his mind.

Tom had little commitment to take Derek to visit Princeton, Yale, and Columbia. Jane offered to take him. Tom didn't object, but he made it plain that he would rather she didn't. This time Jane stood firm. It was her son's life and he should make the decision. On each visit, Derek and Jane talked about life, philosophy, and the world of literature. Derek was excited. It was like old times with just him and his mother.

On their visit to Columbia in New York, Uncle Nick joined him. Nick took them out to dinner at a fancy New York restaurant and then to a Broadway show. They stayed over night at Uncle Nick's apartment in the village. Derek wanted to be part of Nick's world. He told his mother on the way back home that he wanted to go to Columbia. He loved the school and he would be near Uncle Nick. Jane nodded. She was proud of Derek for doing what he wanted to do. She was convinced it was the right thing for him to do, but would Tom be.

With Jane's support, Derek was admitted to Columbia. He expected his mother to tell his father. That was how these things worked in their family. Derek couldn't confront his father, and he never had. Jane talked to Tom about Derek's decision. Tom at first said absolutely not, then said all right if that was the way it had to be but he wouldn't pay for it, then changed his mind and said he would pay for his son's college but he would be no part of it. He wasn't happy about Derek's decision, but he was his son. He secretly wished that he had been able to do the same thing. He told nobody this.

Points to ponder:

So much of who we become is determined by who our parents are and how they treat us, and the messages they convey to us. Equally important is how we see our parents, the bonding relationship with each one, and the overall impression each one makes on us. Typically, the child while growing up and when grown up either desires to emulate the parent or to distance him or herself from what is perceived to be like that parent. Sometimes there is ambiguity creating a love-hate relationship where the child seeks his or her individuality at the risk of losing the parent's approval. Often seeking one parent's approval the child finds the other parent disapproving.

1. Derek's parents, Tom and Jane, were relatively young when Derek was born. Do you think that their young age had anything to do with Derek's growth and maturation?
2. Tom insisted on naming his son Derek based on future advantages when he entered Tom's world of business and commerce. How important is a name to a child growing up and when the child grows up and enters the adult world?
3. Tom and Jane both brought scars from their childhoods into their marriage and parenthood. Tom hiding in his work from social contacts and Jane hiding through Tom from being an unattractive, unpopular child. What effect does the parents' dysfunctional issues have upon their children?
4. Derek looked just like his mother and became his mother's son, while Tom had trouble bonding with him. What importance does

such initial conclusions about a baby by the parents have upon the growth of the baby?

5. Derek bonded easily to his Uncle Nick, but not to his father. What possible issues and confusion can this cause for a child growing up?
6. Tom desired as little contact as possible with his son, hiding in his work. What scars are possible from such rejection by your father and is it possible that minimizing paternal contact could be more favorable to the child than negative contact?
7. Tom wanted his son to have a career in business just like him and become a part of upper middle class society. What affect does such parental pressure place upon a child growing up wanting to be just him or herself?
8. Tom and Jane saw Derek as physically frail and sensitive, resulting in Jane desiring to protect him and Tom placing him in the academic world to deemphasize the physical world. What messages might Derek assume from his parents programming of him?
9. Derek fulfilled his parents' prophecy for him by excelling academically and becoming socially reclusive. Jane tried to offer encouragement if that was what he wanted to be while Tom reveled in his son being just like him. What affect did this have on Derek as he went through school and started to grow up?
10. As his high school emphasized a social program by requiring each student to learn social dancing and attend its sponsored dances, Derek avoided the push toward socialability by bringing a non-threatening date. How do we sabotage ourselves from avoiding positive growth?
11. Derek was raised never having ever really wanted for anything because of his mother's protection and his father's giving him everything but himself. Does such a situation effectively prepare a child for life or provide for a false reality?
12. Why do parents push their children toward what they want for them rather than what the child wants for him or herself? In this case, Jane wanting to protect her son by having him join the world of literature and philosophy just like her, while Tom wanting him to join the world of business and commerce just like him. What pressures does this place on the child? How can parents help their child become what they want to be?

As much as we try not to,
we all become our parents' children—
some for and some against.

The Second Child

Living in the Footsteps

Philip was born two years and five months after his older brother, Larry. By the time he was born Larry was already his mother's favorite. There was not much room left in her heart for another son. When Philip was born, he wasn't given the attention that his brother had been given at his birth. Where she went over six months breastfeeding Larry, only stopping because her milk dried up, she got Philip onto the bottle immediately. Philip was a chubby baby, eight pounds and twelve ounces at birth, with wisps of brown curly hair and a round face. Where Larry had been thin and fair like his mother, Philip was broad and stocky like his father.

When Philip was still an infant, his mother had a mother's helper come in so that she could go out with Larry. The majority of her mothering time was spent with Larry. Philip seemed to accept being alone. When he got into his second year he wanted to come along, but his mother wasn't ready to drag two kids along so she continued to use the mother's helper. Philip would cry and scream and run to his room. He would hide so the mother's helper couldn't find him. Many times his mother would just leave him like this.

As Philip grew up he was always the tag along to Larry. He always looked up to his older brother as he was bigger and seemed more important. As a toddler, Philip wanted to do everything that Larry did. His mother couldn't do anything with Larry without Philip wanting to go along. Somehow she resented him for this. At an early age he sensed this and became a loner.

When Larry was in school his mother would go out by herself during the day and then when Larry came home from school the two of them would go out together. Philip would stand at the window and watch them drive away. He would stand there crying until he could no longer see the car. The mother's helper would try to soothe him by hugging him or getting him a cookie or some milk. He would pull away and run to his room. When he finally realized that it was easier to hate than to love, he wreaked his revenge. For instance, he would go to Larry's room and break one of his toys. He then would go into the kitchen and throw his glass of milk in the air and watch it break all over the floor. He would smile at the mother's helper and go back to his room. The more he hated them, the more they hated him. He was happier that way.

Philip was always a physically healthy child, naturally stocky and rosy. While Larry preferred playing inside, Philip was an outside child and very physically active. At the local playground Larry would play quietly in the sandbox while Philip would play around the swings and gym equipment. Philip would follow Larry around wanting him to play with him, but he seldom did.

When Larry was in sixth grade and Philip in fourth grade, Philip would get on the bus with Larry and want to sit with him and hang out with him at school. Larry didn't want to have to baby sit his younger brother, so he would move away. Philip would try to tag along, but Larry would reject him. After a while, Philip made friends (more than Larry had) with kids in his grade and went his own way. He always considered himself the outsider in the family. As Philip grew older, he became more robust. He would play sports, rough-house with the other kids, and stay outside as long as he could. When he was in fifth grade, he had become a tough kid. He got into a number of fights and always won them.

Larry was now in seventh grade and was easily picked on. One of the seventh grade bullies was harassing him in the school-yard and enticing him to fight. Larry would have nothing to do with fighting and violence. He started to walk away and the bully hit him on the back of the neck. Philip was in the schoolyard when this happened and jumped the bully. He expected Larry to help him. After all, they were brothers, but Larry continued to walk away.

Philip was in up to his armpits and maybe for the first time in danger. The bully started pounding on him, and Philip started pounding back. The schoolyard had filled with kids, who started cheering for Philip, as the bully wasn't well liked. With such encouragement (he had never been encouraged to do anything before), Philip stood his ground. He used all his might to punch the bully hard in the stomach, and the bully doubled over. The kids cheered for Philip to hit or kick him in certain places, but he backed off and waited. The bully got up and ran from the schoolyard. The kids cheered and thus began Philip's reputation. He was never bothered again and neither was Larry. Larry never thanked his younger brother for rescuing him, as he was too ashamed of his fifth grade brother taking care of him.

In the seventh grade when Philip was allowed to go out for sports, he made the junior varsity football and wrestling teams. In the eighth grade he made the varsity in both sports. Where Larry was the academian, Philip was the athlete. In the ninth grade, he was the starting fullback (used mainly for blocking) and defensive end. By this time, he had filled out into a real bull. He was big chested, muscular, and strong; much stronger than his brother. He scared Larry and he stayed away from him and that was all right with Philip.

By the seventh grade, Philip was almost fully developed. He had a powerful upper body with a wide chest and muscular biceps. His legs were like steel. When he and Larry would change in the locker room at the local swimming pool, Larry would look away and turn his back. Philip had more pubic hair than his older brother and his genitals were well developed. Larry was ashamed. Larry would wear swimming trunks that covered his thin legs. Philip would wear a small bikini that barely covered him.

Larry was a swimmer, so Philip became a diver. He would stand at the edge of the diving board, posing, and flexing his body. When he did this, all of the young girls (and most of the old girls) would stop and lose their breath. As he dived, all female (and some male) eyes would be on him. Larry covered himself up in a towel and ran and lay down on a lounger next to his mother. She would dry him off as soon as he got out of the water. Philip would lie on the side of the pool in his swimsuit on his back. The young girls would flock to him.

Philip started running around with the ninth graders from the football team. They were into partying and running with party girls and there were more party girls than good girls. It seemed that the girls were more involved in sex than the boys. Some of them would take on more than one guy in a night. Philip didn't care for that. He preferred a girl of his own. He would single out one girl at each party and go to one of the bedrooms. Quickly, Philip had earned a reputation and the girls waited to be picked by him. He would never pick any girl who pushed herself on him. He tried to be discriminating. There was usually plenty of alcohol and drugs at these parties. Philip would drink some beer, but that was all, as he was an athlete and he had to protect his body.

In the ninth grade when he was the starting fullback, the girls threw themselves at him. He was getting tired of girls. Many times on the weekend he chose to spend a night with the guys, just bullshitting and carrying on. When he wanted sex, it was always available. He was good at that, but not very good at grades.

Philip started hanging out with some of the high school kids, some who were old enough to drive. Philip was bigger and stronger than most of them. He never used his strength to take advantage of anyone as his size alone commanded respect. He had not gotten into another fight since fifth grade, as there was nobody who would challenge him. He was someone on the outside; but he was no one at home. He was used to being alone, and he didn't care. His parents gave him everything he wanted. What else did he need them for?

In high school, Philip started to drift. He still played football and wrestled, but it no longer excited him. He would still party on the weekends, but he was tired of the same routine. He would drink and have sex with girls, a different one each time, but he wasn't enjoying it. He had burned out at sixteen. There wasn't much for him to look forward to. How sad.

When he was sixteen, he was eligible to get his drivers license, and on the day of his sixteenth birthday he passed his test. He knew neither of his parents would take him for the test so he didn't ask them. He went with a friend. He had learned to take care of himself; he had learned to parent himself. He somehow paid for a used MG convertible. His parents never asked him how he bought it; they didn't want to know.

He was out of the house even more now, every night of the week and most of the weekend. He came home to sleep and clean up. His mother was surprised when he showed up for dinner. He was always polite to his parents but difficult to deal with. It was easier to let him have his own way. He was getting acceptable grades in school (B's and C's) and they just cared that he could get into college.

He would drive around in his MG, always with a different girl. He loved to have sex with the rich girls as it gave him the most pleasure. It was like getting back at his parents and it felt good. They always looked pleased when he was with a girl from a good rich family. Each time they hoped that he would settle with that girl. His parents should only know what these girls were doing. They would be sick; it made him sick.

Philip stopped playing football and wrestling in the eleventh grade as he had tired of them both. His father had hoped that he might continue and earn an athletic scholarship to college, as he wouldn't get in otherwise, certainly not on his grades. He spent his senior year as a playboy, mainly taking girls out much older than he was. He had tired of the high school games. By the end of high school, Philip hadn't had a real relationship with any of his girl friends. He really didn't like girls, but there was something that drew him to physically controlling them. He couldn't stop, but he didn't want to continue.

Points to ponder:

The first born, especially a boy, usually gets undivided attention and no matter how old he gets usually remains the favorite child. While the parents may not do it intentionally, the second child receives less attention and his or her needs are sometimes ignored in addressing the needs of the first child. Many times the placing of a sibling by birth order has enduring affects upon the child as he or she grows up and once they have grown up.

1. By the time Philip was born his older brother Larry was already implanted as his mother's favorite. What affect does initial parental attitude and expectations have on the growth of a child?
2. Larry was much like his mother, while Philip was more like his father. How does the parent's perception of which parent the baby looks like and acts like affect the baby's growth?
3. The younger sibling seems to have a longing to be like the older sibling and do everything the older sibling does. When the younger sibling, like Philip, is stopped or rejected from bonding with the older sibling, how does this affect the behavior of the younger sibling?
4. Being rejected by your older sibling as Philip was by Larry creates a trauma in the younger sibling. How would you describe the aspects of this trauma?
5. What affect did Philip being strong and robust and an outside kid as opposed to Larry being non-physical and more academic have on Philip changing his mental position?
6. When Philip beat up the bully who was picking on his younger brother Larry, what affect did it have on each brother? How did Philip feel about Larry not helping him?
7. Philip became fully developed early (by the seventh grade) with a powerful upper body and muscular biceps. What role does physical strength and attraction play in the positive development of a child?
8. As Philip became more physically strong and Larry stayed thin and weak, how did the relationship between the two brothers change? Why is the physical more coveted than the academic while growing up?
9. Philip took the opposite stance from his brother, such as physical to academic, diver to swimmer, athlete to student, and social to reclusive. What do you suppose drove Philip to this opposition of what his brother was?
10. Philip, using his physical attractiveness, became a lure to the girls. Was this really what Philip wanted or was he merely using his attributes to gain expected popularity?

11. Philip started to run around with older kids, using these kids as his family, partying and running around with girls, whether he liked it or not. What do kids do when they can't depend on their families for encouragement and support?
12. Philip tired of sports and worked only as hard as he had to in school to get acceptable grades of B's and C's. How does one understand that they are doing things for themselves and their own growth and not to please or spite their parents?

Free will allows us to be who we want to be, society pressures us to be who it wants us to be— usually society wins.

The Girl Child: Expectations

Cindy was born less than two years (about 21 months) after her brother Todd and five years after her older brother Roy. Her mother, Sally, had grown up with her mother always telling her how wonderful it was to have children—it was the woman's role. And, that was what her husband wanted from her. So she had two children, both sons. She didn't find it too wonderful. She found it constraining as they got in the way of her real life, which she was still waiting to begin. Then her mother told her that the greatest joy was in having a daughter. So, this time she had a daughter. Now her mother might allow her to go on with her life.

While Cindy was still an infant, newly arrived from the hospital, she stayed in the nursery and was fed a formula by the temporary mother's helper. When the helper would bring the baby into the room and hand her to Sally, she would lay the baby next to her, but Sally did little to comfort the baby. Sally would turn her back on the baby and try to sleep. So baby Cindy was alone.

When Sally first brought Cindy home, her two brothers were excited to have a baby in the house. Her older brother, Roy, wanted to hold her and rock her; then he went on his way. Her younger brother, Todd, looked at her, wouldn't touch her, and then ran to his room. As soon as Sally felt fit from the delivery of the baby, she left the baby with a mother's helper while she went out. Todd was so close in age to Cindy she hoped that the two of them would bond as brother and sister. She didn't know it, but the opposite was happening. Todd resented and hated his sister and she was to feel the same way.

When her father came home early (which was very rarely) when Cindy became a toddler, she would run to him and grab him around the legs. Her father would pat her on the head and gently (sometimes not so gently as she held on tenaciously) push her away.

She would then run to her mother and hang onto her skirt. Sally would pick her up and take her into the kitchen for a cookie—the answer to all mother's prayers.

When Cindy was two years old, Roy was six and already in elementary school, and Todd was four and going to pre-school. This was the first time that Cindy had the house and her mother to herself. Her mother joined a playgroup so that Cindy would have children her own age to play with. Sally really didn't know what to do with a girl. The playgroup consisted of about eight other children from the neighborhood—six boys and two girls. Sally expected Cindy to play with the two girls, but she preferred playing with the boys. The other two girls were too prissy for her—the boys had more fun. This was the first indication that Cindy was to be a tomboy, a father's daughter with the wrong father.

Cindy wanted to be on the swings and demanded that Sally push her and be with her like the other mothers. However, unlike the other mothers, Sally was into showing off her figure and attracting men, reinforcing that she was still desirable after three pregnancies. She wore tight mini skirts and tops, with high heels, and her long blond hair flowing behind her. When she pushed Cindy on the swing, she dug her left heel into the sand spreading her left leg so that the bottom of her skirt rode up to the top of her thigh exposing almost her entire left leg up to her bikini underpants.

When Cindy ran off from the playgroup (was it deliberate?), Sally had to chase her in her high heels. As Sally ran, her skirt ran up on her thighs exposing her entire leg. Cindy enjoyed making her mother chase her. When Cindy played in the sand box, Sally sat on the side forcing her skirt to ride up her legs. As she crossed and uncrossed her legs, she exposed her panties. She didn't seem to notice, but of course she did.

The older men playing chess in the park or sitting on the benches and the grounds keepers noticed Sally and stopped what they were doing to watch the spectacle. Male attendance at the park greatly increased on those days when Sally was there with Cindy. Cindy sensed the men moving to get in sight of her mother.

She didn't understand what they were looking at until years later. The image remained in her mind. She never wanted to be a woman like her mother, having to expose herself to men to get attention. She wanted to be more like the other mothers, who came to the park just to be with their children. She wanted to be approved of for herself.

Cindy filled out to look just like her father. She was broad across the shoulders, short and stocky, with her father's round face and curly sandy hair. She was not the kind of frilly girl that her mother was growing up; she was just the opposite. Sally spent most of her time with Cindy chasing after her in her tight skirts and high heels. While she appreciated the male attention, this wasn't the place she was looking for it. It was really too much for her—her sons had been much easier. She let Cindy grow up as much on her own as she could by leaving Cindy alone with the playgroup during the day. Her life was much more important than bonding with a daughter who was a stranger. When Cindy wanted anything, she went to her father. He gave her whatever she wanted, except himself.

It wasn't surprising that Cindy grew up by herself. She needed people, and liked them, but she couldn't get that at home. She grasped onto children her age and made them her friends for life—she collected people. Fortunately, she was extremely likable. When she started school, she spent more time at other kids houses than her own.

Cindy loved all kinds of animals. She found stray dogs and cats, some more stray than others, and brought them home with her. Sally let Cindy feed and play with them during the day. However, when her father was due home she made her take them back where she found them. On those days, Cindy got up on her father's lap and asked him if she could have a puppy; that was all she ever wanted. He said, "we'll see," and put her back on the floor. She ran off happily. She thought, "we'll see," meant soon. She never got her dog.

In school Cindy befriended all the social outcasts; that is, those kids who didn't seem to get the teacher's attention or didn't seem popular with the other kids. She had become the little Queen of the Misfits. She liked that, it made her feel important, and she liked helping kids who seemed to be ignored. Most of her friends were boys. She would run with them, play on the swings and gym, and play ball. The other girls sat around and played with dolls, painted, sewed, cooked and so on. She found them boring. She didn't understand why she had to play with girls who wanted to be like her mother. She wanted to play with boys who wanted to be like her father. She wanted to be a girl just like her father. Cindy would try to play with her brothers, but they pushed her away, so she found her own brothers.

When Cindy started elementary school the teacher encouraged her to play with the girls and leave the boys alone. She hated it, both the girls and the girly things. She would hide in her room when it was time to go to school. Sally was getting exasperated. She punished her by sending her to her room or denying her something (cookies or ice cream), but Cindy didn't care. She wasn't going back to that school. When she did go, she would do something to get herself in trouble, such as tie another girls pigtails together, steal their milk, hide their coats and so on. Sally got a daily call almost immediately upon Cindy entering school to come get her. This couldn't continue.

Sally was successful in getting the school to change Cindy's classroom. The new teacher allowed her to play with the boys if she wanted to. She was happy. The teacher allowed her to do all of the boy activities. She encouraged her to be who she wanted to be. Cindy was excited; she couldn't wait to get to school and never wanted to come home. She had much more fun at school than she could have at home. Her parents were relieved.

Cindy made a girlfriend almost immediately in the new classroom. Her name was Amanda Blake and she was just like Cindy. She loved the boys' games and playing outside. Cindy and Amanda played together with the boys while the other girls would stay inside. Most of the other girls weren't allowed to get dirty or their parents would punish them. If Cindy didn't come home dirty, Sally was concerned.

Throughout elementary school Cindy was extremely popular, especially with the boys in the class. The prissy girls in her class would tease her about being a tomboy. They didn't play with the boys, as good little girls didn't do that and they didn't get dirty. Cindy was always dirty; she just loved it. Cindy's best friend, other than Amanda, was Kent Biddle. Kent was a very shy sensitive boy whom the other boys ordinarily wouldn't play with—they might call him a sissy. Cindy and Amanda fought for his attention. This made him popular with the other boys.

The years between first and fourth grades were the best years of Cindy's life. She played with the boys and some of the girls and everybody just liked each other. The prissy girls were the enemy and none of her friends cared to play with them. The prettiest girl in the school, Pamela Houston, would watch her and Amanda playing with the boys and would stick her tongue out at them. Sometimes Pamela would turn from them, lift her skirt, and show them the back of her underpants. Cindy and Amanda didn't care, but the boys would look at Pamela.

When Cindy was nine years old and in the fourth grade, she started dressing like her father. She wore his old shirts with one of his old ties. She also insisted on having her hair cut short just like her father's. Her brothers found it spooky, but had little to do with Cindy anyway. They thought she was a little strange. Her male friends at school thought it was cool and that Cindy was cool. The girls at school moved further away from her.

In the fifth grade, the boys at school started to notice the prissy girls. Where once these girls were considered the enemy, now they were objects of desire. The boys asked Cindy how to win the favor of Pamela Houston. Cindy was disgusted. Coed dances started in the fifth grade so that the young masters and mistresses could begin their lessons in heterosexual social graces.

At the initial dances, all of Cindy's male friends stayed with her and Amanda on one side of the room while the prissy girls stayed on the other side of the room. The prissy girls snuck looks over to the other side of the room to see which of the boys were looking at them. Cindy and Amanda stared back at them and stuck out their tongues. Some of the prissy girls, including Pamela Houston, asked Cindy and Amanda if such and such a boy liked them or not. Cindy told them that the boys weren't interested in their type of girl.

A number of the girls in Cindy's class had older sisters who were sexually promiscuous. The younger girls learned from the older girls. Some of the girls started to wear lipstick and makeup, short tight skirts, tight tops (particularly those starting to develop) and short high heels. The boys began to take an interest.

Slowly, some faster, the boys stopped playing with Cindy and Amanda and became more attentive to the prissy girls. They were doing things with these girls that they had told Cindy they would never do. One of the boys, Andrew Tilden, stayed Cindy's friend. He was more comfortable playing like a boy than acting like a puppy to the prissy girls. The other boys made fun of him, but he held his ground, as Cindy was his friend. As most of the other boys started bragging about what they were getting sexually from the other girls, Andrew felt he had to do the same. He would tell them what he and Cindy did, none of it true. Cindy had started to develop breasts in the fifth grade, and being heavily built, they were coming in quite large.

While Cindy kept herself quite unattractive from a male perspective, her breasts were the envy of many of the other girls. The other girls looked at Cindy's breasts enviously in the shower at gym while hiding their flat chests. Her breasts were also the objects of desire of all of the boys. When the word spread that Andrew had access to Cindy's breasts, he became the envy of the other boys. Andrew told them that he could set it up for all of them to feel her up just like he was doing. He was getting tired of it anyway. When Cindy heard about this, she cried all night in her room. She never trusted another male again. She spent the remainder of fifth grade and sixth grade with Amanda and Kent. They had become outcasts. Cindy's happy years had ended.

During her high school years, sex, alcohol, and drugs were prevalent for people her age. It was expected that if a female went out with a male, there would be sex sooner not later. Cindy had no interest or time for any of this. She was serious about learning as much as she could from her high school courses and her life experiences.

When Cindy reached the tenth grade she began to develop as an adult. Her body started to solidify. As she trimmed up, her breasts became even more prominent. She had fantastic proportions for a girl her age, or any age: 36-21-36. The boys at her school couldn't help but marvel at her body. As Cindy's overall self-image increased, her self-image as a female increased as well. She became less self conscious of her body and secretly enjoyed the male looks she received at school and outside of school. She still found the physical aspects of a boy touching her body parts or her touching a boy's too uncomfortable and disgusting.

As Cindy's senior year approached, she was being pressured to make a decision as to her college plans. She couldn't decide between a liberal arts education to develop her mind or one of math and science to develop a potential income. She was equally adept in both areas. What she really wanted was a curriculum where she could learn to help people, especially underdogs who couldn't help themselves. She just couldn't hurt both parents; one wanted her to take a liberal arts program, the other a business program. Cindy wanted to make her own decision.

When Cindy told her parents she wanted to attend NYU's social work school, they were aghast. Why would anyone want to spend their lives trying to make life better for less fortunates? Her father had always been a proponent of self-responsibility, and the cause of social workers ran completely against his grain. There would also be a slight humiliation for him, for his own daughter to reject everything he thought he stood for. It was a slap at his life. But, if that was what his daughter really wanted to do, he wouldn't stop her, he never could. And she agreed to work her way through college, which she did. He was off the hook.

When Cindy graduated from NYU she took a job with the parent agency that directed homeless shelters throughout New York City. Cindy was assigned to an agency in the Bronx, not far from where her father grew up. Life can be ironic. Cindy lived in a small dingy studio apartment in the village. She took no money from her family. She got by. Her father saw her once in a while when he was in the city, but she never talked about what she was doing or whom she lived with. Her mother called infrequently, never discussing what Cindy was doing, only what she was doing.

Points to ponder:

Based on whom we are born to our life starts out on a programmed course. Throw in our culture, economic class, neighborhood, and parental desires; and our fate is almost permanently sealed. It takes a strong individual like Cindy to struggle against such a set-up to become his or her own person. Most of us succumb to our parental expectations and subtle, sometimes not so subtle, programming by the society we find ourselves in somewhere along the line of growing up.

1. Cindy's mother, Sally, had grown up with the message from her mother that a woman's role was to have children, especially a daughter, so that was what she did. What happens when one's childhood programming proves to be false?
2. Cindy grew up rejected by her mother, her two brothers, and her father, whom she so dearly wanted to love her. What affect does such rejection have on a child growing up?
3. Cindy preferred playing with the boys rather than the girls as expected, a definite rejection of parental expectations. How does someone like Cindy internalize the message that something must be wrong with her? How does a mother cope with such a daughter who is different, especially from her?
4. Sally was programmed to attract the attention of males through so-called feminine wiles. How does a child like Cindy cope with a mother who is not only at an opposite extreme but behaves in a manner that shames her?
5. Cindy's father wanted little to do with her, other than for her to leave him alone. But when Cindy wanted anything she went to her father—

she wanted him to recognize her—but he gave her everything she wanted except himself. What affect did this have on Cindy as she grew up trying to understand the male and female worlds?

6. Cindy recognized early on that she needed people, and liked them, but she couldn't get that at home, she looked for it elsewhere. How important was this recognition for Cindy in the decisions she made in her life?
7. Cindy befriended the social outcasts in school, becoming the Queen of the Misfits. What factors pushed her in this direction?
8. Cindy was a girl but she felt more comfortable playing with the boys and doing boy activities. In what ways does society push us into conformity with acceptable norms?
9. Cindy made a girlfriend, Amanda, who was just like Cindy in her behaviors. How important is it to have someone who supports your belief system?
10. When Cindy was nine years old she started dressing like her father. What message was Cindy trying to give to her parents and her peers?
11. Eventually society pushes the males and females together. Many times the boys and girls grow up as enemies and then they reach an age when they become attracted to each other. How difficult is it for a female, or a male, to resist such societal pressures?
12. Cindy's mother wanted her to study liberal arts and get married and have children just like her, while her father wanted her to study business and follow in his footsteps. Cindy made her own decision to become a social worker and help people, thought of as a a waste of time to both of her parents. What strengths are needed for a child to make their own decisions as to what they want for their life?

Each of us is able to make the right choices for ourselves,
but rarely does this occur
and when it does we still are not sure.

Caught in Story
Playing out the Script
The Pittsburgh Trilogy

1. Caught in the Mill

The area that they lived in, South Side Pittsburgh, was predominantly a one-company neighborhood, where most of the residents worked at the Steel Mill. Originally it was a Catholic neighborhood with the Catholic Church at the center of activities. There were some other Hungarian immigrant families in the neighborhood when Mikey first came to America from Budapest, but now there were very few, primarily those families who couldn't get out for economic reasons. Their family had become one of those. Mikey's wife Frieda would plead with him to leave the neighborhood as it was turning into a haven for new immigrants.

The steel mill was having rough times, and the neighborhood was getting poorer. Mikey insisted that he was needed at the mill and needed to protect the remaining Hungarian immigrants from the outsiders. Frieda couldn't convince him that the immigrants who could afford to were moving out to the suburbs and those moving in didn't want his help. The neighborhood was always gloomy, with the coal burning smoke stacks from the mill, coal stoves and furnaces in most homes, coal burning trains passing within two blocks of their house coming and going to the mill at all hours of the day and night, and the generally overcast, gray skies. Mikey prevailed, he wouldn't move away from his job and the people he needed to protect. The real truth was that Mikey was afraid to get another job as he had always worked at the mill since coming to America. He was also afraid to take public transportation as he had always walked back and forth to work. And, Frieda could walk to the stores every day. It would be good for the child; they could eat fresh, no need for an ice service. He didn't mention the bars, which were almost three to every block.

Mikey's son Morris grew up playing with the "good" Catholic kids. Morris knew no difference; as to a pre-schooler, kids were kids. When it came time to go to school, Morris went to the public school, while his Catholic friends attended the parish Parochial school. In a short period of time, he lost sight of his Catholic friends. He was forced to make friends with the "new people," those people's kids whom his parents talked despairingly about. Thus, Morris was forced to become a loner, a child without real friends either at home or at school.

Frieda didn't know what to do with Morris, and Mikey was no help. So, Morris drifted away from his parents. Frieda forced him to go to school so she could have some quiet time. She sat in her melancholy state for hours at a time, dreading the time when Morris would come home from school or Mikey from work. At school, Morris had little contact with the other kids. He sat in his class, paying little attention, learning little. He didn't care. When he came home from school, he went to his room and lay on his bed until dinnertime. Typically, it was dinner with his mother, as his father would come home later, many times drunk. Morris was a big boy like his father, and with his inactivity and continual eating he was getting large for his age.

Frieda became concerned, as he was her son and she felt responsible even if his father didn't seem to care. Morris remembered an on-going scenario between his parents that he couldn't ever get out of his mind. His mother would wait for his father to come home, who was usually late and drunk.

"Mikey," she said, "again late and drunk. I take care of the boy, and you go drinking with those people."

"They're not just people," Mikey retorted, "they're my fellow workers."

"Fellow workers, my eye. How many have you had to the house, and how many have had you to their house?"

"Frieda, please, they're fellow workers, not my friends."

"Exactly, Mikey, they're not your friends. So, who are your friends?"

"Frieda, please, don't start. I stop for maybe two drinks, no big thing."

"Two drinks, eh? Me and *your* son have our dinner at five thirty so he can do his homework and you come home after nine. And then you want your dinner. I can't go on like this any more. I can't do it all by myself. I can't, I can't." She clenched her fists, trying to pound on Mikey's chest, but he grabbed her hands, holding them.

"Frieda, please, enough, every night the same thing." He started to leave the room and go into the kitchen.

"Go, go to your precious kitchen. See what you can find to eat. I can't even buy food on the money that's left over after your drinking." She went after him. "Please, Mikey, talk to me. I can't do it by myself anymore."

"Frieda, what do you want me to do? I try; I do what I can. I work hard at the mill. I deserve a little time out."

"You deserve. Well, how about me. I'm a prisoner in this house. There are no neighbors I can talk to, the neighborhood is deteriorating around us, your son is killing my soul, and you deserve. What do I deserve? Please, Mikey, tell me. This can't go on." She was now screaming. "Please, Mikey, talk to me. I'm not some animal that you keep, I'm your wife."

Mikey put some food on a plate and walked past her to the shabby dining room table. He sat down, turning his back to her.

"Mikey, talk to me!" Frieda screamed.

Mikey finished eating got up and went into the living room.

"So, you're just going to leave your dirty dishes there? Who cleaned up for you before? Well, I'm not your slave," Frieda said.

Mikey walked to the couch and lay down.

"Are you going to talk to me or not?" Frieda said again.

Mikey ignored her.

"Oh, what's the use?" Frieda said running upstairs, and throwing herself on her bed, screaming and crying.

Morris was in his bed, crying into his pillow, as his head told him he was not a worthy child. If he were, he would go to his mother and console her, or do something about his father. But, he lay there helpless, crying like a baby.

Mikey heard the crying upstairs, turned over sadly, and was asleep within a few minutes.

As a student, Morris had never been special. He had little interest in any of the subjects. They bored him, put him to sleep. He preferred shop to the academic courses. He was able to make things that made sense to him. His physical strength could be used as an asset, while his mental capacity was less important. He became a vocational tech student, non-college bound.

His mother wanted her son to go on to college, make something of himself, not have to work at hard jobs like her husband. His father saw his son joining him at the steel mill—there was nothing wrong with honest, physical labor. As there was never any extra money in the household, Frieda's dream of college for her son remained just that, a dream. Morris was not doing well at school and Mikey saw no reason for his son to stay any longer than necessary. He was a big boy and should be contributing to the house. It would make things easier for everyone, especially Mikey. Times were hard, Morris was sixteen, and it was time to go to work.

Mikey had little trouble convincing Morris to quit school. Morris would do anything to be with him. Mikey and Frieda fought about it terribly, but they fought about everything, so what else was new? Morris saw school as a waste of time and the other kids had no appeal for him. They were all such adolescents. Morris started work at the mill, moving finished bars of steel. It was hard work, but Morris could handle it easily. It was the first real work he had done. Morris enjoyed the work, working with his father and the older guys, going back and forth to work with his father. He got to really know his father, for the first time in his life. As Mikey talked to him with real concern, Morris began to love him—and to like him. It was his first real recognition.

Getting up early, doing hard work for long hours, and coming home late left Morris little time to lie around and be lazy. He started to get into shape, losing weight, developing his muscles. He was not a good-looking boy, but he was more appealing. Morris settled into a man's life of work and male camaraderie.

Points to ponder:

Life deals all of us a hand to play. In this case, Morris was born to Hungarian immigrant parents in South Side Pittsburgh, a predominantly Catholic gloomy mill neighborhood. Life was hard in that neighborhood working at the mill and just being able to meet expenses. Morris's family was stuck for economic as well as personal reasons. The steel mill was having rough times and the neighborhood was getting poorer with a new wave of needy immigrants moving in. Those who could afford to have moved out leaving Morris with few friends. Morris was left to cope with his situation, one that he hadn't created.

1. Morris grew up playing with the "good" Catholic kids. He knew no difference. What happens when one is different from the others through no other reason than birth?
2. Morris went to public school. His Catholic friends went to parochial school. He was forced to make friends with the new people, whom his parents talked bad about. How does one's parents' attitudes and beliefs impact upon a young child?
3. Morris became a loner, a child without friends. How can a parent cope effectively with this kind of situation?
4. Morris took little interest in school, paying little attention, learning little. Is there anything that teachers and/or parents can do about such a situation?
5. Morris remembered an ongoing negative scenario between his parents related to his father Mikey's drinking and coming home late. How do such scenarios play back to us throughout our life and what affect do they have on an individual?
6. How do couples get into such ongoing arguments that tear them apart and negatively affect their children? Is there anything that can

be done to stop them or prevent them?

7. Such scenarios have a horrible affect on the child. In this case, Morris wanted to do something, but he lay there helplessly. Is there anything he could have done?
8. Morris had no interest in his academic subjects at school; he was more interested in shop courses. His mother wanted him to go to college, his father to join him at the mill. Why do parents push their children into lives they want them to have, rather than support the child as to what he or she wants?
9. Mikey had little trouble convincing Morris to quit school. Why do we do things when we are young that are not in our best interest and have a lasting affect on the rest of our lives?
10. Morris didn't feel very close to his father growing up, yet it was very important for him to work at the mill with his father. Why was that? What pulls us to our parents?
11. Morris fell into a life at the mill similar to his fathers. This was a life that had nothing but heartbreak for Morris. Why would he do this to himself? What factors made such a life appealing to Morris?
12. At the mill, Morris settled into a life of hard work and male camaraderie especially with his father. What messages and needs from his past and growing up years influenced Morris to make this decision?

A bad childhood may beget
a bad adolescence,
which begets a bad adulthood.

2. Caught in the Same Life

Morris had been at the steel mill for over four years and was now twenty years old. While things were getting somewhat better in America, economic conditions were worsening in other parts of the world, particularly Western Europe. His mother's Aunt Sophie had a niece, Alice, who was still living in Hungary. Alice had a daughter, Ruth, a little younger than Morris. Alice was a concert pianist and Ruth was following in her footsteps. However, the Hungarians had restricted opportunities. Ruth couldn't be accepted to a conservatory for study, a university, or a job with a reputable symphony. Her piano teacher since her childhood, when she was considered a prodigy, had recently refused to work with her anymore. She gave no reason; she didn't have to. Alice wanted her daughter to go to America, the land of opportunity; where with Aunt Sophie's sponsorship she knew Ruth would be recognized. Ruth could help take care of Sophie, who wasn't getting any younger. So, Ruth came to America, and lived with Sophie.

Sophie tried to make contacts for Ruth, but the doors in America were as closed as those in Budapest. There were few openings in conservatories or symphonies and they weren't going to an unknown and untried immigrant girl. Ruth practiced with a piano teacher not far from Sophie's, but the costs were adding up with no income other than Sophie's coming into the household. Ruth would have to get a job.

At the same time, Morris's mother Frieda was getting frustrated with her situation. Mikey and Morris were finally bonding as father and son, but she was left out. She was becoming a middle-aged hag and nag. She was either alone during the day trying to keep the house clean for her two pigs, shopping for dinner, preparing the dinner, eating her dinner alone, and then serving and cleaning up the two pigs' dinner. Her life was closing in on her; she was becoming bitter and bitchy. She didn't like herself, but she didn't know what to do.

Sophie was getting older, now in her early seventies, retired from her job about five years. Money was tight and it was becoming more difficult for her to have Ruth in the house. The little money Ruth contributed to the house after paying for her piano lessons made little impact on the additional expenses of having Ruth with her. It was actually costing Sophie to have Ruth live with her. It couldn't continue. Sophie couldn't handle the economics or the additional burden of having someone else in the house anymore. Rather than Ruth helping to take care of Sophie, Sophie was taking care of Ruth. She sought out Frieda's counsel.

They had just finished a lunch of tuna fish sandwiches and tea. This was the time when they talked about their problems.

"So," Sophie said, "Things are good with you?"

"Good," said Frieda, "so who knows from good?"

"At least not worse, eh?" asked Sophie.

"Worse," said Frieda, "how could they be worse? And you?"

"Oh, Ruthie's a wonderful girl." Sophie stopped abruptly.

"And?" Frieda asked.

"And what?"

Frieda looked at her Aunt Sophie. She always knew when Sophie had more to say, but didn't want to.

Sophie hesitated. "Well, okay. She's a wonderful girl."

"Yah, she's a wonderful girl, but?" Frieda probed.

Sophie started. "Yah, a wonderful girl, but...

"But, what?" asked Frieda?

"But, I need to get her out of my house. I can't do it anymore. When you lived with me, I was much younger and you were a big help. Today's generation, they just want to be helped."

"Aunt Sophie, I came later and stayed later. I wasn't ready to go, but you helped me out of the house; you got me married to that Mikey."

"Frieda, you can't blame me for that one. It was time for you leave, to be on your own, but you picked that big palooka."

"Maybe I did, but there wasn't much picking to do. Of all the Hungarian men left in the neighborhood, he was the best of the worst. So, I made my own bed."

"And you lie in it."

"Yes I do, and I clean it too, but now I got two of them, the father and the son."

"And you, the holy ghost?"

"So," said Frieda, "you got Ruth and I got Morris. As long as we take care of them, neither one will ever leave."

They looked at each other and nodded their heads. They started to giggle. They both said it at the same time. "Are you thinking, what I'm thinking?" They giggled again.

Frieda finally said, "and what's that?

"You know," said Sophie.

"And what's that?" asked Frieda.

"The unspeakable," said Sophie. "Ruth and Morris living together."

"Ruth and Morris living together. You mean as husband and wife?"

"What else?" Sophie replied "An elegant solution."

"So it is," said Frieda. "But there is one fatal flaw?"

"And what is that?" asked Sophie.

"They despise each other. Morris calls Ruth a delicate dainty and a pouty pansy. And she has the face of an eight year old Volvo."

"And," said Sophie, "Ruth says he has the face of a Pittsburgh trolley and calls him a rough rider and a what's the name of that flower. Oh yeah, a succulent stinkweed."

"He's certainly that," laughed Frieda. "But the question is can a pouty pansy find happiness with a succulent stinkweed?"

"So," said Sophie, "shall we see?"

"Of course," said Frieda, " more cake?"

"Of course," said Sophie.

Frieda had them all to dinner the following Friday—Sophie, Ruth, Mikey, Morris and herself. She prepared a special Friday night dinner just like Sophie used to do, with bread, roast chicken, boiled potatoes, string beans, with cake and ice cream for desert. She did her best nagging to get Mikey and Morris to clean up and dress properly for dinner. She had to admit that for someone with the face of a trolley, Morris looked impressive when he dressed up. He was a powerful specimen; all of his baby fat had turned to muscle.

The dinner stayed quiet and polite. Frieda had warned her two pigs. After dinner, Frieda and Sophie went into the kitchen to wash and dry the dishes. Mikey started to go into the living room with Morris and Ruth, but Frieda told him, in no uncertain terms, that he was to stay with them in the kitchen. He grumbled, but he did it.

Morris sat at the far end of the living room in Mikey's easy chair, picked up the newspaper. Ruth sat daintily on the edge of the sofa so that her feet reached the ground. She wouldn't have to sit back and her skirt rise. Neither one said anything; they didn't know what to say, to each other or someone of the opposite sex. Ruth could stand it no longer.

"Morris," she said, "so, you like living with your parents?"

Morris stopped reading and looked over. "Did you say something?"

Ruth said nothing.

"Its okay," said Morris. He went back to reading the paper.

"I thought you didn't hear me?"

"I wasn't sure."

"So," said Ruth, "its okay?"

"Not really," Morris said, "but its home, sweet home. And you."

"Its okay, but, " her voice got softer, "Aunt Sophie can be a pill sometimes. Always wanting me to help with this, help with that. I can't risk hurting my hands."

"Why's that?" Morris asked. "Oh, right, your piano playing."

"I'm going to be a concert pianist someday."

"And Aunt Sophie stops you?"

"No, not exactly, but she doesn't make it any easier. And you?"

"I like my folks. I used to hate them, but that was when I was still a kid."

"And when was that?"

"Oh, last week."

They both laughed, Morris loudly at his own joke, Ruth quietly, barely opening her mouth, like a little bird. Morris was holding his newspaper, not reading it; Ruth had leaned closer. They had found a common bond, disliking where they were.

By the time Frieda, Sophie, and Mikey came into the living room, Morris was sitting next to Ruth on the sofa, heavy into comparing whose fate was worse. Frieda and Sophie smiled at each other, and Mikey shook his head. Morris and Ruth looked up at the adults; stopped talking.

"So?" Frieda said, looking down at Morris.

"Nothing Mom," said Morris.

The room was silent; no one dared to talk.

"Ruth," Morris finally said, "would you like to go to Doc Drayton's drug store and get an ice cream soda?"

Ruth hesitated, looked over at Aunt Sophie, who nodded her approval. "Sure," Ruth said. She left quickly with Morris, slamming the door on their way out.

Mikey started to say "But they just had a big dish of ice cream."

Frieda stared at him. "Mikey!" He said no more.

When they left, Frieda and Sophie entwined their pinkies, saying together. "We can only hope." Mikey shook his head, sitting in his easy chair, picking up the newspaper. Frieda and Sophie returned to the dining room, to plot some more.

Some time later, Mikey and Morris were in the locker room at the steel mill getting dressed for work. Mikey dressed quickly; ready to get to work, as he always was. Morris was dressing very slowly, delaying the process as much as he could.

"Come on, slow poke, we'll be late." Mikey was anxious to get going.

"Dad," said Morris, "we're never late. That's why you come in early. If the company had to pay you for all the extra time you gave them, they would be bankrupt by now."

Mikey looked at him, deciding whether to tell him or not. He finally decided to. "They might be bankrupt anyway."

"What? I thought everyone always needed steel." Morris was confused. He didn't understand much about business.

"Not in a recession. They might need our steel, but they can't pay for it. Then the company can't afford to pay us."

"So we might be sacked? I'll have to get another job?"

"Maybe, now you know why I give them the extra time." Mikey looked pleased with himself.

"And," said Morris, "you've got over thirty years in, but what about me?"

"Don't worry about it, you're a good worker. We'll both be the last to go. I'm over sixty, with a little luck I'll retire in a few years. And you'll still be working here."

"I hope you're right, Dad. I really like working with you. You've taught me more in the last few years than I learned all those years in school."

"That shouldn't have been too difficult."

"Thanks, Dad. I was a good student."

"Of what? Remember, I had to sign your report cards."

"Not everything is grades Dad."

"No it isn't son. So, ya ready?"

"Not quite Dad." Morris looked around the locker room; there was nobody within hearing distance. He hesitated. "Dad ."

"Yes, son?"

Morris shuffled his feet, stuttered. "I need to talk to you. I need to talk to someone."

"What is it, son?"

"Uh, uh. I want to get married."

Mikey was taken aback. "Married? To whom?"

"Come on Dad, to Ruth, who else?"

" Well, I guess it's not much of a shock. You just seem to be so young yet."

"I'm almost twenty one, and Ruth's going to be twenty. A lot of kids our age are married. For a girl, being twenty-one and unmarried is a sin. Destined to be an old maid."

"Is that right? I was thirty-eight and your mother was thirty-six when we got married. And look how we turned out. Maybe waiting can be good."

"Dad, I live with you and mom. I don't think waiting is the answer."

Mikey thought. "Yeah, maybe you're right. Okay, so you want to get married. Is this your choice? You know Ruth, your Mom and Aunt Sophie, can be quite persuasive. It couldn't be because Sophie wants to get rid of Ruth, could it?"

"Could be," said Morris, "but this is really my idea."

"How long have you known her? It seems like you just met her that time at our house."

"No, I knew her before, from Aunt Sophie's."

"But, you didn't like her."

"Now I do." Morris was being cautious.

"So, now you do. And what has changed?"

"Well, I've been out with her almost every night and we spend the weekends together. I've gotten to know her."

"I know. I've lost my drinking buddy at the Dew Drop and my weekend helper. So, the delicate dainty is now likable."

Morris hesitated. "I think so."

"Uh, huh, so what do you two talk about? The latest piano concerto?"

"No, Dad. I respect Ruth. She's a good pianist."

"Pianist is it? You're together all the time, you must talk about something."

"No, Dad."

"Then what?"

"Look, we were both lonely. Neither one of us ever had a boyfriend or a girlfriend. It's nice to be loved by someone other than your family."

"So, it's love now is it?"

"Oh, I don't know Dad." Morris hesitated. "I think so."

"You think so. And based on that, you want to get married?"

"Well, yeah Dad." Morris looked away.

"What is it son?"

Morris said nothing, shuffled his feet, buttoned and unbuttoned his shirt.

"Are you all right son?"

"Yeah, sure Dad." Morris looked away and spoke softly. "Ruth is pregnant."

"What's that son?"

Morris spoke louder. "Ruth is pregnant!"

Mikey looked around to see if anyone heard, but the coast looked clear. "Oh boy!"

"But, Dad, it is my choice to marry her."

"That's noble son, but are you sure you want to marry her? You know, you get married quickly, but you stay married a long time. Be sure son."

"I am Dad."

"So," Mikey added,"how did this happen?"

"Come on Dad, you know how this happens."

"Of course I do, but I mean with you and Ruth."

"You were right, we had little to talk about, but we didn't want to be alone again, so we filled up the time."

"And you liked it?"

"Yeah Dad, I liked it."

"I hope it will be enough."

"Me too Dad."

"Okay son, whatever you want to do." Morris looked away. "Let's go to work."

They walked off together, father and son. Mikey became saddened, as he thought how he was able to protect all the others, but unable to protect his own son. Morris thought how nice it would be to have someone other than his mother and father to come home to, maybe escape from that little house, maybe not be so alone and convinced himself that Ruth was really a fine girl—and a pianist.

Points to ponder:

We're supposed to love our spouses, children, and our wards. But sometimes they become too much for us, creating situations that lead us to depression. We want the best for our children, but sometimes we want them somewhere else. Is that so bad? As it may be difficult to talk to the other in such a situation, action must be taken in spite of them. Sometimes it works out well; sometimes it only creates additional problems.

1. Ruth was restricted in furthering her career as a concert pianist in Hungary. However, when she came to America she met similar restrictions. What were the reasons for such restrictions? Could they have been lessened?
2. Mikey and his son Morris finally bonded when Morris started working at the same mill as Mikey. While Frieda might have been joyful at this, she felt even more left out. What did Frieda really want from them?
3. Frieda wanted to get Morris out of the house and Sophie wanted to get Ruth out of her house. Was getting Morris and Ruth together really an elegant solution?
4. Morris and Ruth really didn't like each other. What was it that brought the two of them together?
5. Morris had no one to talk to other than his father, Mikey. Why did he confide in him about Ruth's pregnancy and his wanting to get married? Did Morris really want to get married?
6. Morris saw as his only way out of the situation of Ruth's pregnancy to marry her. Is this always the best solution, especially when the two people involved hardly know each other and probably don't really like each other?
7. Morris tells his father that he thinks he loves Ruth. What is love and how does one know whether they love someone or not?
8. Morris and Ruth were alone and lonely. Why do such negative conditions induce us to take actions we wouldn't do ordinarily?
9. Mikey was saddened about his son marrying Ruth, but he felt unable to do anything about it. What should one do, especially a parent and

a child, to protect them in spite of themselves? What could Mikey have done?

10. Morris witnessed a bad marriage between his parents. Why would he want to get married at 21 and put himself in the same situation?
11. Morris saw his marriage to Ruth as an escape to a lonely life that probably wasn't going anywhere. Does such a decision ever provide the escape that is desired? Can an individual really start over and not bring the same person with them?
12. Morris is a victim of his own environment. Can you see any way that Morris could have avoided this and changed his life?

Loneliness is a breeding ground
for indecision,
creating decisions that may
only make us lonelier.

3. Caught Alone Again

Morris and Ruth were married quietly in a civil ceremony the following week. Ruth had missed three periods, but she wasn't showing yet. It could have been more embarrassing. There was no announcement at work, no wedding party, no celebration, just Mikey and Frieda, and Aunt Sophie. They moved in with Mikey and Frieda. At the end of the month, Morris and Ruth moved into a little apartment that Mikey found for them, two blocks from their house, over Farber's cleaners. It was small, but it was theirs. Morris liked coming home to Ruth in their apartment. He was finally free, on his own with a wife and baby on the way.

With Morris and Ruth gone from their house, Mikey and Frieda were alone with each other for the first time in over twenty years. At first it felt awkward. They had no child left in the house to argue about. They found they had nothing left to argue about, maybe nothing left to talk about. In the beginning, they walked around the house trying to avoid each other. If one of them entered a room where the other already was, he or she left quickly. For the short time that Morris and Ruth lived with them, Mikey returned from the living room couch to the bedroom to sleep. Frieda thought it would look better to Ruth as a newly married, than for Mikey to continue sleeping on the sofa. They had twin beds, so Frieda wasn't inviting Mikey to do anything more than sleep in the same room. Mikey snored horribly, but somehow it was a comfort to Frieda to have him in the same room. As Mikey looked over at her in the other twin bed, he had to admit she was really a remarkable woman.

One night Frieda looked over at Mikey. He looked so adorable curled up in his sleep. He was certainly a giant of a man, but still a big baby. She tiptoed over to his bed, quietly pulled the covers back, sliding in beside him. She held him close to her, his back against her breasts. In the middle of the night, Mikey turned over, pulled Frieda close to him, hugging her into his body. He kissed her lightly on her forehead. "Good night, Frieda," he said." Then he went to sleep.

This became their night time ritual, starting out in separate beds, winding up together in one small twin bed, hardly large enough for Mikey, but somehow large enough for the two of them. They were both amazed that they also had things to talk about, and when one was in one room the other would be too. They both decided that it was all right to want to be together, and they really wanted to be.

They slept together, just hugging, for a number of weeks. One night Mikey woke and found Frieda on top of him. Mikey didn't say a word, just quietly helped Frieda. Once consummated, Frieda rolled over, went to sleep, Mikey did the same. This activity was periodically added to their nighttime routine.

One night, about two months before Ruth and Morris's baby was due, Mikey rolled over on top of Frieda. He was an awfully big man, and she was a little woman. Mikey thrust slowly so as not to hurt her. She always smiled at Mikey while in the act; it still remained a miracle to her. Suddenly, she grabbed him hard around the neck. "Oh Mikey," she moaned. Mikey looked down at her, and again she said "Oh Mikey." Then her body fell from him. She lay still. "What is it? he asked. She didn't respond. She lay too still. Mikey was worried. Heart attack, stroke went through his mind, but she was only 59. What could he do? Mikey got out of the bed; Frieda still lay there, not moving.

Mikey put his pajamas on. He didn't know what to do. It was past ten at night. Mikey had never brought attention to himself; he wouldn't now. No police, no ambulances; they had no doctor; they had never needed one or would not pay for one. Who could he call? He couldn't just let Frieda die. He thought of calling Paul Moleski from work, but would he know what to do, and it would take him a while to get here. He knew whom to call; she was a nurse in the old country.

He let the phone ring. He knew it was late; it would take time for her to get to the phone. The phone picked up after a number of rings. "Sophie," Mikey said, "its Mikey. Something has happened." He was blubbering.

Sophie was still waking up, rubbing the sand out of her eyes. "Mikey, What's happened?"

"Sophie, its Frieda." He was frantic.

"Frieda, oh my God. What is it?"

"I don't know. She's not moving."

"Have you touched her?"

"Of course. I shook her, felt for a pulse, but she's not moving."

"Oh my God! I'll be right over."

"I'll meet you halfway, help you get here."

"No Mikey, you stay with Frieda."

"But what can I do?"

"Nothing Mikey, nothing." She hung up. Men, she thought to herself, what a useless lot.

Mikey didn't want to lose her; he didn't want to be alone again. He thought of life without his Frieda, he was immobilized. For a man of action, he was stuck.

Sophie rushed upstairs when she arrived. Mikey followed her.

Sophie went over to Frieda, trying to find a pulse, in her neck and then in her wrist. She shook her head. "Mikey, how long has she been this way?"

"I don't know. I called you right away. It happened so quickly."

"I'm sure it did. I need to call an ambulance, but it may be too late." Sophie went downstairs to call. She called back up. "Cover her up! Put some clothes on her!"

Frieda was already dead when the ambulance crew arrived. She had died instantly Mikey was told. Her heart had burst. Mikey understood.

Mikey couldn't go back to work after the funeral. Ruth stayed with him for a couple of days, but she was pregnant and didn't want to be away from Morris too long. When Ruth left, Mikey was alone.

Sophie, and Morris and Ruth would stop by once in a while, but he was utterly alone. For the first time in his life, Mikey felt weak. Morris tried to convince his dad that it would do him good to get back to work, take his mind off his mom's death. Mikey wouldn't budge, hauling steel didn't matter anymore—maybe it never did, they would get along without him. He blamed himself, he was too rough, and he had killed her. There was no way he could bring back the years and make it up to her. He would skulk around the house in his pajamas looking in each room for her. When he couldn't find her, he would sit on the floor and cry.

Less than two months after Frieda's death, Ruth gave birth to a baby boy. They named him Bernard, after Frieda's father. When Mikey first saw the baby, he lit up. It was another life, another chance. His mind was already working on how he would do things differently this time. He would make it up to Frieda, through baby Bernard. So, God taketh, and God giveth. Could it be true?

Mikey finally went back to work, to finish out his career, but he didn't care anymore. He did his job, but only so he could see Bernard and take care of him. He went home every night with Morris, played with Bernard for as long as they would let him. He didn't want to go home. There was nothing for him there, but there was no place for him to stay in the small apartment. The baby crib was already crowding Morris and Ruth in the one small bedroom. Ruth felt so sorry for Mikey when they had to send him home. Mikey left reluctantly with his head down, after one last goodbye to Bernard for the fortieth time. Ruth got tears in her eyes. If there were something more she could do for Mikey, she would do it. Her own father had died in Hungary when she was twelve from tuberculosis. She knew what it was like to lose a loved one. She had always had a need to rescue the weak ones, and now Mikey was one of them.

Points to ponder:

When individuals follow the program laid out for them, such as going to school, getting married, and having children many times an individual finds that the program doesn't work for them. Mikey and Frieda got married relatively late in life, -- he was 38 and Frieda was 36—to be with someone after so many years alone. They both disliked the other for changing their lives. Their child, Morris, who was supposed to bring joy to their life produced just the opposite. So they played out their scripts; Mikey drinking more and not wanting to come home and Frieda becoming more depressed with her lot as a stay at home housewife or maid. When Morris left the house they had another chance.

1. Morris and Ruth, after a month of living with Mikey and Frieda, moved into their own little apartment. What did this signify for Morris, Ruth, Mikey, and Frieda?
2. With Morris gone from their house, Mikey and Frieda were alone with each other after twenty years. How do couples cope with being with only themselves after the children have left?
3. Mikey and Frieda continued with their old habits while Morris lived with them. Why do people continue their scripts even when their circumstances have changed?
4. Couples usually get married for a reason. How does that reason evaporate over the years and can it be picked back up after the children have left and they are alone once again?
5. When the negative stimulus is removed for couples it allows them to renegotiate their relationship. How did Mikey and Frieda renegotiate their relationship?
6. Couples seem to get into routines, even around sex. Why was it comfortable for Mikey and Frieda to fall back into such a routine?
7. Mikey, a strong capable man, found himself unable to function when Frieda died. What happens to extremely capable people when an emergency arises?
8. Mikey couldn't go back to work after Frieda died to a job he had cherished for over 30 years. What changed in Mikey and his focus on his job?
9. Mikey regretted the years he had misspent with Frieda. Why does it take a disaster to wake people up to live the life they should be?
10. Mikey, who had little to do with his own son when he was small,

instantly bonded with his grandson, Bernard. What forces pull us to our children's children when we did so poorly with our own?

11. Mikey may have found the opportunity for another chance with Bernard to do things right. Do you think there is a chance for Mikey to do it right this time or will he just do it differently?
12. Ruth felt sorry for Mikey, a grandfather alone. What made her feel sorry for him while at the same time she just wanted him to leave so that she could have her own life?

We don't miss someone important to us
as much as when they are gone
and then there isn't much we can do
but blame ourselves.

Memories Are Made of This

Brad, a rather unattractive, large, bulky young man, successfully isolated himself from girls at his high school by working at the local supermarket through his junior and senior years. It was now spring of his senior year and the senior prom was coming up. Although most of his classmates were excitingly talking about it and whom they were taking, Brad decided to bypass it. It would be too uncomfortable for him; a dance with a girl was no place for him. He had already volunteered to work at the store that Saturday night and he was greatly relieved.

Another student, Todd Haskell, a fellow member of the football team approached him during study hall.

"Brad, old buddy," Todd, said, "how would you like to go to the senior prom?"

Brad looked down at his shoes as if the answer was in his shoelaces. He would love to go like all the other kids, but he was afraid to go, and he had no one to invite without the ultimate fear of rejection. And what would he do with a girl at a dance; he couldn't dance. It was hopeless, and he was hopeless.

"Brad, you still there?" Todd reached up, putting his arm around Brad's shoulders.

"I don't know Todd." Brad continued looking at his shoes.

"What don't you know? You'll be doing me a favor. I'll owe you one."

"I don't know Todd."

"Is there a problem?" Todd bent down, looked him in the eye.

"No, no. I just have to work. I don't know if I can get out of it."

"Is that all, old buddy?"

Brad continued staring at his shoes, saying nothing.

"Brad? Are you still there?"

"Yeah. I mean no. I probably shouldn't go."

"Brad, baby, it would be a favor to me. The girl I'm going with, Gladys Stover, you know Gladys from history class, can't go unless her cousin Cecily Pearson goes."

Cecily was the female equivalent to Brad, hulking, bad complexion, glasses, and ugly. Brad had witnessed the other guys making fun of Cicely; but he had always stayed out of it, he couldn't be that cruel. He felt sorry for Cicely, as he felt sorry for himself.

Todd was pressing him. "Come on, it would be a big favor. This could be the night I finally score with Gladys. You wouldn't want to be the one to deprive me of that. Look, I have my uncle Joe's Chevy for the night; you can have the coveted back seat. Do whatever you want to Cicely. She must be horny." He didn't say as horny as Brad.

After much more pressure, and wanting to be accepted especially by Todd, Brad finally agreed against his better judgment. The date was already set-up by Todd and Gladys. He didn't have to call Cicely and ask her, to face the possibility of being rejected by the least desirable girl in school. Todd offered to buy the corsages and pick up and pay for Brad's formal wear, size 48. Brad only had to go, do nothing if he wanted to, sit in the corner with Cicely or not even come into the gym where the dance was.

On the night of the prom, Todd picked Brad up at his house. Todd had tried his best, but a tuxedo didn't exist anywhere in town that was going to fit Brad. The sleeves on the jacket were three inches above his wrists, the hem on the trousers two inches above his shoes, leaving a large gap showing his orange and blue argyle socks. His only almost black socks could not be found, so he wore his next best socks. The cummerbund that came with the tux had no chance of going around him, so he used his old black studded jean belt. The cufflinks and shirt studs could not be used as he couldn't pull the cloth tight enough to insert them, so he left them off, using bent paper clips to hold his cuffs together, and one shirt stud pulled tight in the middle so that his shirt opened as he moved, revealing his black curly chest hair at the top and his navel at the bottom. He was indeed a sad sack; he looked better in his regular shabby school clothes. There was no way to dress Brad up. When he was ready, his mother looked at him, and started to tear. She never thought she would see her son going to a prom. His younger smaller better looking brother, Rod, came down to see his brother off, he was so proud of him. Rod went over to hug his brother, but Brad was too embarrassed; he pushed him away. Rod looked better dressed around the house than Brad did dressed up. Brad thought if only he could be like his brother.

Todd honked his horn. His mother looked at him and said, "my Brad, so handsome." She pulled him down toward her, kissing him gently on the cheek. "Have a nice time," she said, "just enjoy yourself; forget about the others." Brad kissed his mother, nodded at his brother, who winked good luck to him, and then walked slowly out the door. His father, as usual, was not home to see his son off. Brad secretly wanted to go to his senior prom, it was the thing to do, but he was scared. For a big, powerful boy, he was scared to death. He came slowly out of the house, walking like a poorly dressed Frankenstein monster. Todd and Gladys, sitting close together in the front seat, did all they could to keep from laughing. They were both dressed elegantly. Brad slid sheepishly into the back seat.

"Looking good," Todd said. "I told you everything would be all right."

Brad was silent, trying to get his cuffs and shirt to stay closed.

Gladys tried not to, but she snickered in the front seat. "Hi, Braddie." She snuggled closer to Todd. "Thanks for coming."

Brad said nothing, nodded his head. He thought how dreadful he was, sitting alone in the back seat, being driven to his own disaster.

They stopped at Cicely's house. Brad didn't move.

"Brad, you have to pick up your date."

Brad was still fussing with his shirt and cuffs. They all sat waiting.

"Brad! Come on, we're going to be late!"

Brad was silent. "Can't you just blow the horn?" Brad talked into his shirt.

"What'd he say?" Gladys asked Todd.

"He wants me to blow the horn."

"On prom night," Gladys said, "is he kidding?" Gladys snickered.

"Brad," Todd said. "This is prom night! Go get your date!"

Brad slowly got out of the car, standing by the car door.

"Go!" said Todd. "And here, take the corsage!" Todd handed it to Gladys, who handed it to Brad. He took the box cautiously, walked up the steps. Gladys finally let herself go, breaking into loud laughter. Todd joined her. Brad heard the laughter, always the laughter.

Cicely and her parents greeted Brad at the door, before he knocked or rung the bell. They had been waiting for him. He wanted to die right there. Her parents looked just like her, a mousy father and a chicken hawk mother. Cicely had her hair done; it looked the best it could, and her fingernails polished. She wore a green, organdy, full dress, so that it was open at the bottom. It looked hand made, probably by her mother at much pain and sacrifice. She was not wearing her glasses, but that had not improved her looks much. She looked like a fat, ugly girl in a poorly made dress. Some things couldn't be improved upon; Brad and Cicely were what they were.

Cicely's mother put out her hand for Brad to shake. "Hello, Brad, I'm Mrs. Pearson, and this is my husband Ray."

Brad put his hand out. Ray took it. He was impressed with Brad's strength. "Pretty strong. Cicely says you're on the football team."

Brad stuttered. "Yeah, offensive guard."

"Let's go into the living room." Mrs. Pearson herded them toward the back wall. She lined Cicely and Brad up against the white wall. She picked up a camera from the chair.

"Say cheese!" she said to them.

Brad and Cicely looked blankly at her. She snapped the picture, the flash going into both their eyes. Cicely tottered without her glasses on.

"Now," Mrs. Pearson said, "let's have one of Brad placing the corsage on Cicely's wrist. Brad tried to open the corsage box, but he was all thumbs. "Oh," said Mrs. Pearson, "let me do that. I always had to do that for Ray too. Men are so clumsy when it comes to these things." Mrs. Pearson tried to get the corsage around Cicely's wrist, but her wrist was too large. She gave up in frustration. "Oh, heck," she said "I'll just pin it on her dress." She took a large hatpin from her sewing box, pinned the corsage crudely to the top of Cicely's dress. She now looked like a dressed up pig with a corsage on her chest. Mrs. Pearson picked the camera back up. Mr. Pearson stood in the back smiling. This was a very important night for Cicely's parents, her first date and the senior prom, with such an imposing date.

"Now, lets say cheese again." Mrs. Pearson was insistent.

Brad tried his best to smile, Cicely did the same, but both of them knew that they were not photogenic. They looked as uncomfortable as they felt. Brad couldn't wait to get of there. He nudged Cicely on the back, moving her toward the door. She shuffled along with him.

At the door, Mrs. Pearson kissed Cicely on the cheek, trying to do the same to Brad, but he pulled away. She settled for a limp handshake. "Now, have a good time, kids. Don't worry, we won't wait up for you." Cicely was mortified; she still hadn't said a word. As they went down the steps, Mrs. Pearson yelled at them, "have a good time," as she waved to them. Mr. Pearson stood in the back waving meekly.

Mrs. Pearson turned to her husband. "She makes me so sad. She's such a nice girl, and he's such a nice boy. I hope she has a good time."

Mr. Pearson shook his head. They went back inside.

Brad opened the car door for Cicely; she slid to the other side, as her dress came up over her underpants. Brad and Todd looked away at the same time. Todd and Gladys had been laughing all the time Brad was in the Pearson's house. They snickered all the way to the high school. Brad and Cicely said nothing.

When they arrived at the prom at the high school, Todd and Gladys left Brad and Cicely immediately. Brad didn't see Todd and Gladys the rest of the night. Todd and Gladys went back to Todd's Uncle Joe's Chevy, making out in the back seat. Afterwards, Todd bragged that he did it three times that night with Gladys, but Todd had always been known at school as a bullshitter. Gladys's reputation, of course, was ruined. It didn't matter to Todd; he had already picked out his next possible conquest.

As Brad stood awkwardly with Cicely, he heard the undercurrent of talk and laughter as some of the other kids pointed at them. He heard them saying "the hulk and the bulk," "the beast and the least," "the diarrhea duo," "the blob and the glob," "Porky and Portia," and so on. Kids could be so clever and so cruel at the same time. Cicely ran from the gym. Brad, after standing there awkwardly, went looking for her, finding her in the cafeteria. He sat down next to her. She had her head in her hands, crying into her glasses. Brad lifted her head, and removed her glasses.

"Cicely, it's okay. I'm used to being made fun of by girls."

"Well I'm not." Cicely cried harder.

"I'm sorry. I never should have come."

"Neither should I. Gladys talked me into it. Said you liked me, but were too shy to ask me. I wanted to go to the senior prom so much. I wanted to be just like other girls."

Brad patted her on the shoulder. "But, Cicely, I do like you."

"So, you wanted to take me to the prom?" Cicely sat up; her crying subsided into dry heaves.

"Well yes, no. That is, Todd said it would be all right, that you would go with me. I wasn't going to go. I'm not good at this."

Cicely started crying again. "Neither am I. I knew I shouldn't have come. All the other kids have fun and make fun of me."

"Me too. Would you like to dance?" The music was heard faintly coming from the gym.

"No, Brad I can't dance. I never have."

"That's okay, neither have I. Come on, let's try it." Brad

helped Cicely get up. They held onto each other, moving slowly to the music. Brad leaned against Cicely, she smelled terrible, her hair and body odor. Cicely smelling Brad, was just as repulsed. But, they kept on dancing; it was the thing to do.

"Do you want to stay?" Brad asked Cicely.

"I couldn't go back in there." Cicely held onto Brad as she had seen the other kids do.

"Me neither," said Brad. "Let's go."

"How about Gladys and Todd? I can't just leave them." Cicely was genuinely concerned; Gladys was her cousin.

"I don't think they'll miss us. They have other things on their minds." Brad didn't tell her that he came as a favor to Todd.

They walked two steps apart down the road. As latecomers passed them in the other direction going to the high school, they waved, and as they went past, they whispered. Brad and Cicely kept on walking. Brad took her to the only place he knew, Drakes drug store. They sat in their formal clothes at the counter. Doc Drake came over to serve them.

"So, Brad," Doc said, "who's the lovely young lady? Prom night, eh."

Brad looked down at the counter. "This is Cicely."

"Well," Doc said, "hello Cicely." He said nothing about her tear-streaked face or how she looked. "So, what will it be?"

Brad had a tough time getting the words out; he choked. "The usual for me."

"And you, Miss Cicely." Doc had his ice cream scooper ready in his hand.

Cicely couldn't speak; she looked over at Brad.

"How about a chocolate fudge sundae?" Brad said.

"Sure," Cicely was able to say.

"With wet nuts, whipped cream, and a cherry on top?" Brad asked her.

"Sure," Cicely said.

"Okay," Doc said, "one Brad special and one Cicely special coming up."

Doc placed Brad's cherry vanilla milk shake and Cicely's sundae in front of them. Doc went into the back of the store. There was nobody else in the pharmacy, on a Saturday and on a prom night. Doc kept the rubbers behind the cash register, and when a young fellow asked for one, Doc had his wife wait on him. This kept the young guys from buying something they shouldn't and kept them out of trouble and out of his store. It also made for a slow Saturday and prom night.

Brad and Cicely ate in silence. When they were done, they got up and went to the cash register.

Brad called out to Doc. "How much, Doc?"

Doc called from the back room, he was sitting with his wife. "For you Brad, it's on the house. My treat, for the lovely prom couple."

Brad didn't reply; he walked out of the store pulling Cicely along.

When they left, Doc turned to his wife and said, "what a nice boy, what a shame, always they make fun of the nice boys, never the rats."

His wife took his hand in hers. "You're a nice boy. I don't make fun of you."

"No you don't." Doc kissed her hand.

Brad walked Cicely to her house; they stood there awkwardly. Cicely reached over; trying to give Brad a kiss, but he didn't stoop down, so she kissed him on the chest. She ran to the house, crying. He watched her sadly go in her front door. He felt sad for her and himself. He had never felt so bad, no more girl things for him. He walked around the neighborhood in his formalwear; he was too embarrassed to go home yet, so early from the prom. He knew some of the kids would stay out all night. He vowed to have nothing more to do with girls; it hurt too much.

When Brad got home, Rod was in his bedroom, waiting up for him. He had fallen asleep on Brad's bed. Brad had tried to sneak in, but he woke Rod up anyway.

"Brad, is that you?"

Brad sat on the edge of the bed, looking down at his younger brother.

Rod rubbed his eyes to wake up. "Did you have a good time?"

Brad didn't want to lie to his brother. "Fine," he said.

"I'm glad."

Brad looked down at his brother. "Thanks," he finally said.

Rod got up to go to his room.

"No," Brad said, "it's okay."

Rod looked at him. "You mean I can stay here tonight?" Brad had never allowed anyone to stay overnight in his room.

"Sure," said Brad, "you're my brother."

Rod smiled. "I'll always be your brother." He started to go to the smaller bed.

"No," Brad said, "tonight I'll sleep in the little bed, you stay in the big bed."

Rod smiled at his brother. Brad had never shared his bed with him before.

Brad undressed and got into the small bed. "Good night Rod. Thanks for waiting up for me and for being my brother."

"I love you Brad." Rod started to doze off.

As Rod started to sleep, Brad whispered to himself. "I love you too." He fell asleep with tears in his eyes. He would never be alone as long as his brother was alive.

Points to ponder:

Childhood can be a cruel time especially for those kids who are considered less desirable and become the butt of the other more popular kids' jokes. Brad was one of those kids who seemed to exist solely to give the other kids someone to poke fun at. High school is a time when permanent memories are formed, fond ones for those who are fortunate enough to be considered popular and traumatic memories for many of the others like Brad and Cicely. These are life-time memories that tend to shape the remainder of one's life.

1. Brad had decided, even though he wished he could go and be comfortable, not to go to his senior prom. His football teammate Todd convinced him to go mainly for his own purposes, to seduce his girlfriend. Why do popular people such as Todd always think that they can manipulate others like Brad assuming that they want to be like them?
2. It was apparent, even to Brad, when he tried to get into the tux that Todd had gotten for him, that he was not meant for proms and dances. Why did he go anyway?
3. Brad's mother tried to encourage him knowing that he wasn't made for dances, while his brother Rod, who looked up to his older brother, was proud of him. His father was not there to see his son off. What roles do family members play in our story and what impact do they have in our growing up?
4. Todd and Gladys couldn't stop from laughing at Brad and then at Cicely. Why are other people so cruel to those who need understanding the most but are the easiest to treat as inferiors?
5. Cicely's mother tried to make Brad and her daughter's prom date into something normal, hoping that Cicely wouldn't be hurt again. Her father said nothing while he stayed in the background, knowing that it wasn't normal. How do parents support their children and which parent do you think was right?
6. When Brad and Cicely arrived at the prom, Todd and Gladys left them immediately, and the other kids made fun of them, forcing Cicely to run from the gym. Why can't the others leave the less social functioning alone rather than using them to support their superiority?
7. Brad ran after Cicely into the cafeteria, two misfits running away. For what reasons was Brad kind to her, dancing with her when he didn't want to, and trying to make her feel better?
8. Brad took Cicely to the only safe place he knew, Drakes drug store. Doc Drake treated them like they were special people. Was it pity or something else?
9. When Brad and Cicely left the drug store, Doc said to his wife, "what a nice boy, what a shame, always they make fun of the nice boys, never the rats." Do you think the experience with Brad and Cicely raised some of Doc's own memories?

10. Brad came home early and found his younger brother Rod lying in his bed, waiting up for him, and sincerely wanting his brother to have had a good time. What are the ties of family and siblings that far outweigh the judgments of the rest of the world?
11. What affect do such traumas as Brad's senior prom have on the rest of one's life? How do such traumas play out in one's continuing tale?
12. How do you think one makes up for being treated cruelly growing up? Do they typically treat others kindly to make up for their poor treatment or do they tend to reek revenge on others?

Without a safe harbor
we may never feel safe.

Dreams Unfulfilled

Bob Sterling was a drama student in the Theater Arts department at Manhattan University in New York. He was raised in the Midwest in a small town in Iowa where he had not been exposed to diverse populations, minority groups, or a variety of entertainment possibilities other than the local movie theater that played only family type pictures. As an only child in a small town he had few real friends. He created his fantasy world through assuming various roles from the movies and books. His life was one of acting out. So, it came as no surprise to his parents that he wanted to go to acting school, but did it have to be New York, that city of sin?

The Theater Arts department at Manhattan University was small compared to other departments within the university. This allowed Bob to be a part of all of the department's theater productions, sometimes as part of the acting cast, sometimes on the production end. In effect, this allowed Bob to learn everything there was to know about theater. This is where he met Anne Bernstein, his wife-to-be. Anne was in the music department, a fairly accomplished flutist as well as a more than acceptable vocalist, with a choral quality rather than a popular musical voice.

Anne Bernstein was the daughter of a Jewish doctor, who was more interested in serving humanity than making money. He had become a doctor as it was at that time an occupation more open to Jews, even with medical school Jewish quotas, than the restrictions imposed on hiring Jews by the gentile controlled corporations. He had no interest in the law or becoming a neighborhood merchant, or working for one; the other occupations open to Jews at the time. So he became a doctor, as a way of quenching his thirst for doing something meaningful. He turned down the opportunity to join a prosperous Jewish group practice in the burgeoning affluent suburbs upon medical school graduation to open his own small office in a low-income neighborhood of New York. Rather than live in a predominantly Jewish neighborhood, he bought a modest single home on a half acre of land in a mixed ethnic and religious area. He thought this would be best for his children, to know other cultures and religions than segregate them in a self-imposed Jewish ghetto.

His daughter, Anne, grew up with little religious ties, other than the harassment about her being Jewish from some of her gentile neighbors and kids at school. She couldn't run from her name or her predominant Jewish nose. Anne was slight, with dark black hair, large brown eyes, dark complexion slightly north of olive, and that nose that would make Jimmy Durante proud. As a Jew, she would be considered Sephardic or Semitic; without that nose, she would be considered an extremely attractive Italian or Greek girl—a little bit of an upgrade without the Jewish slur. When she was thirteen, her father asked her what she wanted to do from a religious standpoint. At this time, Jewish girls were rarely Bat Mitzvahed, and it wasn't very important to her or her parents. She decided that instead of a Bat Mitzvah she wanted her nose fixed, and that was what she got. At the same time, she had started to develop breasts and a shapely figure. With her new pug nose and newly developed breasts and shape, she was a teenage knockout, and she knew it. She would spend hours just looking at herself in the mirror, marveling at her transformation. She could now go into the world and be anyone she wanted. Now, all she had to do was take care of her name.

Anne met Bob Sterling when she tried out for a vocal part in a musical, *Pajama Game* that the theater department was putting on. Her voice didn't have musical comedy star quality, but her dark looks and build got her a supporting role. Bob, on the other hand, had the looks of a matinee idol, tall, dark, and handsome, but Midwestern shy, especially with girls. However, he was one of the stars of the theater department in spite of his shyness; all of the girls were after him. He was the catch of the theater department. Subconsciously, such unconditional acceptance and adoration in spite of his shyness, especially from the girls, was one of the major reasons he was in the theater department rather than learning something else that might actually get him steady employment upon graduation. Anne saw nothing particularly attractive in small town Bob, except that all the other girls seemed to think he was something special, a real dreamboat; so she got interested. It wasn't difficult for big city Anne to land small town Bob once she made up her mind to land him.

Bob and Anne were married in their junior year, against the advice of both sets of parents; neither one wanting the other in the family. But Anne didn't care, she was no longer a Bernstein with a Jewish nose: she was now a Sterling with a pug nose. She could be anyone she wanted to be without the stigma of having to live as a Jew in America was expected to live. Once they had children, their parents came around, as they were all just people, and they weren't going to miss spoiling their grandchildren. Small town or big city, grandchildren took precedence.

Points to ponder:

We are all victims of our own circumstances, such as who our parents are, where we grow up, the presence of other siblings, relationships and acceptance by our peers. Bob grew up as an only child in a small town in Iowa that consisted of a homogeneous population. Anne grew up in the New York area that was a real melting pot of various cultures. As a Jewish girl living in a mixed neighborhood, she grew up not being accepted by the gentile population. Bob wanted to expand his small town roots; Anne wanted to shed her Jewish identity. Such are those parts of our lives that carry scars into our adult life.

1. Bob, coming from a small town, wanted to expand his horizons by going to college in New York. Why do people desire the opposite from what they have?
2. Many times, children like Bob, growing up in a small town as an only child, resort to a fantasy life. How does this play out for them in their growing up and moving into adulthood?
3. Anne's father was a Jewish doctor who decided on opening an office in a low-income neighborhood rather than practice in the more afflu-

ent suburbs contrary to the expected stereotype of the Jewish doctor. What possibly could have motivated him to make this decision?

4. Anne was born with a Jewish name and a predominant Jewish nose, bringing her harassment from her gentile neighbors and kids at school. What forces create the need to harass the other and where do kids learn such behavior?
5. When Anne was thirteen, rather than opting for a Bat Mitzvah (a Jewish ceremony for girls of thirteen welcoming them into the Jewish adult community) she decided to have her nose fixed. What pressures push us away from our religious roots (especially a Jew in America) and towards the desire to be like everyone else?
6. Anne didn't see Bob as attractive, but the other girls were after him. How does this stimulate someone such as Anne to go after him herself?
7. Bob, coming from a small town and being shy, chose to attend college in the Theater Department in New York City. What were some of the reasons that he made this decision?
8. When Bob and Anne were married in their junior years, neither set of parents approved of their marriage. What might be their respective reasons?
9. What were some of the reasons that Anne would marry someone such as Bob, coming from two extreme upbringings? What did she hope to achieve by marrying Bob?
10. Anne and Bob, coming from two diverse places, eventually had children that brought their parents back into their lives. What experiences and traumas do you think their children are in store for?
11. How easy is it today for a couple of diverse and religious backgrounds such as Anne and Bob to assimilate easily into society? Are there still prejudices and biases affecting such couples and their children?
12. Do people and children still separate themselves based on ethnic, cultural, and religious backgrounds? Are such issues still as prevalent in today's society? Can you cite some examples pro and con?

You can be anyone you want,
but will the others let you?

Social Pressures

Betty was now twenty-eight, a little older than her new boyfriend, Sidney. She had been at her job, the same job, in the accounts payable department for almost ten years, from the time she graduated from high school. In the beginning, her job was her life. She was going to go somewhere in the company. Over the years as she watched college graduate males coming in to the company and quickly being promoted while she stayed in the same position, she formed her own routine knowing she was not going anywhere in this company. Although she knew she was smarter than most of these college educated bozos, this would never be recognized. So, in time her work became just a job and was no longer the center of her life. Work was only a means to support her weekly routine.

Monday night was drinks and dinner out with Terry, her oldest girl friend from the parish grade school, who had been married for almost ten years to Barry Burdo, with three kids. After the weekend, with Barry and the kids, Terry needed to unwind. Monday night with Betty saved her life. Tuesday was beer and bowling night with the office girls team. Betty with her size was the kingpin of the team, averaging in the one hundred and eighties. Wednesday night was girl's night out, shopping, drinks, and dinner with her work friends. Thursday night was card night, usually Poker, at one of her married girl friend's house. This was always a short night for Betty, as she got tired quickly of hearing how wonderful married life and having kids was, and why wasn't she married as yet. She ran as soon as she could to the nearest neighborhood bar, hoping for her ship to come in—it was still out at sea.

Friday night was happy hour night with the company drinking club, an informal group of fellow female worker whiners without mates or partners. This depressed Betty until after her third scotch and soda, then she joined in, becoming one of the loudest whiners –life sucked and so did the company. Saturday was shopping, not necessarily buying, day, either with one of her girl friends or alone. This got her out of the house, avoiding another confrontation with her parents; why wasn't she married like her sisters, when was she moving out to be on her own; and killed the day with nothing else to do. Saturday night was the worst and loneliest time for Betty. Saturday night to her was still date night, not a night to be seen out alone or with "the girls." Betty felt that she couldn't go out and that she couldn't stay in, not without her parents nagging her. So this had become babysitting night for one of her younger sister's children.

When Betty grew up, it was expected that a girl would be married by the time she was twenty; otherwise she was destined to be an old maid. Those of the female persuasion were not expected to work, but to be married, be unpaid housewives, and raise children, many children in the Italian Catholic tradition. Betty was too big (almost six feet tall) and bulky (almost 160 pounds) to be attractive to boys as she was growing up. She was the one other girls talked to about their boyfriends, she was the girl friend but never with a boy friend of her own. She went through high school never having a boy friend, rarely dating, and mostly one-time blind dates. She was called "moose."

After high school, like all good girls of the Catholic persuasion she expected to be married within a couple of years. As college wasn't an option in her parent's economic position, she took the job with the company as a short-term fill-in to make some money. She paid board to her parents, but saw it as a temporary situation until she got married or was able to move out on her own. With her self proclaimed winning personality it was only a matter of time. Most of her friends got married quickly, within two years of high school graduation. Betty's time had to come, but nine years later it still hadn't. In the meantime, her two younger sisters, Grace and Connie, had both gotten married to their high school boy friends within a year of graduation. In those days in their community sex was saved for marriage. Grace now had three children and Connie four, making Betty an aunt, but not a wife. Betty had little envy for her sisters. She wasn't looking for an auto mechanic or a printing press operator.

She was holding out for a college graduate, hopefully Catholic, and larger than her. Sid wasn't perfect, but he looked good to her as a prospect, and two out of three wasn't bad.

Sid was twenty-seven (well, going to be twenty seven), never married, still lived at home with his parents, a college graduate, even larger and bulkier than her, and her boss in the accounts payable department. He was easy-pickings for Betty; she just had to make him seem smarter than her. Sid was one of the few non-Catholic employees. Sid was tongue tied from the first time he saw Betty. There weren't many women of any persuasion that were large enough for Sid. Betty was the perfect size. He would work on honing down her Catholic edges.

Sunday was Betty's one real day off, a day to herself. Her parents, Al and Maria, still attended Sunday mass at St. Anthony's in the old, Italian section. They expected Betty, while she still lived in their house, to attend with them. Betty, however, had lost interest in the Catholic religion and it's nonsensical rules the moment her parents and the priests lost control over her, the day she graduated from her confining, all girls, Catholic, high school. She felt that they hadn't prepared her for life, only for a Catholic life. She wanted more for herself; she wouldn't be told how to live, not by her parents, not by other people. Betty saved Sunday for special activities like reading the newspaper in bed with her coffee, walking in the park, and visiting museums. She would usually go with another single girl friend, but there were less and less of them. She didn't like going alone; she would stay home if there were no one else, hiding in her room from her parents. Sometimes she would take one or more of her nieces and nephews with her for company. She was always on the alert for her special "soul mate." She was tired looking, she wasn't getting any younger; thirty was the threshold to old maiddom. It was downhill from there. Sid was looking better all the time, if she could only get him away from his overbearing mother and into her lair.

Betty decided one Friday night to take matters into her own hands. She took Sid, who rarely drank, out to the Purple Chicken, their near work haunt, to get him drunk—and she was successful.

Once outside of the Purple Chicken, Betty led him away. They walked aimlessly; only Betty knew where they were going. She wanted him a little drunk, but not too drunk. Three scotch and waters did it. She, herself, hardly finished her one drink. They stopped in front of Betty's and her parents' house. Betty walked them toward the front door.

"Betty," Sid said, "you forgot something?"

"No, Sid, this is our dinner date."

"At your house, with your parents?" Sid was sobering, getting depressed. He had never met Betty's parents; he had hoped he never would.

"Of course, they've been dying to meet you."

Sid was dying too. "Do we have to?"

Betty looked at him from the corner of her eye. "You don't have to do anything you don't want to, only if you want to see me again. We can't keep hiding. My parents want to meet you. You'll meet them. Its up to you."

Sid was confused. "You mean if I don't meet your parents, you don't see me anymore?"

"And the girls think your not management material. You sure got that quick."

Betty pulled Sid up the stairs, opened the door with her key, pulling him into the vestibule.

"Mom!" Betty called, "we're here!"

A little, round woman came from the kitchen area. She wore a full-length apron smeared with red pasta sauce that said on its front "Italians do it with pasta." The small, round face had some of Betty's features, but she was not large boned like Betty. She was a miniature; Betty was a giant. She held a spatula in one hand, waving it up and down. She rushed to Betty, hugging her around the waist. "Bettina," she said, "just in time, the gnocchi, almost ready. Come sit." She led them to the living room. It was thickly carpeted, with elegant looking furniture, sofa and chairs, all covered with plastic slipcovers. A room to be looked at, admired; but not lived in. Betty was surprised that they were being allowed into Momma's sanctuary, but she said nothing.

Betty stopped. "Mom, this is Sidney."

"Of course, Sidney, who else?" She looked at Sid. "You're all Bettina ever talks about. Sid did this; Sid did that. So, of course its Sidney." Sid extended his hand. Mom ignored it, hugging him around the waist. She was a strong, little woman. Mom looked up at Sid. "Another big one! My Bettina likes you, I like you!"

Sid hesitated; he didn't know what to say. "Mrs. Cascorella," he began.

"No, no," Mom said, "Maria. You call me Maria, that's my name."

Sid started again. "Mrs. " He hesitated. Mom waited.

"Sid's happy to finally meet you," Betty finished for him.

"So, sit!" Maria left them in the living room, went back to the kitchen.

They sat together on the sofa, the plastic slipcovers making it difficult not to slide off, especially for people the size of Sid and Betty.

Sid whispered, "Don't you live here?"

Betty whispered back, "Of course, but my Mom is embarrassed that I still live at home. She makes like I'm a visitor when I bring someone home."

"Like your other boyfriends?" Sid looked at her.

"No, Sid, you're the only boyfriend I've brought home." She kissed Sid on the lips.

"Ah, ha! So, you're here. And what's this, on our couch?" Betty's dad, Alphonse, had quietly entered the room.

Betty quickly moved away from Sid. "Hi, Dad," she said. "When did you get home?"

"Oh, I've been home. Waiting for youse, so we's could have dinner."

"So, here I am."

He looked at Betty, then at Sid. "So, I see."

"Oh," she said, "This is Sid."

Sid once again extended his hand, but Al ignored it. "Of

course," he said, "who else." He moved closer to Sid. "You're all she ever talks about, Sid this, Sid that. You must be something special. Betty doesn't usually like boys."

Betty blushed with embarrassment. "Dad, stop it!"

"See, even her own father she doesn't like."

"Dad, please!"

"Dinner!" Maria yelled from the small dining room. The table was set with the Cascorella's best tableware, the holiday and special guest treatment.

"So," Al looked at Betty and Sid, "let's eat!"

Sid and Betty sat across from each other while Al sat at the head of the table and Maria sat at the other end near the kitchen. Maria brought in the first course, an enormous antipasto. She served each of them and then returned to the kitchen. Al began eating, Sid waited for Maria to return. Al looked at him.

"Whatsa matter? A big boy like you don't eat?"

Sid didn't know what to say. Betty saved him. "I think he's waiting for Mom."

Al banged his forehead with his hand. "Momma mia. Maria never eats with us, in the kitchen or after we're done. She's watching the chicken scaloppini and the spaghet. Mangia. Please, Sid, its fine."

Betty nodded to him, to start eating. They ate in silence. Dinner was serious business to Alphonse Cascorella. He was about Betty's size, but wore his bulk well. With black wavy hair and mustache, broad shoulders, muscular arms, twinkly eyes, aquiline nose, and expressive lips, he was a handsome man—a smoothy and a dandy. He was always well dressed, tonight in an Italian knit shirt finely pressed, black silk slacks; and black polished loafers. One could easily mistake Al for a very successful businessman. The truth was he had always made a living by his wits, in legal, somewhat shady scam type jobs; such as used car salesman, low end furniture (little down, so much a week), home improvements (some needed, some not), and now aluminum siding (specials for widows and older people). Al had a low opinion of people, except for himself.

Maria continued to bring dishes to the table. Al reached over, forking what he wanted. Sid waited for the dish to be passed, but it didn't happen. Betty eventually passed the dish to Sid, after she had taken hers. As they finished each dish, Maria cleared the table, removing the dirty dishes to the kitchen. As they continued eating, Maria washed and dried the dishes in the kitchen. Finally, Maria cleared the last dish, and set a large plate of her home made spumoni in front of each of them, including her. She sat down with them, started to eat.

"Mrs. Casco," Sid began.

"Maria," she said. "Its all right, Sid, I eat in the kitchen. Come, we all have desert together, then coffee in the living room."

Betty looked up. "In the living room, Mom?"

"Sure, in the living room. Sid's our special guest."

Al had finished his spumoni. "So, Sid, now we talk. You like our Bettina?"

"Please Dad! Let him finish his ice cream." Betty rubbed Sid's thigh with her foot under the table. She smiled at him.

"Sure, sure, let him finish, plenty of time to talk. For a big man, he doesn't eat much, and so slow."

"Give him time, Dad. This is his first meal at the Cascorella's Italian smorgasbord. It takes growing into."

Sid looked up at Maria. "Mrs, Maria, this was wonderful."

Marie blushed, looked down at her spumoni. "Thatsa nice Sid."

"Wait until you taste her veal parmaganie. Umm!" Al smacked his lips. "And her cannolis."

"Al," Maria said, "he came to dinner. He's not moving in."

"Maybe he is, maybe that's why Bettina finally brings her Sid home, to meet her parents." He looked over at Betty. "Eh, Bettina!"

"No, Dad, it was just time."

"So, Bettina, you got news?"

"No, Mom, just dinner."

"Eh, Sid?" Maria looked up at Sid.

Sid said nothing. In some strange way he liked these people, a family he never had. Sometimes a dinner is more than just a dinner.

When Sid left, Betty asked her parents what they thought of him.

"A nicea boy," Maria said, "a big boy, but he doesn't eat much, and so slow."

Al sat in his lounge chair, with his fingers laced across his belly, fully satiated and bloated with good Italian food, puffing on a cigar. "I like him." I just hope Bettina knows what she's doing, he thought to himself. Betty thought the same thing.

Sid was grateful to have survived the dinner with Betty's folks. He was still angry about being surprised and tricked into going there, but he had to admit he liked her parents; they made him feel comfortable and important. It also brought him closer to Betty, a big hurdle cleared. He wasn't sure what love was, but he couldn't get Betty out of his mind. She was as forceful as he was meek. He could hide behind her strength. On her parent's stoop, outside of their house, as they kissed good night, out of sight of Al and Maria, Betty had breathed in his ear, saying softly, "I love you" for the first time. Sid felt the same way, but he couldn't say it. Instead, Sid asked her to go out with him the next night, their first Saturday night out together. Saturday was usually his night to spend with his mother. For Betty, it was like Sid saying I love you.

Sid made reservations for seven at Betty's favorite, neighborhood Italian restaurant. Sid dressed in his best suit, shirt, and tie. Betty wore a tight, knit dress, which emphasized her ample curves and breasts, without making her look too large. Sid never felt so proud to have her on his arm, as they walked in heads turn, especially the male heads. Sid had pre-ordered all of Betty's favorite dishes; antipasto, mussels in red sauce, cheese ravioli, veal parmigiana, and spumoni for desert. After a quiet dinner of holding hands and looking at each other, the waiter winked at Sid as he placed the spumoni in front of each of them. Betty took her first bite, made an awful face. She put her fingers into her mouth, pulling out something hard. She wiped it off on her napkin.

"My Gawd, Sid! Its a ring!"

Sid smiled. "Try it on."

Betty put the ring on her finger. It fit perfectly She looked over at Sid. He was smiling; he was the thief who had eaten the lasagna. "Sidney! What is this?"

"Its for you if you want it?"

"Oh my God! Of course I want it. Oh, Sid, you made me so happy." She went over, kissing him harder than she ever had. Sid floated on clouds, knowing she liked it.

"So, what does this mean? Engaged, Sid we're engaged?"

"You want to be engaged?"

"Oh, Sid, of course."

"Come on. I got to show my parents." Betty walked around the room, showing everybody her ring while Sid paid the bill.

On the way out, the waiter who conspired with Sid to hide the ring in the spumoni came up to Sid. He whispered, with a heavy Italian accent, in Sid's ear " in bocca al lupo." Sid thought he was calling him crazy but the waiter meant to wish him luck—in the wolf's mouth.

Betty was on air as they walked fast toward her parent's house. Sid was not as much in a hurry. He just hoped he could go through with it.

Points to ponder:

Parents try to raise their kids so that they internalize their values and beliefs. There is a desire to have their children follow in their footsteps, to live like them as a way of justifying their own lives. While they may wish the best for their children, it is important that the best encompass their own standards of righteousness. Betty was raised with an Italian Catholic upbringing, with the expectation that she continue living that way. Sid was raised with no cultural or religious upbringing. He was still affected by other's religions if only through other's prejudices and his parents' prejudices. Could love, if this be love, conquer all? What social programming creates the pressure that brings us to conform?

1. Betty was twenty-eight years old, working in the same job for almost ten years. She had grown-up expecting to be married within two years after completing high school. What pressures did this expectation place on her?
2. Betty developed a routine for the week that kept her occupied but also kept her thinking about her plight. Is this a normal reaction when one isn't happy with their real life?
3. Betty still lived with her parents while her girlfriends and younger sisters were married with children. Why did Betty believe that she had to apologize for her position in life?
4. Betty's expectations of getting married young had not happened. She was approaching thirty years old and getting tired and depressed looking for her special soul mate. To what extent did this condition have on her decision to accept Sid as her boyfriend?
5. Sid was a large, bulky unattractive male who still lived with his parents and never had a girlfriend. He was extremely scared of girls, but most of them found him too scary. He took a non-threatening job, especially for a male, so that he could hide from more embarrassing social situations. What was his attraction to Betty?
6. Betty, out of frustration, took Sid to dinner at her parents, to move the relationship along. What did she really expect? Was it acceptance or rejection of Sid by her parents?
7. Sid was greeted warmly by Betty's parents, showing him a family life that he had never had. Did this bring him closer to Betty or increase his feelings of trepidation?
8. At dinner, Sid was surprised to see that Maria didn't eat with the family, not like his family. How does one deal with a clash of values between cultures?
9. Having cleared the hurdle of meeting and being accepted by Betty's parents, Sid takes Betty out to dinner and gives her an engagement ring. Was this really what Sid wanted to do? If not, why did he do this?
10. Betty seemed elated to have the engagement thing leading toward marriage over with, but did it have anything to do with Sid specifically? Did Sid really want to get married to Betty? What doubts might be in both of their minds?
11. Based on the scenario presented, do you really believe that Betty and

Sid will go through with the marriage and have children? What pressures do you see getting in the way?

12. Coming from two divergent backgrounds, as Betty and Sid did, do you believe that its easy and even possible to overcome such differences in today's society so that the couple and their children can live in social comfort?

Free choice is a wonderful thought,
but most of us can't exercise it.

Ethnic Connecting

Doris and Sam had worked together for over five years, never getting closer than a work relationship. Sam was a manager; Doris was an administrative assistant. Last weekend they had finally been thrown together at a party. They found out they had much in common, both coming from similar working class backgrounds, and liked each other. Doris became closer to Sam now that the office and position barrier had come down somewhat. Sam felt freer to talk to her about his situation at home with his mother. It had been a long time since he had had someone to talk to about his life outside of work. Doris and Sam started to share coffee together in the morning, in Sam's office under the guise of work, even though Sam had already had his morning coffee with his mother. Sam really didn't like coffee.

At lunch, Doris brought them both food from the cafeteria, which they ate in Sam's office, another work meeting. With Doris staying an hour later, Sam and Doris left work together. Doris waited with Sam at the bus stop until his bus arrived, then walked home alone.

The office rumor mill started up, matching Sam and Doris romantically, already planning the wedding. With her husband dead, Sam's mother Jean resurrected the tradition of the family Friday night dinner, just her and Sam. He stopped at the bakery for a fresh bread and desert cake on his way home. They ate in silence. It was not a festive occasion; it was observance and remembrance.

Jean insisted that Sam bring home that nice girl he talked about from work, what was her name? Sam promised he would, but he never did. One Friday night, Doris walked him to his bus, waiting with him, getting on the bus when it arrived. Sam turned around to look at her as he dropped his payment in the exact change machine.

"Doris, where are you going? You never take the bus. You always walk."

Doris smiled at him as she dropped her change in the machine. "Tonight, I take the bus."

Sam usually didn't notice. Tonight he noticed that Doris was dressed up, a straight, black skirt, a white Angora sweater, and black high heels with stockings. Sam was impressed. He had never regarded her as a woman, only as a work friend. They walked to the back of the bus together, Sam stepping aside to let her sit down first by the window, he sitting next to her in the aisle. At each stop, Sam looked over to see if Doris was getting off, but she didn't move. At his stop, he reached up to pull the cord to notify the driver. As he started to walk toward the front of the bus, he turned around to say goodbye to Doris. She got up as well, followed him off. At the curb, as the bus pulled away, he confronted her. "Doris, are you following me?"

Doris smiled slyly. "Why Sammy, why would I do that?"

"Doris, I don't know, but you're scaring me."

"Little me?"

Sam looked down at her; she was not quite so little in her high heels and tight sweater. "Yeah, little you. Where are you going?"

"I told you on the bus, dinner with a friend of mine."

Sam shook his head. "Okay by me. I'll see you Monday." He started to walk away; she followed right behind him. Sam turned around. "C'mon Doris, what's going on?"

"I told you." Sam walked to the trolley stop, Doris right behind him.

Sam waited for the trolley, Doris right beside him. "So," Sam said, "where does your friend live?"

"Oh," Doris said, "on the East Side."

"Uh, huh," Sam said, "what's going on? Who's this friend?"

Just then the trolley came, Doris jumped on. Sam stood there; she looked down at him. "Well, are you coming?"

Sam looked at her. "I don't know; this is getting creepy. You sure you're not following me?"

The driver looked at them, ready to shut the doors. He looked down at Sam. "You coming or staying."

Sam got on the trolley as the driver started up. He lurched into Doris, having to grab onto her to keep from falling. He quickly took his hands off her. This was the first time he had ever touched her. Doris smiled at him, moved toward the back to sit down. Sam sat next to her. Once again, he expected her to get off at each stop; but she got off with him. He walked toward his house; she followed. He stopped at the bakery to pick up the bread and cake; she waited outside. They continued toward his house. At the steps leading to his house, he turned to Doris. “Well, good bye again, see you Monday.” Sam walked to his front door, opened it with his key, and walked inside, leaving Doris standing at the bottom of the stoop. His mother waited at the door, smiled at him, took the bread, continued smiling like the dog that had swallowed the drumstick.

The doorbell rang. Neither one moved. “Well,” Jean said, “aren’t you going to answer the door?” Sam didn’t move, so Jean went to the door. “Why look Sammy, it’s your friend from work, what’s her name.” Jean moved aside, Doris entered. Jean hugged her. “Thank you for coming. Friday dinner has been so lonely, with just the two of us.”

Jean and Doris went into the kitchen, clucking like old friends, leaving Sam alone at the front door. He finally closed the door, sat at the dining room table, waiting for dinner to be served, trying to hear what they were saying. He finally realized that the friend of hers was his mother. He wouldn’t invite her, so his mother did. Sometimes good intentions produce good results. Doris became a regular Friday night visitor.

After some time, Doris invited Sam and Jean to her parent’s for dinner. Jean met them outside their office building. They walked to Doris’s parents’ house from there. The house was a small row home on a well-kept street in a less desirable section of the city. Doris’s parents turned out to be small, rotund, jovial people; almost look alikes and act alikes. One of them started a sentence; the other one finished it. They both laughed, this is what became of living with the same person so many years. Sam couldn’t help feeling good with these people. Even Jean smiled. As they sat down to dinner, a young lady came down the stairs. She was not happy. She was sad, depressed; she did not want to be here.

"Sammy," Doris said, "This is my sister Sue."

Sue looked savagely over at Doris. "That's Suzanne!"

"I'm sorry, your highness." She turned to Sam. "Sammy, this is Suzanne."

Suzanne looked pleased; she smiled at Sam. She was a younger version of Doris, semi-attractive and drab, obviously not liking her life. She didn't find her parents funny.

Doris's parents tried to make the dinner light; Suzanne kept it heavy. They tried to keep Sam and Jean later. Her father promised to drive them home, but Sam couldn't wait to get out of there. Suzanne had sucked the air out of the house.

At work, Doris explained to Sam. She was the oldest child, going on thirty-three, her sister was twenty-nine. Her parents were not overly strict, but they held on to the old country traditions. Female children didn't leave the house of their parents until they were married, and the younger daughter didn't marry until the older daughter had married. Doris loved her parents, wanted to get married, but wouldn't just marry anyone. Suzanne hated her parents and her sister, had a boyfriend, and wanted to get married, but she couldn't. Honor your father and your mother she was told. She said "bullshit" to herself. She obeyed them but hated them.

This was the first time Doris had mentioned marriage to Sam. He liked Doris. She was a good friend, had become a good friend of his mother's, but he didn't want to marry her. She was too much like his mother. He was afraid she would make him like his father.

One night after dinner, Doris asked Sam to take a walk with her. They walked down the street, Doris taking his hand. Sam chilled, pulled his hand away. She put her arm through his; he let it be. Around the corner was an old storefront; the lights were on. Doris pulled him toward the building.

"Doris," he said. "Where are you taking me?"

"Come on," she said, as she pulled him toward the door. There were cryptic letters on the door and sides of the building.

"Doris," he said as he pulled back. "What is this? Some kind of church?"

"It's our neighborhood church. They have nightly services here. I thought you might like that."

Sam froze up. "No! I can't go in there!"

Doris looked at him; she had never seen him like this. "Sam, you are religious, aren't you?"

Sam was choking, his nose and head clogged; he tried to breath, making snorting sounds through his nose.

"Sam, are you all right?"

"Doris, please, I can't go in there." His face was flushed, his breathing severe.

"Sam, what's the matter?" Doris envisioned horrible experiences in another church.

"It's religion."

"What about religion?" Doris was frantic that Sam was going to faint. He was too big to handle. What would she do?

"I can't do it. I'm sorry."

"But Sammy you are religious? You do believe in Jesus Christ?"

"I'm American, proud to be Amrican, but not religious. The religion scares me. Ethnically, culturally I'm American. It's a heritage, a proud heritage, to be American, not a religion. My grandpop taught me. Live as a model to others; show the world a different kind of person—moral and ethical but not religious. Organized religion makes me feel too much like the others. I just want to be myself, no labels, no attachments."

"Sam, do you know what you're saying? You want to be like the oppressor, don't dare to show your difference." She tried to pull him toward the door.

"No, please Doris, I can't. Roy took me to his church. I got sick. Religion, all religion, makes me sick. I'm sorry Doris." He walked back toward her house.

Doris caught up to him, holding his arm. "It's okay Sammy."

But it wasn't. Doris had less to do with him at work. No more

Friday night dinners. She wanted to get married, but to a religious boy, a real church going Christian. She started spending more time with Ralph, an adjuster in the claims department. Three months later, Doris was showing everyone the two-carat engagement ring Ralph had got her. The wedding was to be in June. There would be a wedding after all, but not Sammy's.

Points to ponder:

Those born into similar cultures and/or religious systems tend to want to be with those who share that culture with them. While there are many wonderful people out there, such cultural thinking tends to limit the possibilities. We expect the other person coming from the same cultural background to share the same value systems. So even within the same culture we tend to separate people out. Doris and Sam were both born into working class families and communities. However, each of them came out of a similar heritage with a different set of values.

1. Sam and Doris worked together, but until they shared their working class upbringings they remained merely fellow workers. Once the barrier came down, they found they had much in common. What is it that brings us closer to those that share the same background?
2. Many times a shared heritage brings people closer together, allowing them to become closer than they can with other people. What are the artificial barriers that we put up to keep other people away from us?
3. Sam stayed living with his mother after his father died even though he was uncomfortable living with his mother. What do you think kept him there?
4. Sam's mother Jean resurrected the tradition of the family Friday night dinner for just her and Sam, an uncomfortable experience for both of them. Why would she do this?
5. Jean insisted that Sam bring home that nice girl from work although

it was obvious Sam didn't want to and that Jean didn't want Sam to leave home. What internal pressures could have motivated Jean?

6. Doris followed Sam on the bus and the trolley to Jean's dinner based on an invitation from Jean but not Sam. What could have possessed her to do that?
7. Doris's parents had a different value system than Sam and his mother coming from the same working class heritage, especially in their values towards their two daughters. What pressure is created when parents dictate their own values such as daughters don't leave the house until they get married and a younger sister doesn't get married until the older sister gets married?
8. Sam and Doris were pushed together in some part by their shared working class upbringing. Is this a basis for making a relationship? Is love saved only for those sharing a similar heritage?
9. Sam had a difficult problem with religion and its trappings. Is there a difference between heritage and ethnic culture and religion?
10. Doris held out to get married to a religious Christian boy, pushing Sam aside as not religious enough. Are such barriers always to the benefit of the individual?
11. After giving up on Sammy, Doris quickly found another male who more closely met her criteria. Did Doris make the right decision or should she question her criteria?
12. Doris, who wanted to be married, found Ralph at the company where she worked. Was it Ralph or getting married that she really wanted? What kind of a marriage do you think they will have?

Beware of those who judge others,
as they may be judged as well.

Decision Making

Thelma pressured her husband Joe to start looking for a house. She didn't get pregnant for nothing, anything to get out of that inner city hovel, living with *his* mother. They looked after work, on the weekends. Joe was glad for the activity, getting out of the house, but he had little commitment to actually finding something. They agreed that they didn't want to live in a homogeneous ethnic neighborhood like the one they now lived in. This made it difficult to find a house in their ethnically segregated city, making it easier for Joe to go through the motions.

Thelma concentrated on the lower end of Muskrat Hill, once a sanctuary where the wealthy could live comfortably without harassment, but now becoming more economically and ethnically integrated as many of the original wealthy families fled to the suburbs. Some of the older previously wealthy families still lived here, while younger less affluent families were moving in. These were desirable, fairly spacious homes, well kept by the previous families; now affordable to the next generation to raise their families. As a house went on the market, a young couple grabbed it, sometimes within the same day. Thelma kept in constant contact with the realtors (old line realtors trying to sell to young conservative families, they didn't like their parents' houses going to the hippy class) and scoured the real estate section first thing in the morning. She let everyone she knew know that she was looking for a house in this area; she had to get away from the inner city and her mother-in-law, Estelle.

One morning she got a call from a friend at work, Rhoda Gerber. Friends of Rhoda's parents had lived in their house all of their married life, the husband had just died, the wife was moving in with her son in a fancy suburban development. The house was right in the middle of the neighborhood Thelma was eyeing. She was assured it was a creampuff, it wouldn't last more than a few days. Rhoda had made an appointment for Thelma to see the house that morning; the family would like to avoid the realtors and the lawyers, both a set of thieves. They had set a price, reasonable, without a realtor involved. Thelma knew as she had looked at everything on the market. The wife was ready to sell. Rhoda cautioned Thelma to get out there immediately before the wife changed her mind, you know how old people are. Thelma knew only too well, she was living with Estelle.

Thelma called her school where she worked as a third grade teacher, pulled in a favor, getting Penelope Hastings to take her class until she could get in. She rushed to the bus station, as fast as her chubby, pregnant legs could move. She saw the bus approaching when she was within a block of the stop. She pulled up her skirt and scooted, arriving just as the bus came to a stop. She breathed hard, held her sides waiting for her body to stop heaving. The driver noticed her distress, came down to help her up, waiting until she was ready. Transit workers were not known for their courtesy. Thelma wondered if she weren't pregnant, would he have left her standing there. Pregnancy does have its privileges.

The house was two blocks from the bus stop. Thelma hurried from the bus stop, arriving at the house completely out of breath, body heaving. She stopped at the door, trying to calm down, looking over the outside of the house—it was perfect. She rang the bell, no answer. She fought her anxiety, rang again, putting her ear to the door, thinking she heard footsteps. "My God," she said to herself, "I hope Rhoda got a hold of her. She's gotta be home. I want this house."

Thelma heard the look-through open; there was an eye in there. "Oh God, she's home." She breathed away, gained her composure, straightened her skirt, and ran her hand through her hair. My God, what am I doing? I'm only buying a house, not auditioning for a job, she thought.

The door opened. A little, old lady stood there. Thelma's heart thumped, she looked too much like Estelle; this was going to be trouble.

The lady looked at Thelma, smiled. "Pregnant? Rhoda didn't

say." She spoke with the remnants of a middle European accent, German probably, maybe a survivor.

Thelma shook her head, slightly embarrassed. "Yeah, pregnant, sixth month."

The lady stared, small tears forming at the corners of her eyes. "I remember my first, a boy, Stanley. Kicked my sides something awful, until I got him out. Wouldn't wish it on Eva Braun." She laughed at her own joke.

Thelma fidgeted on the steps. "Yeah," she said, "I got a little kicker too, but not so bad. Next time my husband carries."

The lady started to tear. "Just lost my Al. You got a good one?"

Thelma smiled. "Yeah, I got a good one, a real keeper."

The lady looked down at her feet. "What's the matter with me, leaving you standing on the stoop. Come in, come in." She opened the door wider, allowing space for Thelma to enter. "Carrying big, I always carry big, three kids, all gone. Thank God, my Stanley has room for me." She started to tear again, she didn't want to leave here, move in with her Stanley. Thelma felt bad for her, mustn't let it get in her way. She wanted this house.

Thelma put her hand out. "Thelma Jordan, Rhoda Gerber's friend."

"Ya, I know, Rhoda call. Vera Gold, call me Vera. You professional?"

"Yeah, sure. Schoolteacher, third grade. Joe, my husband, lawyer, two years out of law school"

"Good, house stay in nice hands."

Thelma didn't know what to say. They looked at each other, one not wanting to sell, the other over anxious to buy. "Uh," said Thelma, "can I see the house?"

"Ya, maybe some tea? You look, I make." She went into the kitchen.

Thelma went from room to room. The house was beautiful, every room tasteful, immaculate. The downstairs had a vestibule where you walked in, with a separate door to the living room that was large and airy with a big bay, front window. Behind it was a formal dining room with doors front and back, large enough to seat twelve. She left the kitchen for last, not wanting to confront Vera until she had seen the rest of the house. The stairs to the upstairs came off the side of the living room, unobtrusive, richly carpeted like the other rooms. The upstairs had three large bedrooms, even the smallest one was spacious, each one with two windows. The master bedroom, looking out at the front of the house was immense, with its own private bathroom with a stall shower, large enough for two. Joe was going to love this house. There was a large well-decorated hall bathroom as well, between the other two bedrooms. Closets and wall space galore, everything large enough for her, Joe, and the baby. No more walking into furniture and walls in that Lilliputian inner city shanty.

Thelma composed herself as she walked into the kitchen, not wanting to look too eager. Vera looked up from the kitchen table. "Oh my God?" Thelma thought to herself, "a large kitchen, large enough for a table." "Ah," Vera said, "there you are. Please sit." A pot of tea, a basket of cookies, with two places set surrounded Vera at the table. Vera motioned to a seat next to her. "Please sit close, the hearing you know."

Thelma looked around the kitchen as she sat. There were plenty of counters, a large refrigerator, top freezer, and a dish-washer? No more washing and drying by hand. She had to have this house.

"So," Vera said as she poured the tea, "you like?"

Thelma nodded. "What's not to like? You have a lovely house."

Vera dabbed at her eyes. "Al, my handy man, he do a lot."

Thelma patted her on the arm. "He did a good job."

Vera sobbed softly. "Yes, he did. So, you saw everything?"

"I think so."

"The attic?"

"There's an attic?"

"Of course, Al fix up. Good for the mother-in-law, no?"

"In this case, definitely no."

"I see, no mother-in-law."

Thelma said nothing, shaking her head.

"And powder room, Al also do." Thelma looked at her. "Powder room?" she said.

"Powder room, downstairs, between living room and dining room."

"I thought that was a linen closet. I didn't look in."

"Used to be, now powder room. And Al's room, downstairs?"

"Downstairs?" Thelma asked.

Vera nodded toward a door at the back of the kitchen. Used to be basement, coal originally, now oil. Al make room, for kids, now Al's room. You look."

Thelma got up, opened the door; walked down the stairs, looked at the room. It was a paneled room, with a little bathroom off to the side, nicely furnished, and with the oil burner closed off in its own separate room. Again, it was a perfect mother-in-law room, but not for her mother-in-law. It would be the kids' playroom.

Vera looked down at the table. "Laundry room in the back, washer, dryer, stacking table, easy to do clothes, almost brand new, I leave for you."

Laundry room, washer, dryer, Thelma thought to herself. Estelle still did the wash by hand, using a hand wringer over an old, original laundry tub, in that filthy basement; hanging the clothes outside or in the basement. God, I have to have this house.

"Anymore surprises?" asked Thelma.

"Surprises, no more surprises. Oh, maybe garage, you have car?"

"No," Thelma said, "no car. Joe doesn't drive. Neither do I."

"Ya, today women drive, maybe later. Garage big, for big machine. Now, Al's workshop." Tears welled up, she dabbed at them. "So, you like house?"

Thelma couldn't contain herself; this was perfect.

"I see you like, you buy. Rhoda tell you price. Stanley set, he say fair."

"Price is fair. I know I've been looking."

"Ya, get house before baby. Stanley say get deposit, sign papers." Vera took the papers from the pocket of her housedress, passed them to Thelma.

Thelma looked them over. She couldn't wait to sign before Vera changed her mind. They were asking for a two thousand dollar deposit, almost the entire amount she and Joe had saved. She hurriedly wrote the check, signed the agreement, and handed the papers back to Vera.

Vera looked at the check. "Same bank we use, me and Al." She dabbed at her eyes. "I move next month, you move after that?"

"Sure, that would be fine."

"Good place for baby, we raise our three kids here, now all gone."

Thelma couldn't stand the sadness anymore. If she stayed longer, she would start to feel sorry for Vera, talk her into staying—even if it was with her and Joe. She got up to go, extending her hand. "Thank you. We'll let you know when we get our mortgage."

"No see garage."

"I don't have to, the house is perfect, thank you." Thelma moved toward the front door.

Vera sat at the table, sadly sipping her tea from the glass. "Big garage," she said as Thelma let herself out.

Vera said to the closing door. "Glad professional couple. Al will be happy. Always says too many working class moving in, spoil neighborhood, undo what we do, not clean like us."

Thelma didn't hear her; she had already left, hurrying off to work. Joe will be so happy, she thought, a nice clean neighborhood. He can be the model for the other professionals and the working class. Can't be a model without the others. Thelma smiled to herself, patted her stomach. A nice place to raise you, you'll be happy too.

Thelma got home before Joe. She sat at the dining room table, sipping tea, with a grin on her face. She was quite satisfied with herself; she had bought her dream house.

Joe entered the house with a flourish, with his size he couldn't help but be intrusive and noisy. Thelma looked up, smiled at him, a self-satisfied smile. Joe knew that look. It was the same one his law partners used when they had just screwed a client.

Joe went over to Thelma, kissed her on the cheek, rubbing her belly, a habit they had gotten into. Thelma smiled. She never felt better.

Joe looked at her; he was the luckiest man alive. "Okay, Thelma, what have you done?"

"Guess?"

"Thelma, I'm not good at this."

"Please, try to guess."

"Okay. The baby is fine, going to be a boy."

"No, Joe, how would I know that?"

"A girl."

"No, Joe, we bought a house! A beautiful, wonderful house, smack in the middle of where we wanted."

"A house? How could we buy a house? I was at work all day."

"I saw this house, friends of Rhoda's parents, the husband died, the wife is selling, moving to the suburbs, ugh! going to live with her son. Joe you're going to love it, three bedrooms, two baths, a powder room, finished basement, laundry room, dishwasher, garage, can you believe it?"

"Whoa, slow down." Joe sat beside her.

"Joe, I had to do it. A creampuff, we could move in tomorrow. A nice old lady, Vera Gold, her husband Al did all the fixing up, workshop in the garage. Oh, Joe, I'm so happy. Let's go out and celebrate."

"Thelma, shouldn't I see the house first, and my mom."

"Your mom?"

"Sure, she'll be living with us, won't she?"

Thelma's glee turned quickly to devastation. Her face sunk.

"Thelma, what's the matter? Are you all right, the baby?"

Thelma stopped to catch her breath. "No, Joe. I just never thought of your mother living with us."

"Where else would she live?"

"Why here. This is her house."

"Thelma, she can't live alone, here, in this house."

"Joe, she's lived here all her married life."

"Yeah, with my dad, with me, never alone. She's just a little lady, a little, old lady."

"Joe, she can take care of herself. She may be little, but she's tougher than the both of us. Still does everything for herself, won't let me help her. She's in the basement now, doing our clothes by hand, hanging them on that ratty line, after she insisted on making me tea. Believe me, she'll be fine on her own. Let her have her own life."

"What life? She watches TV all day, soap operas and quiz shows. Her biggest excitement is getting the answer before the contestants. All she has left is taking care of us. No, I can't leave her here. She's still my mother."

"Your mother! She still thinks she's your brother Tom's mother, that you're your father's son. I catch her sitting at the piano fingering "Ring Around The Rosie" and "Pop Goes The Weasel," like Tom is still sitting there with her. Joe, I hear her talking to him, crying. It's eerie!"

"Thelma, I know. But, how can I leave her?"

"Joe, most of the time she doesn't even know we're here. She passes her days waiting for her Tommy to return, keeping the house clean for him. She won't leave this house as long as she believes he'll return here."

"I know, but she's still my mother."

"Joe! She doesn't want you; she wants her Tommy. She thinks her Tommy graduated Harvard with honors, as an economist. That he won't come home until he's successful. That he's doing it for her. How could he lie to her like that?"

Joe hesitated, looking at the floor. "He didn't."

"What do you mean?"

Joe looked down at the floor, trying to hide the tears forming in the corners of his eyes. He dabbed at his eyes with his finger, avoiding looking at Thelma. "I told her."

"You told her! Why!"

"Why? She's my mother. It would break her heart to know that Tommy never went to Harvard, that he's not a successful economist, and that he's a plumber in Steubenville, Ohio."

"She really doesn't know?"

"No, she only knows what I tell her. She thinks Tommy is ashamed to write her directly, for leaving her. She forgives him, she will always forgive him." Joe was sobbing.

"Oh Joe, I didn't know. And you, you're trying to be the son she misses."

"No, I could never be Tommy to her. I just want what she gave to Tommy."

"Unconditional love?"

Joe hung his head. "Is that too much to ask for, from your mother?"

"No, it's not. But Estelle can't do that for you."

Points to ponder:

For some individuals it's difficult to leave your parents. For Tommy, given unconditional love by his mother that resulted in suffocating him, it was easy to leave home and run for his life. However, for Joe, who was always second best striving for his mother's recognition, he was unable to leave his mother, not until he got what he wanted from her. Enter a third party, Joe's wife Thelma, who sees the situation for what it is. If she doesn't get her husband Joe out of his mother's house, they will both die there.

1. When one partner, in this case Joe, is resistant to an agreed upon action such as buying a house, why does the other partner either back off or get more interested in making it happen like Thelma in this situation?
2. When one is committed to make change as Thelma is to get out of

her mother-in-law's house she will intensify her efforts even when six months pregnant. Why is this so? What issues encouraged Thelma to take such action?

3. Thelma spent considerable time looking for the right house in the right neighborhood. Was the house that Thelma saw really her dream house or was she more motivated to get out of the situation she was in?
4. Thelma wanted the house she saw, Vera Gold's house. Although Thelma felt sorry for Vera and her situation, why was she more concerned about herself and her situation than Vera's? Why can't we see the future and that one day we may be in a similar situation?
5. Thelma was extremely eager to buy Vera's house quickly before anyone else had a chance to make an offer on it. What possessed Thelma to pay the deposit of two thousand dollars, almost their entire savings, without first consulting with Joe?
6. Vera was moving due to pressure from her children. She didn't really want to sell and move form the house that gave her so many fond memories. Why did Vera rationalize the selling of her house to a professional couple when she really didn't want to move from there and her memories?
7. Joe was supposedly working with Thelma to buy a house for them and their coming child. Why was Joe angry over Thelma buying the house without him and what was the real reason for his resistance?
8. Joe had always lived with his mother even when he married Thelma. What really was keeping Joe tied to his mother and his insistence that his mother move with them?
9. Joe's mother, Estelle, took care of Joe and Thelma, in spite of her missing her favorite son Thomas. How did she value Joe and Thelma? Why do you think she took care of them? Why was she unwilling to believe anything bad about Thomas but not about Joe?
10. Joe lied to his mother about why his brother Thomas left home and his lack of success, protecting a brother that he really didn't like or respect. Why would he do this? Was he protecting himself, Thomas, or his mother?
11. How do we ever successful move away from our parents? Do they follow us even when we move far away? What is it that holds us under parental control?

12. Do you think Joe will be able to move away from his mother and if so will he be able to overcome his feelings about her and her favored son, Thomas?

Are we to be forever tied to family,
while friends may come and go?

The Good Life

Danny was finishing his latest movie musical score project, his twelfth, all winners—the scores, not the movies. He had time before his concert tour; he would like to spend it with his wife Alice, in Los Angeles, proving how wrong she was about the city and its people. The director of the movie, Reggie Roland, mentioned the possibility of a house, really an estate, coming up for sale. It was in the exclusive Bella Moola section, the closest Los Angeles came to upscale and uptight Connecticut. The owner, Jack Forest, who was a big star in the seventies, was now a has-been in the nineties. He couldn't get work, not even on a sitcom on TV. He had to sell the house to pay alimony to his three ex-wives. While at the top, he was caught in bed with, and worse, the studio head's 22 year old, bubble headed, trophy wife, in her bedroom. Unknown to him, he was being video taped, a video that made the rounds. She was thrown out, so was Jack, and blacklisted, Hollywood style. The video was a hit; but he was not.

Danny went out to see the house with Reggie, a favor from Jack to Reggie, prior to listing. It was everything Danny wanted, his own estate in Bel Air. Reggie walked around the house with Danny. Reggie had been there many times. He had directed Jack Forest in many of his hits; they had stayed friends. He knew all the secret chambers and hiding places. They stopped in the immense living room, thirty-by-fifty, with sixteen-foot ceilings, overlooking the impeccably landscaped grounds.

"So," Reggie said, "what do you think?"

Danny was floored. "What do I think? It's magnificent. But can I afford it? The upkeep alone."

Reggie came closer, talking quietly, confidentially, even though there was no one else there. "Danny, its a steal, at three eight."

"Three hundred and eighty thousand?" Danny still thought as a poor boy from the Bronx.

Reggie laughed. "How long have you been out here? You sound like a rube from the east."

"I am a rube from the east."

"Touché! That's three million, eight hundred thousand."

"Whew!" Danny sighed, "That's a lot of musical scores."

"I thought you were rich, all those movies."

"That's right, but I'm not an actor, only a poorly paid musician."

Reggie looked querulously at him. "Its not the same? Actors, directors, and musicians?"

"Well no," he said, "I want to surprise my wife."

"Good investment, she'll love it here."

"She hates it here."

"Oh, I see. I think you can get it for three, three two. Jack is desperate. I'll talk to him on your behalf. He's got the bank and three wives breathing down his pants." Some friend.

Danny walked around the living room, into the other rooms. "I don't know; that's a lot of money."

"Danny," Reggie said, "You don't pay the three two, only the required down, maybe ten, fifteen percent, about half a mil."

"Five hundred thousand!"

"About that. Then you pay the mortgage every month, just like rent, with ownership."

"And if you can't pay the mortgage?"

Reggie pondered. "Eventually the bank throws you out. Then you take the money you made on the deal and buy a bigger house."

"Like Jack?"

"Exactly. You learn quick for an east coast rube."

"I've been out here too long. This is starting to make sense."

"Believe me, you can't lose."

"As long as I have half a mil, and prices keep going up."

"They always have." Reggie smiled at him. "Can't lose."

Danny shook his head. "Can't lose."

As they left, Reggie whispered to him. "The neighbors will be happy. Jack is an actor; not well thought of in this neighborhood."

Danny shook his head. "No, you never know. Actors can be so tacky.".

Danny bought the house on his own, not telling Alice. When it was fixed up, gentrified ala east coast, un-Hollywooded ala west coast, Danny invited her out. He used the guise that he would be receiving an award for his latest movie score. It was true but it was a minor award from the sound engineers association. He assured Alice she would love where they were staying.

Danny picked her up at the airport in a limousine, the best for his Duchess. He had the driver take them directly to the new house. Although she looked nonplused as they drove through the gate to the house, he knew she was impressed. Nothing like what she was used to, impressive Hollywood style.

"Danny," she said, as he led her around the house, "this is magnificent."

He was pleased; it was east coast acceptable. He took her to the master bedroom suite; it was a replica of the bedroom suite from their New York honeymoon at the Waldorf.

"Oh, what is this? Something looks very familiar." Alice was cold, she didn't joke; this was as close as she came.

"It's our master bedroom."

"Ours?"

Danny nodded. "I bought it for you, it was Jack Forest's."

"The actor? You met him?"

"Of course. I bought the house from him, the bank, and his three ex-wives."

"Oh I love it. I still hate Los Angeles, but I love this house. So secluded, so elegant, amongst all the Hollywood stuff." She patted the mattress on the bed. "Nice and soft, just like my husband." She lay down, kicked off her shoes; motioned for him to lie next to her. She kissed him. "Thank you, Danny, this is wonderful."

"The house? You like the house!"

"No, a house is just a house. You are wonderful." She didn't tell him how distasteful she found the house, so LA, so Hollywood.

Danny snuggled against her; he was home.

He knew Alice would never like living in Los Angeles, but he hoped she would do it for him. The house would remain his. As Alice said, "it fits your ego." Danny needed the constant recognition and adoration he could only get in Los Angeles, phony, insincere, but necessary. Danny had a large gold piano, with his caricature, installed on the gate. This way Alice would know which house was theirs, as would all of the neighbors. "Thank God, he wasn't an actor."

Points to ponder:

We go through life wishing and fantasizing about the things we don't have that we're told we should want. There are many pressures in our society—the media, advertisements, wannabe and quasi celebrities, entertainment magazines and so forth that make us feel inadequate and envious of the lives of other people. It has become increasingly more difficult to be satisfied with the life we have fallen into and with what we have. Danny, a poor lower middle class boy from the east coast, has had some luck scoring movies in Hollywood. This is a world that Danny has always wanted to be part of. However, his wife Alice was quite happy with her life on the east coast, the Hollywood life style sickened her—a basic conflict of values.

1. Danny was somewhat successful in scoring music for the movies in Hollywood. What was the lure to him that made this more important than a concert tour?
2. His wife Alice was opposed to Los Angeles and the lifestyle it represented. What were the deterrents that made her feel this way?
3. When Jack Forest's house in the Bel Air section of Los Angeles came up for sale, Danny was interested. He compared the property to estates in Connecticut. What do you think were the inducements for Danny?
4. Jack Forest, a big star in the seventies, was now a has-been in the

nineties, having devastated his career and life by acting out the stereotype of the Hollywood heel. What is it that makes such successful people self-defeat themselves?

5. When Danny saw Jack's house he was overwhelmed. Something in him triggered the need to have this house and the accompanying life style. What were those factors?
6. Danny came from an east coast value system as to how to live and how to buy a house and pay off the mortgage. Why was he convinced by Reggie to buy the deal ala Hollywood style?
7. Reggie's statement that Jack Forest as an actor wasn't desired in this neighborhood to the chagrin of the neighbors didn't seem to bother Danny. Why was that?
8. Danny bought the house on his own, not telling his wife, Alice, who he knew hated Los Angeles and what it represented. Why would he do that?
9. Danny did everything he could to make Alice like the house, but she still found it distasteful. What mental messages might be getting in her way?
10. Alice told Danny that the house fit his ego. What did she mean by that?
11. Danny's need for constant recognition and adoration was achievable in Los Angeles. Was this sincere or phony and why do people want this?
12. Danny placed a large gold piano with his caricature on the front gate. What was his need to do this?

How do we know what to wish for,
is it for us or others?

Growing Up in the Wrong Place

Michele and Robert, as brother and sister, tried to be just like the other kids. But they were poor kids in an upper middle class neighborhood. In the early years they were all just kids. Michele didn't want to be different from the others. Robert, as a boy, was less readily accepted. The other boys, due to his size, were scared of him. But his passive nature made him easy prey, someone to pick on, which they did. His mother, Rita, found him in his room a lot. She suspected he had been crying, but Robert said no. Rita talked to her husband Bob about moving to a less affluent suburb; it would be better for all of them. They could get another car; Bob could commute to work. Bob didn't want to leave the neighborhood; he liked living in a rich neighborhood. He didn't want to become a commuter. He was not a deserter. He did not want to live like "those ordinary people."

Michele got through elementary school as one of the popular kids. Robert had a tougher time, a loner. Michele tried to protect her brother, but her tendency was to distance herself from him. Due to the closeness in ages, Michele was only one grade above Robert. Many times, Michele's acceptance by her classmates had saved Robert from being picked on and called names. When Michele was in her first year in Junior High School, Robert was still in his last year of elementary school. He was now more open to bullying by the kids in his grade. The fact that Robert was extremely large and bulky for his age only made him more of an object to be picked on. Robert was not physically aggressive. He took the verbal derision and physical abuse without fighting back; he became a punching bag for the bullies.

Rita watched her son come home from school in a beat-up, physical or psychological, condition almost every day. He said nothing to her, ran directly to his room, stayed there until dinner. Rita tried again to approach Bob about moving, but he was adamant.

This was their home. She tried to console Robert, but he pushed her away. He was no momma's boy. When Robert reached Junior High his sister, sometimes by reputation alone, once again protected him. As an active, athletic, girl, she was still popular with the other kids. She was now in the eighth grade, at an age when girl's attention turned to boys. As some of her friends started to take an interest in boys, their interest in Michele ebbed. The boys interested in girls socially were not interested in Michele. She was too large for them; they called her "big mama." She quickly became a piranha to both the boys and girls. Her close friends from the neighborhood and elementary school moved away from her. She was an outsider, an unappealing female. Her being poorer than them became more an issue of derision.

Michele bonded with Robert. They walked to school together, lunched together, came home from school together. Michele was forced to become friends with the less popular girls, those that she had rejected all through school. She felt that she was the same person; the others made her feel different. Robert still kept to himself, hiding behind his studies, earning A's, except in gym. They had done nothing to be branded as outcasts, it didn't matter; they were not as rich as the others and lived differently from the rich.

Michele graduated the public high school with academic honors. Every college she applied to accepted her, all out of town. She couldn't wait to leave this place, her place as an outsider. She decided on the University of North Carolina, in the Chemical Engineering program. She had always liked the sciences; it was one field that was equal for both genders. She just wanted to be judged for who she was, not for whom she was born. It was her decision. Bob, as a good father, had put money away for both of his children to go to college. No night school or community college for them; they could go anywhere they wanted.

When Michele left for college, Robert was alone at school once again. He somehow got through his senior year, ostracized by his classmates, ostracizing his classmates. He graduated near the top of his class academically, his constant studying paying some rewards. Rita, and Bob, had been quite concerned for some years, at their wit's end as to what to do with Robert. Bob said, "Robert was a late bloomer like him." Rita sighed and said, "I hope so." She wasn't really sure he was a bloomer at all.

Although most colleges would probably have accepted Robert, he only applied to two local colleges. He was accepted to both of them, but decided on the more academic, smaller one, a better place for him to hide. He was deathly afraid to be on his own. This way he could still live at home, study and hide in his own room.

Michele found herself at North Carolina, accepted as just another Chemical Engineering major, a tough program. Most of the other students were brainy like her, not particularly attractive, some large like her. She was accepted for what she knew, not who she was. The other students bonded together as a study unit, each one helping the others. In her second year, she became friendly with a fellow student, Boyd Dalton, from Atlanta. He was big and unattractive like her. Sometimes likes attracted. Michele was happy, after so many years of sadness, not understanding what was wrong with her. With Boyd, she became just another person, without a specific label.

At graduation, Michele, like most of her classmates, was offered a number of job opportunities. She decided to stay in Chapel Hill; it had been good for her. She accepted a job at a large pharmaceutical company in their research lab. Boyd was being pressured by his parents to come back to Atlanta, work in the family meat packing business, or take another job in Atlanta. His parents had never said anything about his relationship with Michele. They knew she wasn't rich, and not religious. They would rather he marry in the Baptist faith. There were plenty of nice Baptist girls. Michele and Boyd had visited both sets of parents. Bob and Rita knew he was Baptist. They would rather she marry a non-denominational, non-religiously affiliated boy.

At the last moment, Boyd decided to take a job offer from the pharmaceutical company as well. He and Michele would be working side by side. Neither set of parents was happy about this, but what could they do? After three months, Rita got a call from Michele. She and Boyd were moving in together. Rita cried herself to sleep for the next week. Bob tried to console her, with no success. Finally, Rita turned to him. "At least we know where she is, who she's with." Bob smiled at her. "Yes, we do." In another three months, Michele called her mother to tell her that she and Boyd were married. Rita cried for another month, finally said to Bob, "maybe now she'll be happy."

Robert got through college keeping to himself, going to classes, coming straight home to study. He graduated cum laude in the civil engineering program. He was a sad boy, who made his parents sad to see him like that. He had always stayed to himself, or with Michele. Now he seemed to be alone in the world. Robert tried to get a job locally, so he could continue to live at home. There were limited opportunities for a civil engineer at home. The good jobs were with large engineering firms, working in far away places, building bridges, chemical plants, refineries, and the like. Most of his classmates had gotten jobs, but Robert persisted in working close to home. One of his classmates, Roberta Swenson, had accepted a position with Global Engineers. She had recommended Robert to them, as a top flight graduating civil engineer.

Robert accepted the position, even though it was far from home, assuming he would be working with Roberta, that she liked him. When he started the job in St. Louis, he learned that Roberta worked in the Dallas office. She had received a bonus for bringing Robert aboard. Robert was alone once again, but away from home, out of the house. He tried to quit his job and move back home, but both parents were solid for once, try the job for a year. By the end of the year, Robert had been assigned to four major contracts. The family work ethic had stood him in good graces. He was recognized as a hard, diligent worker, in demand by project management. He had been working in South America, on a chemical plant contract, for the last four months. He was accepted for himself, for his work. He had found a new home. His parents sighed with relief. Robert never married; he had found a friend, Stephen. His mother thought that was nice, Robert wouldn't be alone. His father thought that he must be gay, but he said nothing to Rita. It was enough that Robert had found someone.

Points to ponder:

This is a story of two siblings, Michele and Robert, one female and one male, a year apart in age, but so different. They were relatively poor kids living in an upper middle class neighborhood that put them at a handicap. Michele as a youngster was outgoing, athletic, and popular; Robert was passive, large and scary, and unpopular—easy prey to be picked on. Two siblings living together in the same house and neighborhood winding up developing differing stories.

1. In the early years of our life we assume that we are all just kids. Is this true and when does the social separation between kids start and on what basis?
2. The other kids readily accepted Michele, but Robert became easy prey to be picked on by the other kids. Robert came home and cried in his room. His mother Rita wanted to move, but her husband Bob wouldn't hear of it. Why are some parents willing to sacrifice for their children while others are not, pampering to their selfish needs with little regard for the effect it has on their children?
3. Robert who was large in size but unpleasant to look at took the verbal and physical abuse from his peers. What affect does such passive behavior have on the development of one's self image?
4. Through the eighth grade Michele as a popular athletic girl tried to protect her brother Robert. What might have been her motivations?
5. In the eighth grade, the boys' attention turned to physically attractive girls, and away from big athletic girls like Michele. Why would her girl friends move away from her as well?
6. Michele and Robert didn't see anything of value that branded them as outcasts. Robert remained alone while Michele was forced to become friends with the less popular girls she had always rejected. What were the values that made them outcasts?
7. When college decisions came Michele wanted to get as far away from home as possible while Robert wanted to stay in town? What

were their respective motivations?

8. Michele found a fellow student at college, Boyd Dalton, just as big and unattractive as she was. What attracted her to Boyd?
9. Michele had grown up with no religious affiliation while Boyd grew up as a southern Baptist. Why does such artificial barriers, including parental pressures, make it difficult for two people to get together?
10. Both Michele and Boyd tried to be happy in spite of their respective parents. Do you think that parents want the best for their children or is it only if they meet their own wishes?
11. Robert continued to keep to himself through college, living a lonely life at home with his parents. How do bad patterns and habits learned in our early years continue to affect our later life?
12. Robert was tricked by one of his classmates to take a job with an engineering firm in St. Louis. He tried to quit and return home, but his parents persuaded him to stay on for a year. Robert was accepted as a peer by his employers and considered a hard diligent worker. He found a friend, Stephen, on the job and settled in. What was it that Robert was looking for all those years?

Living in the same house,
with the same parents,
living different lives.

A Life Examined

1. The Early Years

Terry was born at three o'clock on Christmas morning at the Women's Hospital; of which birthplace his mother periodically reminded him, as if this had some significance. As his mother, Dorothy, said to him later, "He was an early Christmas turkey right out of the oven." She thought this was very cute, as cute as his mother could be. While he was there, he was an infant not quite a witness to his life as yet—that would come later. In the meantime, he had to depend on hearsay, some maybe accurate, some probably slanted and embellished. His father, Danny, had to be called to come to the hospital, as this was his sacred sleep time when he was home, any time from ten at night to noon the next day. This was also prophetic, as he was never around when he was needed or at other important events in Terry's life. He certainly wasn't needed during the delivery as he would only be in the way and make matters worse. As it turned out, he seemed to always be just in the way and make matters worse.

The doctor was prodding Terry's mother. He needed to put a name on the birth certificate. He didn't want to record "baby Christmas." Terry's parents needed to provide a name for him. His mother had named his older sister Colleen, but she did not want to name the baby boy by herself. Boys were the responsibility of the father. Unfortunately, his father was never responsible. Terry was told later that there was an argument over the naming right there in the hospital room, three hours after his birth. His mother wanted to name him Peter after her father. His father insisted on the name Terrence, which was his father's name, who had recently died. Terry was rooting for his mom and Peter, but his dad prevailed, he seemed to always prevail when he cared. He very rarely cared. He won on the argument that if they named the baby Terrence, his father's mother would look favorable on the boy, endowing him with riches. His dad was the master of the easy road even to the point of using his new-born son. His mother would give the baby things and he would be the heir to the Donahue fortune. Terry's grandmother died relatively penniless some years later in a nursing home. Some fortune. Some name. Some turkey. Some Christmas. This was the first turning point in Terry's life, given a name not wanted, named after an old man who was also known to be lazy and irresponsible. Like father, like son, but hopefully not like grandson.

Terry's first real memory was one of lying on a blanket on a hill with his mother and other mothers and their babies. He was maybe two or three years old. Some of the mothers chucked him under the chin and said how cute he was, and he was. His mother left him lying on the blanket while she talked gossip with the others. Some of the other mothers held their babies, but not Terry's. He was alone on his blanket. Somehow, he felt relieved. This was to become a prevailing theme in his life; the rugged individualist who needed no one. Better to be alone, than to be suffocated by others. Who needed that?

The Donahue family lived in an area called Dunkirk, a predominately Irish Catholic neighborhood. The section of Dunkirk where the Donahue family lived was a relatively newly developed area for first time buyers. The houses were row homes, called town houses by the builders, of a modest nature. The neighbors were mostly working class, that is, working for someone else for wages. If you earned $300 a week, you were rich in that neighborhood. You could afford to pay your mortgage, pay off a car, and take your family out once a month and so on. Some of the fathers were away in the military during the war, but not Terry's dad. Danny told everyone that he was contributing by working for a company connected to the war effort, but no one knew how. Terry never knew what the company did or what Danny did there, but it can be assured that it was no effort. The other kids bragged about their fathers and how they were saving America. Terry said nothing.

One of Terry's uncles, Jimmy, was away in the military. Terry bragged about him. It seemed like an okay thing to do. From the beginning, he sensed that he was placed in the wrong family. He resisted his father holding him and so did his father. His mother treated him as an object; an entry ticket to be one of the ladies with babies. His sister Colleen he never really knew; she was too much like the family. He still doesn't know her. Colleen was always his opposite and will always remain that way. For his first few years, he thought of himself as alone without a family. He was sad when his father came home. Any element of fun left the house.

Terry's neighborhood had always been predominantly Irish. But now there were a number of newly arrived immigrants. Many of them didn't speak English or spoke broken English. Some went to the elementary school to learn English and become citizens, others in the country illegally hid their identities. When Terry got older he laughed at them with the other boys. Other kids who had such parents tended to be ashamed of them. They all just wanted to be part of America. They had foreign sounding names. Terry didn't think that these were the names of America. He thought the rest of the world was Irish like his world. He had a lot to learn.

The first day of school, kindergarten, and Terry's mother walked him the three blocks to the elementary school. Terry made her leave him at the gate. He could find his way from there. He had always played with the older kids as well as kids his age. He was embarrassed to have them see him coming to school with his mother. The next day, he refused to let her walk him to school and back. He was a big boy and would walk with the older kids. That was the last place Terry remembered his mother taking him. He was a big boy, five years old. Who needed a mother tagging along in your life?

Terry started to have a secretive life. What he did in school and after school was his business. His mother tried to evade his secrecy by asking him and his friends probing questions. Terry told her little, his friends told her stories that she believed. Terry learned early on to get out of the house. When he was home, his mother wanted to know his business. The more she wanted to know, the less he told her. When his father was home, he ignored Terry. His father came alive when Terry's friends came over. Otherwise, he had no time for Terry or the family. However, his father had all the time in the world for others; this was the way it would always be. Terry wished he could be a stranger to get his father's attention. Ironically, he became that stranger.

Terry remembered only a few times that his father paid attention to him or played with him. His father lay on the threadbare sofa, with his hands in his pants, too tired to get up. Except when Terry's friends appeared; then he was ready to play. His father tossed a ball around with Terry's friends, while Terry watched from the sidelines. Terry wanted nothing to do with glamorizing him as the wonderful father. Terry's friends thought he was the greatest, but Terry knew better. Terry learned to never trust an adult. He had no desire to ever be part of that world. The world of kids was so much greater; and it was easier to get their attention.

Terry's mom had four sisters and his dad had two brothers. They saw very little of any of them. When they did, it was usually for some occasion, a birthday, anniversary, holiday and so forth, and they were invited as a courtesy. Terry's dad, Danny, was a glad hander, a four flusher, a braggart, and a bullshitter supreme. Terry always had the feeling that his mother's relatives would rather not see him. His father treated them like they were long lost friends. They humored him, but did not encourage him. Terry always felt that they pitied his mother and felt sorry for him and his sister. She was the poor sister who had married the good-looking catch of the day; they thought she should have thrown him back once he had started to smell.

Terry's dad's brothers, thought the sun rose and set on his dad. Danny had always been the favorite son as the first-born. His mother did everything for Danny. He was going to be her Irish doctor or lawyer, her Danny boy. While her Danny dressed in nice clothes and stayed clean, the other two brothers worked at dirty jobs as soon as they could to contribute to the family's household expenses and Danny's college. The brothers were the workhorses; Danny was the thoroughbred. The two brothers always worked hard for their money. Danny neither worked hard nor had money. When Danny did (or didn't) work he treated everybody; that is everyone but his family. Danny was the first to reach for the check. Uncle Jimmy once told Terry that Danny would borrow twenty dollars from you so that he could take you out to dinner. That is as close as Terry can describe his dad to this day.

Terry's grandmother, Danny's mother, came from a small village in Ireland when she was about thirteen years old on a boat all by herself. She married Terry's grandfather a few years later by arrangement. She never read or wrote English very well. She owned and worked in a produce store with her husband, and now without, for most of her adult life. She could locate any product in the store by sight and calculate the bill using pencil and paper to the penny. Her Danny was going to get her out of all this. She worked to save pennies to have him go to college. He was able to get accepted into a pre-med program. No mean feat for a second generation Irish immigrant. He contacted a minor form of disinterest in college in his second year and dropped out. His mother had saved him from work; and he was now saving himself from work.

When Terry was younger, the family visited grandmother's store. When Terry got older, his dad took only him to visit his mother about once a month. Terry knew that his grandmother and his mom didn't get along. Dorothy wasn't good enough for her Danny, shanty Irish. While Terry liked his grandmother, as she gave him things, this wasn't his favorite way to spend time. He had more important things to do on the corner with the guys. He was persuaded anyway. While Terry's dad talked to his mother in the apartment behind and on top of the store, Terry ran the store. Many times when he went back into the apartment he found his grandmother with her back to his dad, reaching between her breasts to pull out her purse. When she saw Terry she hurriedly took some money and snuck it to her Danny. She offered Terry a dollar for being such a good boy. Kids bribe easy.

Terry never saw himself as one of the overachievers or most popular kids, nor did he see himself at the low end of kiddom. He was always in the middle, getting along with other kids from all sides of the popularity spectrum. He was always small and wiry as a kid.

He couldn't overpower the other kids with his physical strength, so he adjusted by getting along as best he could. He was never (well, hardly ever) picked first or last for pick up sports. He was a true medium and still is. He played boxball, stickball, handball against a wall, punchball, halfball, touch football in the street and so forth. He was happy, he had his friends, he didn't need a family. Ugh!!

Terry grew up through elementary school in a predominantly Irish world. He thought the world was Irish. Most of his neighbors either worked in small neighborhood businesses or had their own businesses. Not all of the men were hard working class; some were hustlers, scammers, get rich quick dreamers, gamblers, and gangsters. Danny avoided the hard working class but stopped just this side of gangsterism. Terry never knew quite what his dad did as he was growing up. He only knew that his father and mother talked a lot about money, or the lack thereof. Terry tried to be out of the house. His mother seemed to take pride in his father's good looks and affability with others outside of their family. She seemed to like the role of housewife and the pride that came with having a husband who can take care of you. However, she couldn't depend on her husband, as he was too selfish and undependable. Danny always dressed well, had a new car at least every three years, and had money in his pocket. Dorothy didn't dress so well (she had gotten heavy being in the house), didn't drive, and had little money in her pocket. Danny seemed to revel in being the man of the house, the king of his castle.

Dorothy had to embellish her world to survive. She bragged to the neighbors and her sisters as to how well her Danny was doing. Danny started to not come home under the guise of working hard and late to support his family. Terry thought he was avoiding his mother and the arguments over money. Fortunately, in their neighborhood, most of the neighbors also had money problems. Terry's family didn't seem any worse off than most of them.

Terry's life of supported independence moved along smoothly. He was protected in his neighborhood and school. It was an Irish world and he was Irish. What a wonderful feeling to be in the dominant ruling class. He knew very little of the outside world. Even the television stars like Conan were Irish. The sports stars that he rooted for weren't all Irish, but they were only there for his entertainment. As far as he knew, everyone was either Irish or wanted to be Irish—and not just on St. Patrick's Day.

When Terry was ten or eleven, in the fifth grade, his world changed. He was told that his mother was going out to work. This wasn't considered good as the husband was supposed to be able to fully support the family. The better he could provide support, the better husband, father, and man he was. If he was able to send the family away for the summer to get away from the heat and humidity he was a god. However, Terry spent his summers at home, hanging out at the playground in the schoolyard or on the corner with the boys. Having to go to work was not only another embarrassment for Dorothy but also the ultimate shame. Their neighbors didn't live well, but very few of the other mothers worked. Terry noticed his mother changing. Where there once was pride, even if it was false, there was now shame. It shamed Terry some too, particularly when he sensed the pity of some of the other mothers and their relatives, but his greatest feeling was one of liberation and freedom. He was willing to give up the cookies and milk that awaited him after school for the freedom of the streets and the weekly allowance that allowed him to buy whatever he wanted at the corner luncheonette. He was cool; he had money in his pocket, and was independent. Who needed family anyway?

Points to ponder:

We talk about a life unexamined; an ordinary life that seemingly has no impact or significance. These lives are unknown to society other than to family, fellow workers, and ordinary friends. However, when we examine a life such as the story of Terry we find the messages, experiences, turning points and life shaping decisions that form a life. It is the individual's strengths and effective use of their free will that frees them from their backgrounds and allows them to become whoever they want to be and to have a life worth examining.

1. Terry was born on Christmas morning at the Women's Hospital. His mother Dorothy made sport of this throughout his life telling him "he was a Christmas turkey right out of the oven." What impact do such comments by one's parent have on their self-image?
2. Terry was named Terrence by his father, Danny, his own father's name, assuming that his mother would look favorable on Terry and endow him with riches. How does the name a child is given affect them throughout their lives, especially when it is a name that the child despises?
3. His naming was the first turning point in Terry's life, even though he had nothing to with it. Being given a name not wanted, named after a man who was known to be lazy and irresponsible just like his father. Can a child overcome such a turning point?
4. Terry's first memory was lying on a blanket with his mother and other mothers and babies, being left alone while his mother talked gossip. How do such early memories create prevailing themes in the individual as they grow up?
5. The Donahue family lived in a predominately Irish Catholic neighborhood of modest low priced row homes. Although the child doesn't have much say as to where the family lives and the choice of neighborhood, such a decision does have an impact on the messages the child takes with him or her as he or she grows up. What messages might Terry receive and retain growing up in this ethnically isolated neighborhood?
6. Terry's dad found a way to avoid going into the military during the war, which created shame and embarrassment for Terry. Why are children so tied into who their parents are and the need to be proud of them?
7. Terry was not proud of his father and resisted him, felt treated as an object by his mother, and felt he didn't know his sister Colleen. What does such family alienation do to a child growing up, feeling alone, without a family?
8. Terry started to have a secretive life away from his family. His mother

tried to invade his secrecy, while his father ignored him. What action does a child take when he can't get attention or support from his own family? What is the purpose of family?

9. Terry's father Danny always had time for Terry's friends and strangers but never time for the family. What affect does such lack of attention by one's father have on a child growing up and once they become an adult themselves?
10. Feeling that one's father is not someone to be proud of has an adverse affect on a child. What messages does the child take with him or her into their later life?
11. Danny's mother, a hard working Irish immigrant, wanted the best for her son, Danny, the first born and her hope for a better future, while at the same time delegating her two younger sons to a life of hard work. Danny would take Terry with him as an incentive, when he visited his mother for money as an adult. What affect did Danny's mother have on his life and attitudes, as he became an adult, a husband, and a father? Did she contribute to his selfishness and irresponsibility?
12. Terry, being small and wiry as a kid, didn't see himself as an overachiever or popular. He was content to just be accepted. Is there any relationship to Terry's accepted role with his peers to his family life?
13. Dorothy took whatever pride she could muster in Danny's good looks and affability, ignoring his undependability, lack of making a living, selfishness, and so forth. She was content in her role as a housewife, allowing Danny to be king of his castle. Why do wives allow their husbands to dismiss their responsibilities and make like it isn't happening?
14. When Dorothy had to go out to work to save the family financially, Terry noticed her changing as well as his life. What happens when a family needs to adjust to adverse changing conditions? How did Terry react and rationalize the family changes?

Changing conditions,
changes lives,
of ourselves and others in our life.

2. The Middle Years

Dorothy worked so that Terry and Colleen could have basic things like the other kids such as food, clothes, and school supplies. Terry saw no real change in the way they lived, no new furniture, no more going out, no extras—and nothing for his mother. She took care of the family; Danny took care of himself. It bothered Terry to have to ask his mother for his weekly allowance. He figured out ways to provide for his own money. He would flip coins against the wall on the corner with the older kids. He would usually win to the tune of up to five dollars a week. His mother had been giving him a dollar weekly allowance. He stopped asking her, she stopped giving it to him. She never asked Terry where he got his money or whether he had any money. Terry also became an arcade game hustler, playing for money—another few dollars a week. Gambling for money was risky as he didn't always win (he hated to lose) so Terry and his hoodlum friends looked to other avenues such as shoplifting, banging open vending machine coin boxes, opening game machines and other coin boxes. Terry was now making real money, sometimes twenty to thirty dollars a week. Probably more than his father brought home, after his selfish indulgences. Terry was twelve years old, rich and resolved to stay that way. He would always be financially independent. He didn't need anyone.

Although his given name was Terrence, from his earliest memories he was called Scooter by his parents, relatives, friends, and at school. He guarded his real identity as Terrence. Scooter was freedom and fun; it was cool. Terrence was stuffy and stodgy; it was a drag. Terry felt sorry for some of his friends with names like Nelson, Brian, Thomas, and Seth. Scooter could soar. He was always small, skinny and scrawny, wiry, and tough—and a real street kid. After school he either hung out at the schoolyard or on the corner. Most of the other kids his age and some older, the momma's boys, had to go home around five or six to eat dinner and do their homework.

Once they went into the house they stayed there for the rest of the night. Terry stayed out as long as possible, even after his mother got home.

Dorothy had to take a bus and a subway to get to work. As she had no real business skills, she had to take the best job she could find. She worked in the office of a small manufacturer of ladies apparel. The owner did her a favor as a referral from a friend. Danny drove her sometimes (very infrequently), especially when he needed money from her. She usually got home around six-thirty and then made dinner for Terry and Colleen. She usually stopped for bread and cakes, possibly as a treat for her not being there. She didn't need the treats and neither did the kids. Terry ate little dinner, as he didn't like much, particularly vegetables. Dorothy didn't push him to eat much. She seemed pleased that he ate the bread and cakes. He tried to leave some cake for breakfast and after school. However, the next day it was gone and so was his father.

When the kids Terry's age went in for the night, he stayed on the corner with the older guys from junior and senior high school. He became part of their discussions and the mascot of the gang. They pitched coins, played cards, played the video machines, and generally harassed the owner of the luncheonette. Some of the guys smoked cigarettes and allowed Terry to grab a drag sometimes. It was awful, but he played it cool. Terry stopped identifying with the kids his age as they still did baby things. The older guys were into more mischief, and he liked that. They harassed the girls in the neighborhood including Colleen and her friends. The guys talked about what they would do to these girls and their body parts. Terry listened; he was learning more from these guys than he was at school.

They yelled out things like, "Hey Cookie" When the girl looked their way, they would yell, "Not you dog biscuit." These were real clever guys; at least Terry thought so then.

After dinner, Terry went back out to be with the older guys; those that could get out. His mother asked about homework, but he always had it done. He did it in school so it didn't interfere with his outside life and he didn't have to carry books back and forth like the momma's boys. They spent the night pitching coins, shooting the shit, or playing handball against the wall until it got dark. Then they went inside the luncheonette and harassed the owner and his wife; maybe order one cheeseburger and a coke to share with all of them. They moved to the video machine for major competition. They never paid, either using slugs or a wire to advance the granting of free games. They didn't rifle the coin box since the owner was a friend—lucky him. Sometimes when the owner got angry or ornery with them, they played pranks on him. Like unscrewing the table legs so that the table would fall on the next customers, or loosening the stools at the counter so that they would slip off easily, or when he really got to them one of them snuck into his back room and urinated in his pickle barrel. The gang of course never had pickles. They laughed while others ate them. It was just good clean childish fun. Terry loved the kid's world; he hated the adult world.

Terry usually waited at the corner for his mother to come home. She walked the three blocks from the bus stop, sometime between six and six-thirty at night. She always had packages with her; bread and cake and sometimes something special, like tapioca pudding, for Terry. Terry grabbed the packages and walked home with her. While he loved his independence, he also loved the cakes she brought. When she didn't show by six-thirty, he got worried. He didn't want to go home and wait with his sister, so he went to a friend's house, usually right at dessert time. What great timing.

Sometimes he missed his mother when he was busy with the guys. She called him when dinner was ready or sent Colleen out to get him. Colleen hated doing this, as the guys on the corner teased her unmercifully. She blamed Terry for this. The guys were always trying to find out Scooter's real name. One time Colleen must have been really mad at Terry because she told them "his name is Terrence" and ran off. After that Terry was teased unmercifully. He hated her for that.

Eventually the euphoria of elementary school ended. Sixth grade was over and Terry was destined for junior high. While the elementary school was only a short three-block walk from the house, the junior high was over two miles away with no bus service. Terry was able to walk to school with his older friends. This would be his first real venture out of his Irish neighborhood. Kids from other non-Irish adjoining neighborhoods attended the junior high. He didn't look forward to that. There were Italian kids and some Polish kids. The Irish kids were no longer in charge; they had to share the power. Terry didn't like that. The tough Italian kids were always looking to fight with the tough Irish kids. They used to have rock fights across a large pit that separated the Irish neighborhood, little Dublin, from little Italy. The Irish kids played "hit the dago" from their side and yelled and screamed when an Italian kid was hit. Later Terry found out that they played "hit the mick" on their side. Now he had to face these faceless people in school. He found that some were cool, some not so cool, just like his Irish friends. But, it wasn't acceptable to be friends with them, so he developed some sneaky friendships. It was the same with the Italian kids. There weren't enough others to make a difference. They just kind of blended in without making much of an impact. Terry's world now consisted of Irish and Italians. It was expanding, but the Irish still ruled.

In the middle of seventh grade, Terry's parents lost their house. Danny was supposed to pay the mortgage and Dorothy was to pay all the other household expenses. Evidently, Dorothy took care of her part of the bargain, but Danny hadn't paid the mortgage for over a year. Terry heard his parents arguing. He got out of the house. They had to move in a hurry. Danny had a friend in a newly developing suburb. It had become the envied place for upward mobile Irish families to want to move, those who had the money to afford it. While Irish Catholics were not entirely welcome, the window of respectability was opening up a crack and the richer Irish families were rushing through. Danny's friend found them a lower end rental. They were probably the only family who had lost their house for inability to pay the mortgage and were able to move up into the desired suburbs. Terry was not happy.

Terry missed his old friends. Terry and Colleen agreed that

they would continue going back to their old neighborhood and keep their old friends. This required taking two public buses, but they avoided the unfriendly richer kids for as long as they could. Terry brought some old neighborhood friends home with him. They were impressed with his living in the suburbs. The Donahue's must be rich. Terry sometimes went back to the old neighborhood after school. On the weekends he would ride his bike and many times sleep over with one of his old friends. He spent as little time as possible in the new neighborhood, avoiding the kids in the new neighborhood. They were strange. No corner to hang out at, no luncheonette, no game machines, no fun. They were serious about going to school and talked about going to a good college in the seventh grade. In his old neighborhood, it was expected that as soon as a boy was able he would get a job and contribute board to the household. After high school, he would get a job (college wasn't even a consideration) and if he still lived at home, his board would be increased. This seemed more like life. Terry didn't understand this new neighborhood where the kids did nothing but play and spend their parents' money. He didn't like these kids; he liked his old friends. Fun had gone out of his life, and learning had entered. It changed his life and focus and things became too serious. He was still trying to recapture that free feeling of being a kid.

In eighth grade Terry found some suburban kids who played cards for money. Terry got into one of their games. He won a little money, not too much at first, and was welcomed back. He started playing cards seriously, after school and on the weekends. He was averaging between thirty and fifty dollars a week in winnings. He now had money in his pocket, but he wasn't going to waste it like his dad. He was going to hold onto it so that some day he would be rich like these suburban kids. He certainly deserved it more than these spoiled brats. He would be financially independent some day, no more rich kid stuff for him—he wouldn't need them.

By the time Terry reached high school everyone wanted to buddy up and travel with him. How sweet it was. He was always used to traveling with an older crowd; the kids his age always seemed too infantile. Some of the older kids in eleventh and twelfth grade already had their own cars or the use of a family car. A group of tough, older girls who Terry hung around with became his pick up buddies. They picked him up in the morning to take him to school, and hung around in the halls and in the smoking area during school, cruise around after school, and then drop him home. They also got together at night to carouse, sometimes make out, and try to get into trouble. Terry was the envy of the other kids. Another of life's lessons learned. He who could provide the goodies became the good guy.

Somewhere during this time, Terry started to drink alcohol and smoke pot. One of the older girls could always sneak a bottle of liquor or some joints from her house. He became the slave to a good bottle of gin or vodka and a fine toke. Only the best for this poor kid. Terry quickly fell into a life of alcohol, blowing grass, parties, card playing, girls and fun. He forgot who these kids were; he was becoming one of them. The more they provided the niceties of life, the more he accepted them as a way of life. He became their social equals (if not superior) without the cost. He always enjoyed the good things of life when the other guy was paying. He was a suburban kid by association, if not by fact.

By the end of the tenth grade, because some of Terry's friends were old enough to drive and had been given their own cars or had the use of the family car, they didn't need Terry as much anymore. They shifted back into their safe lives with their safe friends. Terry stayed with his crowd, but it started to thin. He was forced to melt back into his poor boy roots. He tried to fake being part of the suburban scene, but he never really could do it. This was the end of his reign as "cool." Life became more serious as the pressure increased to get into the right college. Terry felt no such pressure, so he continued to try to have fun, but it was becoming more and more difficult. He had become imprisoned in a world of academic achievement where he saw no benefit. He was not destined to go to the best college or the college of his choice. He was free to have fun, but with whom. Once again he was alone.

It was around this time that he started drinking and smoking more heavily. This brought him in touch with a different crowd, some older, some poorer, but all cooler. They found the bars in the neighborhood that would serve them and they became regulars. When they wanted a private party, they would chip in money and have one of the bigger guys, never Terry, buy the booze with a false ID. Pot they bought at school. This kept them high during school, after school, on weekday nights, and weekend days and nights. Such behavior also brought Terry in touch with older guys and girls. These were some of the tougher kids in the neighborhood. They became Terry's new friends. He was alone no more.

In the last half of eleventh grade, Terry started to think about college. He knew he couldn't go to one of the fancy colleges, but maybe some college. It could be his way of ultimately equalizing things. He always had gotten acceptable grades without doing much work. He typically completed his homework quickly during school, so that he could play after school and at night. He got mostly B's with some C's and a rare A thrown in. He knew that if he really applied himself (or so he told himself) he could get mostly A's, but he would have to work much harder and what was the use. Some of his classmates studied all of the time to get their A's and stay in the running for a good Ivy League school. He made the honor roll (a fluke?) once in spite of himself and his unruly classroom behavior. He knew he was smarter than most of these people. He didn't need to prove it. That would come later on.

Terry knew there was no money from his parents to go to college. If he wanted to go, he had to do it himself. He really didn't want to become part of "their" world. His suburban high school was geared to college preparatory. It had a general, business, and technical curriculum, but they were for the dumber kids. For self-esteem reasons Terry stayed with college prep. He liked the other so-called dumber kids better, but he liked the idea and status of being college prep. For some reason, he found it important to identify with these kids. He didn't like them much, but he was drawn to them. He still didn't know why.

Terry wasn't looking for a job as he was doing okay playing cards and selling a little dope. But many of his card-playing friends with wheels started going out on dates on the weekend. His universe was diminishing. He was talked into going out on a few dates, double dates where he got the back seat, but he quickly realized the return on investment wasn't worth the lack of fun. He could do better on his own, merely going over to the girl's house for a make out session. It more than met his needs and the cost to benefit relationship was much more to his liking. He also found it difficult to declare himself as going with only one girl. It not only killed his need for independence but it also laid him bare for evaluation and approval. He couldn't make a commitment to a suburban girl that would glorify his mother and bring her back into his life, or a poor Irish girl which would be bad for his self image and make a statement he wasn't ready to make. In many ways he believed they were much easier to deal with, but yet he hesitated. So, he had put myself into another box.

On Friday nights Terry went out drinking and carousing with his remaining lower life friends. On Saturday, he had to make his own plans if he couldn't hook up with any of these friends. He would go to the bars and sulk. On his own, he reduced his availability and shut down his social life. He was alone, depressed, and stuck, but inside he felt he was still the same cool person. He only had to wait for him to surface again. He moved away from his suburban college bound friends and they moved away from him. They had their own lives to live that didn't seem to include those of the poor persuasion such as Terry. He worked to isolate himself. Misery might need company, but he didn't.

Terry was now almost seventeen years old and felt that he had done everything worthwhile in his life. There was little to look forward to, certainly not high school life. At the beginning of twelfth grade, it was time to make decisions about college. At his high school, each student met with a guidance counselor to discuss his or her college plans and which colleges to apply to. His guidance counselor looked at Terry's grades and wrote down a selected list of colleges in terms of entrance requirements and costs. Terry looked at the list quizzically. There was no way he could afford to go to those schools even if he got in. He was flattered by the recommendations, but what was the use. He took the list and left. The counselor set up a follow-up appointment to prepare admission applications. Terry's parents wouldn't even give him the money for application fees. It was only later that others told him that this counselor gave a similar list to all of his college prep advisees.

Terry waited as long as he could to make a decision about college. He knew he couldn't afford to go away to school and there really wasn't a local school that interested him. College seemed like a social step backward. He was leaning toward getting an entry-level job and staying in his present lifestyle. It seemed to suit him and it left him alone with little social pressures. Early in the spring of his senior year, the others started to get accepted into colleges. Some got into the top schools, others into prestigious small liberal arts schools. Terry wasn't really envious as much as he was angry. He knew that he was much more academically smarter then they were. He helped many of them with their homework and through the math and science classes. His anger coerced him to apply on his own to the local state-supported college. This was a school that he knew he could get into easy. He really didn't want to go to college, particularly this school, but he also didn't want to be left behind. He never really believed that he would ever catch up to them, but at least this way he still had a chance.

That summer was one of the worst Terry had ever spent. It was hot and humid and he was mainly alone. He worked part-time at a supermarket and was a regular at the neighborhood bars. While most of the other kids were excited about going off to college, he was still deliberating. His sister Colleen, who had always got A's in her academic subjects, had lived through the bitterness of not going to college while she watched her dumber friends go. She was now a data entry computer operator at a large company. Some use of her smarts. Terry wasn't going to let the same thing happen to him. He bit his anger. He would pay his own way—screw the folks. He would do what he had to do to not wind up like any of them. He would get away from them as soon as he could afford to.

Terry got through college as a loner, bemoaning his fate. Upon graduation he took a job with a large corporation. He behaved himself and moved up the ladder. He got married, had three children, two girls and a boy, and moved to the suburbs. He found that he never fit in; he was just ordinary. He was no longer cool. When he was fifty-four he was downsized. His life was over. What was it all for?

Points to ponder:

While it is said that it is in the early years when most of our beliefs and attitudes are formed, it is the middle years where they are reinforced and set in our minds. It is these years when we move from young childhood through adolescence and then toward adulthood that our peers start to become more important than our parents and it is their approval that we seek. In Terry's case he was already estranged from his family and taking care of himself, and needing nobody. It is in such an environment that our life's messages are etched that serve us through the remainder of our lives unless we are strong enough internally to change our course.

1. Dorothy went to work so that her children could have the things that kids need growing up. She took care of the family and Danny took care of himself. In effect, what roles did Dorothy play in the family?
2. Terry saw no real change in the way he lived except now he had to ask his mother for money. Instead, Terry found his own ways to get money, by flipping coins, hustling, shoplifting, and stealing from vending machines. Were these things Terry really wanted to do or did he feel forced by necessity? What other factors played upon Terry?
3. Terry guarded his real given name of Terrence as it had bad connotations for him. He enjoyed going by his family nickname of Scooter, as it was cool. What affect does an unwanted name have on an individual and is there anything one can do about it?

4. Dorothy had to take a bus and a subway to get to work, which required her to leave early and get home late. She would bring breads and cakes home with her. Terry would eat little dinner, but he would eat the bread and cake, leaving some for breakfast and after school, but his father got there first. What do you think was her reason for doing this?
5. Terry became a street kid, playing with the older kids on the street corner. He became the mascot for their gang. He stopped identifying with the kids his age, they did baby things, the older guys were cool. What transformation was Terry making in his life?
6. Terry started to do his homework in school so he could spend his time at home with the older guys. School became less important; doing mischief with the older guys became his life. He loved the kid's world and he hated the adults' world. What values were being implanted in Terry that would shape his later life?
7. Colleen was sent out to get Terry for dinner, but she hated doing this as the older guys teased her. She blamed Terry for this. One time in spite she told them that Scooter's real name was Terrence, which resulted in his being teased. What was Colleen's motive for doing that to Terry?
8. When Terry started junior high school, it was the first time he had ventured from his Irish neighborhood. There were now non-Irish kids, and the Irish kids were no longer in charge. The Italian kids who were always the Irish kids natural enemies were now his classmates. What changes did this trigger in Terry's thinking?
9. In the middle of seventh grade Terry's parents lost their house through Danny not paying the mortgage. Danny rented them a lower end row home in a newly developing suburb where richer upward mobile Irish families and others were moving to. Terry was now a poor Irish kid in a rich neighborhood. What effect does such a situation have on a kid Terry's age?
10. Terry never really adjusted to the new neighborhood as he missed his old neighborhood. The kids in the new school were serious about school and getting into a good college and didn't care about having fun. How does such an abrupt change in values affect a youngster just starting to grow up like Terry?

11. In eighth grade Terry found some rich kids to play cards with for money. He usually won which put money in his pocket. He vowed not to waste it like his dad. Someday he would be financially independent like these rich kids' families. How do values such as this one become part of an individual's value system?
12. By high school Terry had become very popular with the rich kids due to his being different and cool. Poor little Terry from Dunkirk was controlling the rich suburban kids. What did the rich kids see in Terry that appealed to them?
13. When his rich friends became sixteen and started to drive they didn't need Terry any more. Life became getting into the right college for the rich kids. Terry had no hope for this. When values change as we get older someone is left behind like Terry in this case. What could Terry have done other than except his exclusion?
14. Terry didn't want to go to college or was it resentment towards his rich classmates. He got accepted to the local state supported college, which he got through as a loner, bemoaning his fate. What was his motivation to get through college, which wasn't part of the life he really wanted?
15. Upon graduation from college, Terry took a job with a large corporation, got married and had three children and moved to the suburbs. He walked through this life that he never fit; he realized he was just ordinary, no longer cool. At fifty-four, after moving a good ways up the corporate ladder, he was downsized. What was it all for? Why did Terry do this to himself?

We try to live within our own convictions,
but sometimes it's us who are convicted
to someone else's life.

Hiding from Life

George grew up in a typical middle class suburban neighborhood, single homes on an acre or more of ground, two cars, two intact parents, both working, and one sibling. George's parents, Horace and Hilda, were computer programmers, he on the scientific end, she on the business end. George grew up with mother's helpers, neighbors, and relatives keeping an eye on him. When he was six years old, his parents got him his first computer, an Apple. From that day forward, George spent all of his non-school time on the computer, learning how it operated and eventually programming it himself. At school, he paid little attention as he was daydreaming about a new program for his computer. Due to his quiet nature and desire for isolation, his teachers let him be. The school, both teachers and the principal, talked to his parents, who expressed minimal concern—he was just like them as they grew up.

George hid through most of his childhood, locked in his room working on his computer. He became so proficient that his parents used him to consult with them relative to their jobs. All through school he stayed by himself with few friends, only those nerd types similar to him. In high school, he won a number of awards related to his computer work that resulted in his receiving an academic scholarship for computer sciences to a prestigious technology college.

For his first year at college, George spent most of his time in the computer lab or in his dorm room working out computer problems, the same as his roommate. He had little to do with anyone, remaining a loner. He went to classes and worked in the computer lab as a work-study, using his room as a place to sleep for a few hours. His work-study allotment together with his now infrequent computer consulting for his parents provided enough money for tuition, books, meals, and so forth. George had never had a real date (either male or female) and still wasn't ready to throw money out on a date that he didn't enjoy, clothes that he didn't need, and a car that he didn't want. He had no real desire to get rich, just to be able to do his computer work—his way. He was having his own fun, doing what he wanted—the old equalizer. He would find some of his nerd-like fellow students to work with on the weekends. He would stay around the computer lab, and then go back to his room. It helped him make it through the rest of the week. Technology school was not a place for fun.

Two of his computer geek classmates were kind of going with similarly leaning girls that had become steady sex for them. They brought them to the computer lab. George cringed at the idea. The girls were semi-attractive for computer types, but not really social types. George didn't care. He thought it might be good for the anal-retentive uptight computer geeks, but not for him. His classmates tried to persuade him to go out with one of their girl friend's friends. George had no desire to do so. She might get the idea that he liked her and she might even like him. The thought gave him the willies. He also wasn't comfortable with a female, even a computer type. He might actually like one of these people and want to be friends with them afterwards. Fat chance.

When one of his class dances came up, some of his classmates pressured him to go. He was tired of being made fun of as the "computer monk" so he agreed to go. One of his classmates, Jim, had been going around with a girl, Tracy, who was very quiet and seemed to pay attention to George. He felt he might be comfortable with someone like her as neither one needed to say anything. She had kidded around with him and she seemed to kind of like him. She seemed easy to get along with and unwilling to do most normal things—a good match. Jim was no longer seeing her, so George called her. She was available and expressed interest in going with George to the dance. His good luck?

George and Tracy stayed at the dance for a while for as long as they could. His classmates and their girls wanted to stay. George resisted. He thought that maybe it would work out. He had to go to school with these people. When it became obvious that the excitement level was not to exceed that of George's first uncomfortable spin-the-bottle-type fifth grade party, he agreed to leave with Tracy. They walked quietly back to their rooms. George quietly shook her hand as she went into her dorm. He washed the memory of his first dance from his mind. Working on the computer made it easy for him to forget life's little horrors. They returned as nagging flashbacks later on.

George ran into Tracy in classes and at the computer lab. She seemed to bear him no ill feelings about their unpleasant dance date. In fact, when she saw him she always had a ready smile and tried to talk to him about a computer problem she was having. He met her in the school cafeteria after classes and in the evenings some times to help her. Sometimes they went out for a soda afterwards, both sitting there but saying little. She was easy for George to get along with, not demanding like most of the other so-called "nice girls." She allowed George to stay in hiding from any real life. They started to go out during the week and sometimes on the weekend. They went to out of the way coffee shops, teahouses, and small casual restaurants. They started to make-out a little, that is hold hands and touch lips, on campus benches and sometimes continued in her dorm house waiting room.

Eventually, George and Tracy started having sex. It was her idea and they had little else to do. She wasn't very personable and they had quickly run out of things to say. Eating, making out, and sex helped pass the time and make each feel less lonely. They did it in an empty classroom or dorm room. It became an easy release for both of them, and kept them isolated. It helped George get through the year. They continued during the summer while George worked for his dad's employer as a programmer. This provided George more space to nurse his depression. Sometime in the early fall of the next school year, Tracy informed him that she was pregnant. None of George's computer programs were able to prevent it. Somehow, it didn't greatly affect him. If that was the way it was, then that was the way it was. His life had never really begun so what difference did it make. He took Tracy home to meet his mother and discuss the situation. Hilda sat at the kitchen table with her head down. It wasn't that she felt for George. It was more that he had killed her dreams of his marrying a smart rich girl that would afford her bragging rights. His dad thought it was funny, his son the computer geek getting a girl in trouble—only he could find humor in this. Such a family reaction increased George's isolated sense of rebellion. He said to Tracy, "let's just get married. I can't wait to get out of here."

They were married in a small ceremony, just the two of them and both sets of parents. Their parents had to sign for them, as they were both under age. Horace saw it as an occasion to glad hand George's new father in-law. They actually got along, both scientific types. Small miracles. George's mother and new mother-in-law looked like there was a death in the family. It made George feel better. Tracy had a miscarriage two months later. It was a golden chance for George to get out of the situation, but where was he to go? He was imprisoned in a world that he wouldn't have ever chosen, but it was a safe place to hide, so he stayed in the marriage.

Through George and Tracy's work-study jobs they were able to afford tuition and other college expenses. Tracy took on another part-time job and George did more tutoring that allowed them to rent a small apartment. It was a safe place for the both of them to hide away in. Time went by slowly, sometimes by the minute, sometimes by the second.

They both graduated from college with excellent credentials. George had to make a decision as to what to do. His last part time job was with one of the big software development firms. They made him an offer to come to work for them. It would be easy for George to accept their offer. However, he just couldn't see himself in that world of uptightness and politeness, working hard as an obedient child to move up in the firm. He really wanted to go on to graduate school as he had bonded to good education and learning. But, economically that wasn't easy and he wasn't a great sacrificer. He was tired of under-living. He decided to find a job that did some good for society where he could do the world some good. A couple of guys that he had known at college had taken government related jobs. They made it sound just like what George thought he was looking for and he liked the interviewer. He accepted their offer. If he couldn't be rich quick, he would use his technology skills to be a do-gooder. Tracy had no such conflicts so she took a higher paying job at a computer-consulting firm.

While George was at college, he was safe from the world. Then, when he got married, he was doubly safe. In December after graduation Tracy got pregnant again. While it wasn't entirely planned, this worked for both of them. George could concentrate on his job and Tracy would be able to stop working. It was a pregnancy of mutual convenience. George had seen the industrial world at college. It scared him and he knew that the corporate world was one form of imprisonment he could live his life without. Tracy had now been working for over six months and knew that full-time corporate work was something she could live without.

The baby was born in July of the following year. George was now the proud father of a son they named Timmy. They brought the baby home from the hospital and settled in to the cloistered life of young parents. This was the last nail in making his life's hiding place safe. Tracy left her job for motherhood and part time at-home projects. It was not exactly the role George had auditioned for, but there he was. He was now twenty-three years old and life, as he knew it and fantasized about was over.

He stayed at the government job for a year. It wasn't anything like he expected. Within three months, he was already retired in place. If he just did what was asked of him as a project programmer, he could easily move up the payroll ladder. He would never be rich, but he would be job safe. There was little opportunity to spur on great world changes; there was little opportunity for personal growth or learning. He was able to develop three proprietary computer programs on his own and a scientific programmers guide while employed there. He was still put in for promotion. He took his programs with him on his next job.

George shunned the promotion; it was a death knell to oblivion. He was ready to be challenged and make some money. His government contractor experience taught him to look out for himself. He took a job with a start-up software development firm as program specialist. Luckily, he was assigned to work with a wonderful older man, Vince, who became his mentor. The other members of the staff made fun of Vince and his elderly manner. However, he and George became close work friends, developing George's programs into sellable commodities. This made him feel important again, made him feel challenged and important for the first time.

George's real life started to take shape at work. He was accepted as a respected peer not as a computer geek. His programs were making big money for the company and he was earning royalties and bonuses. He did his job well and was quickly promoted to a management position. The project team that worked with him was wonderful. They laughed, had fun, but got the job done. He was beginning to rise from the dead. He was once again included as part of a group that he wanted to be a member of. He was still wary of distrust and betrayal, but he felt safe for the time being. The contrast of his life at home was starting to become too great of a chasm. Tracy was a nice well-meaning person; she just wasn't company for the emerging George.

George started going out after work with some of the project team, some males, some females. He started to drink for the first time in his life and actually had some fun. He got involved with some of the females at work, strictly on a work basis. He was realizing that there was more to life than martyrdom. He didn't have to be a rat like his father. He could be himself and still enjoy life. After about three years of living like this, his main project was finally coming to an end. He would become a maintenance project leader. He realized that he liked creating and designing state-of-the art computer software systems, but he had no interest in maintaining them.

The company he was with agreed to promote him to head client contact representative. This new job required considerable out of town time. At first, he found it to be a burden to be away from home. But slowly he adjusted to the lifestyle of first class travel, first class hotels, meals on the client, and drinking and carousing out of town after work. This also allowed him to start accumulating money. He left on Sunday and returned on Friday night. He would come home on the weekends to get his clothes cleaned. He didn't miss his life with Tracy and Timmy. Being out of town during the week was like being out on parole. He also found that he liked what he was doing, software problem solving for clients. He was living a hidden life out of town, but he had no other real life to speak of. He was waiting for something to happen. He could hope, couldn't he? George had always been a passive observer of his life letting things happen and accepting them. Now he knew he had to take some action, but he couldn't make movement. Just go with the flow and something would happen

Points to ponder:

When we have children we have expectations for them to be a most exceptional child. Very few meet those expectations. So the parents either have to make up fantasies about their children or accept them for whom they are. The parents who saw themselves as popular as kids expect their children to be the same and those who weren't popular expect their children to be the opposite. George's parents were both computer types, good at their work, bad at social interactions. When they realized that George was going to be just like them they weren't concerned. They smiled to each other; George was going to be all right.

1. George got his first computer when he was six years old and spent his time learning how it operated. At school, he daydreamed about getting back to his computer. While his teachers were concerned, his parents weren't. Why was that?
2. George hid for most of his childhood locked in his room with his computer. He stayed to himself with few friends. In high school he won a number of awards for his computer work and received a scholarship to a most prestigious technology college. Is the way that George was allowed to grow up by his parents a healthy one for growth?

3. In his first year at college, George continued his life as a computer recluse. He rejected material things as unimportant such as dates, clothes, and cars. He had no desire to get rich only to be able to work on the computer. Life wasn't a place for frivolous fun. Where did George get these values?
4. George refused dates that his computer nerd classmates tried to persuade him to go on. He wasn't comfortable with females or socializing. Where did these feelings come from?
5. Eventually he got tired of being called the "computer monk" so he agreed to go to a dance with Tracy, who seemed to be very quiet and attentive to George. It didn't work out and George went back to his computer. What got in George's way to eliminate any chance of the dance working out?
6. Tracy persisted in trying to make a relationship with George with a ready smile and willingness to talk. She became easy for George to get along with, allowing him to stay hidden from any real life. What attraction did George have for Tracy and where did it come from?
7. George and Tracy started to go out to out of the way places and make out a little; that is holding hands and touching lips. They were two lonely people trying to find themselves. What were George and Tracy hiding from? What did they really want out of life? Did it really include the other?
8. Eventually, George and Tracy started having sex; it was Tracy's idea. Neither one was very personable, they both had little to say and they had run out; so screwing helped pass the time and made them feel less lonely. What do you think was the motive for Tracy to start having sex with George?
9. Tracy got pregnant the following year. Somehow it didn't greatly affect him. His parents' reaction increased his isolated sense of rebellion. So he married Tracy. Why do you think he married Tracy?
10. Tracy had a miscarriage two months later. It was a golden chance for George to get out of the marriage, but he didn't. Why was that?
11. George and Tracy graduated from college together. George took a job with a government entity and Tracy with a large software firm. They then had a child so Tracy could quit her job and George could become the man in charge. How do external situations such as having

a baby affect our choices and decisions, sometimes decisions that we wouldn't make otherwise?

12. George finally left his government job and went to work for a start-up software development firm. George's real life started to take shape at this job. He did his job well, made money for the company, and was promoted to a management position. He liked what he was doing, software problem solving for clients and being out of town that released him from the drudgery of being home with Tracy and his son. He was having fun at work but not at home. He was waiting for something to happen. Why do people like George stay in a bad family situation waiting for something to happen rather than to take action?

While I waited for something to happen,
my life went on without the real me.

The Last Affair

One of Bill's best friends at work had left the company and there was to be a going away party for him on a Friday night after work. Bill arranged to be in town for the party. Festivities, drinking, dinner, and more drinking, ended sometime after midnight. One of Bill's fellow workers, Herb, offered Bill and another colleague Tom a ride home. Herb was of Irish derivation and single handedly kept up the Irish tradition of continual drinking. He suggested they stop off at one of the places still open for a nightcap, something for the road. The gruesome threesome was on their second or third round of drinks when two girls walked in and looked over at them. Tom was aware of Bill's preference for female body parts and so was Bill. As they say, Bill was in love.

Herb made the first move once the two girls had sat down. He, of course, offered to buy each of them a drink. They refused and ordered their own drinks. Tom sensed that Herb might be having trouble as an older guy and that maybe young blood was required. He offered to buy the two girls another round of drinks. They refused again. Bill was observing all of this, resisting getting involved, as he had enough troubles at home. He didn't play around and was brought up to honor his commitments, marriage being one of them. *You make your bed, you lie in it.* Divorce wasn't a consideration in his family. Eventually, however, it became apparent that maybe he had to come to the rescue of his colleagues, once again. There was something about the girl in the tight slacks, other than the obvious, that seemed very familiar and pulled him toward her. Bill, being of the cheap persuasion, was also attracted to any girl who bought her own drinks. He had learned that it didn't pay to invest in the cost of a drink if you didn't have to; wait until the girl ordered and paid for her own drink. It never diminished the possibilities; it only increased the possible return on investment. He sat down next to the tight slacks. She looked at him with her big seductive brown eyes. Bill was seduced in spite of himself. He started to stroke her shoulders while Herb continued to proffer his proposition. They turned him down for the night. Possibly it was the pictures of his six kids that turned them off. Herb gave his card to tight slacks. She looked over at Bill, who had told her he was recently separated; he didn't know why; it just seemed like the thing to do. Always keep your options open, leave the door open a crack, he had been taught at work She told Herb her name, Ellen Janek. Bill made a mental note, one never knows. He didn't tell her his name.

The following Thursday Bill got a page in the office. It was Ellen. This was out of his league. She wanted to get together. Bill resisted, but he was only mortal. He caved and agreed to meet her later that night. There was something pulling Bill toward her. Was this what he was waiting to happen, while he went through the motions of being a husband and father? Doubtful, but one never knows. He met her at a downtown hotel. She was smart enough to wear the tight slacks. This time Bill was smart enough to buy the drinks. His chance of a good investment return was increasing. Unfamiliar as he was with dealing with single girls, it had been so long, he came clean and told her that he was still married. She said she knew this all the time. Maybe so, maybe not. They decided to meet again—and then again. They became a steady Tuesday night twosome. Bill was able most weeks to adjust his schedule. Eventually, it led to the hotel room. Oh my god! Bill was in his first real affair. His week revolved around seeing Ellen on Tuesdays. The rest of his week was merely commentary. Ellen tried to get downtown as often as she could for lunch or happy hours. Eventually, they added Friday nights to their repertoire. Then Bill took her on a business trip with him. She was the only business. The customer would survive without his input, maybe even better.

Bill learned that Ellen was still married and had a young child, but she wasn't ready for Bill to meet her daughter, and neither was Bill. Why complicate a good affair. Eventually, Ellen wanted more. She claimed her marriage was over, but not final until her husband moved out. He was presently sleeping on the sofa. Maybe so, maybe not. Her husband worked nights. She finally invited Bill over. After that, they would meet regularly at her house. Bill was relieved to stop paying for motel rooms. He came early and stayed late. One time her parents stopped over. Her mother greeted Bill warmly, obviously with prior knowledge. Her father merely grunted at Bill. Her father told Ellen later that *a man doesn't buy the cow if he's getting free milk.* All of a sudden Bill realized that this was someone else's daughter, and it was getting more serious than he wanted. His upbringing brought guilt into the equation. He might wind up with another family after all. Jesus Christ, what was he doing? But, Bill couldn't stop it. He really didn't want to. He didn't know if he could do it; leave his present wife and kids, especially to live with someone else's kid. Besides, Bill was living at a much higher level than Ellen. Could he really take such a giant step backward? Bill felt that he was on the road to wealth and wasn't sure he could afford the detour. But, maybe, he couldn't afford not to take it.

After living like this for over a year, Ellen finally put the ultimatum to Bill—move in or ship out. It scared him. Up until now, he had let life make his decisions. Things just happened. He wasn't equipped for making personal decisions. He didn't know why they just couldn't go on the way they were. He had no idea of the female perspective. He didn't even know there was such a thing. He had always seen the female as the object to the male. None of his "girls" had ever questioned that wisdom. He should have known better than to start with a strong willed girl. He agonized, he anguished, he pleaded, he cajoled, but the decision was still there. He knew what he had to do, to run toward life and stop hiding. But he couldn't leave where he was, as bad as it was. It was his world. He procrastinated as long as he could, but he knew the claws of truth were increasing their grip. He finally told his wife about his affair with Ellen. She took it as unemotionally as she took everything, as if he had asked her to pick up his dry cleaning. He knew then that his decision was right; he would move in with Ellen. He would run toward his life. He felt his sentence coming to an end; now his real life could begin.

He moved in with Ellen with three matching trash bags with

ties (a leaving husband's set of matching luggage) filled with his clothes. That was the sum of his accumulations for 12 years of a bad marriage. His wife got the rest, as freedom has its cost. It hurt Bill to start the game of accumulation over, but in the end he thought it would be worth it. Sometimes in life, you have to pay to move forward. Bill cried inwardly and outwardly during this time about leaving his family and starting over. This was quite a show of emotion from someone who had never cared or cried before in his life. His parents stopped talking to him. How could he leave his wife and family, and divorce didn't happen in their family. They offered to get him help. If they wanted to help Bill told them, don't help. It was the worst time and the best time in his life, but strangely he was finally feeling alive again. His senses were slowly returning. Bill and Ellen told themselves that they didn't need to get married. Marriage didn't hold good memories for either of them. Denial of reality was always better than facing the truth. It had always worked well for Bill in the past—hadn't it?

Bill's search for himself brought him to the realization of what his prime mover had been. He had always had a problem with mainstream conformity and the pressure to be like everyone else. He always looked at this as his curse. Why couldn't he just accept the basic norms and levels of life like everyone else? He accepted his solitude and aloneness and kept it to himself so that he wouldn't contaminate those around him. In his life's goal not to be like his father, who failed at everything he tried, he put himself in extremely uncomfortable positions at work and at home. He finally realized that he not only wasn't like his father, but also never would be and this was all right. He was now himself and it finally felt good. Once he stopped the self-punishment, he could start the search for himself.

One of the things Bill realized about himself was his quest to have all human beings as part of his community. He resented being labeled as anything; that is, a husband, a father, a professional and so on. He just wanted to be himself without the burden of what those labels forced him to be. He just wanted everyone to be themselves, but the system was against him.

He recognized that another prime mover of his life was to get everyone else to understand what he thought came to him naturally. That is, that we are all in this together. That it is humans themselves that have made up this script of separateness, cultural differences, national and religious superiority, materiality and the quest for money and so on. He had been a one-man band of tolerance. He had tried to dispel stereotypes from his own persona and from others. He had been mildly successful. He had started to question his motives and ask some questions. Was it worth changing a few minds when his goal was to change all minds? Was it worth distancing himself from the unpleasantness of stereotypes? Was it worth trying to live a parallel life as a husband, father, and employee to show the others? Was it worth staying with his principles that made his life lonelier at times? Was it worth fighting for his individual identity in a world that needed to label and classify? Was it worth living a life on his terms, trying not to compromise, in a world of compromises? Was it worth attempting to bring some humanity to an inhumane world? Was it worth trying to know himself and who he was rather than knowing the others better? You be the judge.

Bill lived a life of mistrust and betrayal. He expected the world to remain safe and comfortable for him, but he found out that he couldn't control it. He worked to make it safer for himself, but he only made minor and individual changes. Is this enough for a life? He looked to the outside as the agents of change. He now realized that change comes from the inside, from the individual.

Bill saw such changes since his life with Ellen began. He felt that he would continue working on them, continue to stay with the positions that he still believed were right. He continued to change where he saw the errors of his ways. He joined with others, but remained himself, sitting by himself when he had to rather than be crowded together with the others. He thought this was enough for one life.

Points to ponder:

1. Bill, Tom and Herb were fellow workers at the same company. They were all respected family men in their communities with wives and children. What possesses such men when they are out drinking together to resort to their adolescence especially around drinking and womanizing?
2. Herb, who was of Irish derivation, took it upon himself to maintain the Irish tradition of being a heavy drinker. Why do individuals tend to take on the values and cultural habits of their ethic roots in an effort to reinforce the accepted stereotypes?
3. Bill resisted getting involved with the two girls while watching Herb and Tom ineptly attempt to pick them up. Bill was brought up to honor his commitments such as marriage being forever and divorce not an option. What possessed Bill to finally "rescue" Herb and Tom from their ineptness?
4. Bill felt that there was something familiar about the girl in the tight slacks that pulled him toward her. Have you ever experienced such a feeling yourself and can you describe the feeling and how does it affect you?
5. Bill was also attracted to a girl who insisted on buying her own drinks from a return-on-investment philosophy. How do such areas of learned behavior creep into our value system and become part of our essence?
6. Bill sat down next to the girl in the tight slacks, who looked at him with her large seductive brown eyes, which seduced Bill in spite of himself. Why do some people have that affect on you in spite of your knowing not to get involved?
7. Bill told the girl that he was recently separated, knowing full well that he was married. He didn't know why. It just seemed like the right thing to do. What were Bill's motives to lie and keep the door open?
8. The girl, Ellen, called Bill at his office the following Thursday, wanting to get together. Bill resisted, but finally agreed to meet that night. What was pulling Bill into this situation with Ellen?
9. Bill, who was unfamiliar with dealing with single available girls, came clean and told Ellen that he was still married. Why would Bill do that and risk losing Ellen?

10. Bill and Ellen became a steady Tuesday night twosome. Tuesday used to be his night out with the boys, and as far as his wife knew it still was. What was Bill hoping for in this new relationship with Ellen?
11. Bill learned that Ellen was also still married with a young child. She told Bill that her marriage was over and that husband worked nights but was moving out and he was presently sleeping on the sofa. What do you think Ellen was doing with this relationship?
12. When Bill met Ellen's parents he finally realized that Ellen was someone else's daughter and that this wasn't merely an affair but was real life. He couldn't stop himself but he couldn't go back on his family values. What conflicts were preventing Bill from taking action?
13. When Ellen finally gave Bill the ultimatum to move in or ship out, Bill didn't know what to do. For a successful businessperson he was stymied and immobilized. He wanted things to continue the way they were and he wanted to run toward life and stop hiding. What factors kept Bill immobilized from making a decision?
14. Bill finally moved in with Ellen but he still agonized over leaving his unemotional wife, and divorce didn't happen in his family. His parents stopped talking to him. It was the worst time in his life but he was finally feeling alive, that his life had finally begun. What are some of the difficulties that keep us in bad situations and prevent us from making changes that we know are best for us?
15. Bill had finally left his programming from his upbringing and was trying to live his life for himself, not be like everyone else. Why is it so difficult to know ourselves and to live the life we want contrary to societies rules?

It's extremely difficult to remain you
when everyone else is trying
to make you more like them—
but I'll continue trying to find the real me.

Authors Note

A sincere thank you for reading this book. I hope you thoroughly enjoyed the stories and thinking about the points to ponder related to each as much as I did in compiling them. Hopefully, by analyzing the tales of others and examining the corresponding points to ponder the book helped you to understand how life develops in all of us and how we construct our own tale of self. Using the development of others' tales and the experiences and messages that form those tales helps us to understand the development of our own tales. Through this understanding, we can identify areas for change and work toward becoming the person we want to be and the person we were meant to be before influences started to take over—creating an authentic life.

Well that's all for now. You'll have to excuse me
but I must get back to living my life.
Here's to the storyteller in all of us
and the ability to change our lives.
Really, when reality comes will I be able to see the real reality?

www.ingramcontent.com/pod-product-compliance
Lightning Source LLC
Chambersburg PA
CBHW020608270326
41927CB00005B/228

* 9 7 8 0 8 6 5 3 4 6 5 7 4 *